Beyond Advertising

Creating Value Through All Customer Touchpoints

Yoram (Jerry) Wind, Catharine Findiesen Hays,
and The Wharton Future of Advertising Innovation Network

WILEY

Why *Beyond Advertising* is a Must-Read for CEOs, C-level Executives and Change Agents

The core message in this compelling new book is that 'everything communicates.' Advertising, once the realm of marketers and agencies is now a core business strategy, requiring fluid and silo-busting orchestration of innovation, customer service, corporate reputation management and more. The authors effectively argue that brand equity today is in continuous flux. And if there is any daylight between what a brand says and does, customers will short it like a poorly performing stock. The only answer is to put customers at the center of the organization and 'Beyond Advertising' will teach you how.

— John Gerzema, *Chairman & CEO, BAV Consulting*

Rarely can you find such a comprehensive, cogent, and compelling look at how to market in the future. For those of you open to new models, new media, new ways of managing brands, you'll find innovative and lively thinking from an all-star list of people who are living and breathing the changes every day.

— David Sable, *Global CEO, Y&R*

Beyond Advertising *is a must read for any Business person because it is like a good whack to our existing mental models waking us up to think a new.*

— Rishad Tobaccowala, Chief Strategist, Publicis Groupe

The traditional form of mass marketing is mass suicide. Beyond Advertising *charts a clear pathway to engaging the empowered and hyper-connected consumer through a thoughtful and holistic approach that recognizes the many ways we experience brands, companies, people in our social spheres of influence, the media, and the incredible power of predictive data."*

— Jim Speros, *EVP, Corporate Communications Services, Fidelity Investments*

Beyond Advertising *sets the scene and provides valuable practical help for all in the industry who are grappling with the challenges ahead.*

— Kate Sirkin, *President, Global Digital, Data and Analytics, SMV Group*

A comprehensive and diverse look at a world where what we used to call advertising is evolving into something far more personal & ubiquitous. You may not like it, but you'd better be ready for it.

— Chuck Porter, *Chairman, CP+B*

The book is enriched with easy to understand frameworks and many examples. The authors stress the importance of storytelling and use it through the book to illustrate the key points, making this an easy to follow primer for anyone in the marketing space who wishes to have a chance to stay ahead of the technological waves confronting us.

— Saul Berman, *Chief Strategist, VP & Interactive Experience Partner, IBM*

What we are experiencing now is arguably the biggest change in the history of advertising and marketing. This book offers a superb guide to the changes every marketing practitioner, every advertising/PR professional, and of course every CXO needs to understand.

— Akihiko Kubo, *Chairman, Group Representative, Ogilvy & Mather Japan*

Finally, a comprehensive view into the future of how brands will grow. The Wharton Future of Advertising Program has already been tremendously influential in the industry, and this book synthesizes years of learning into an enjoyable and immensely valuable read.

— Barry Wacksman, *Global Chief Strategy Officer, R/GA*

Virtually all aspects of consumer behavior that are important to businesses are being impacted, causing companies to have to rethink their entire approach to marketing. Fortunately, a roadmap needed to safely navigate a seemingly ever-changing and challenging new terrain is contained in this truly impressive book.

— Gian Fulgoni, *Co-Founder & Chairman Emeritus, comScore*

For the first time Jerry Wind and team tell us why and how we must change our mental models to see the future of what we used to know as marketing. They make sense of all the digital changes and provide a holistic framework to enable future marketers to redefine their role and see how they can be successful in the future.

— Shelly Palmer, *Managing Director, Digital Media Group, Landmark|Shelly Palmer*

As our industry's pace of change accelerates, this book provides a terrific road map for embracing the myriad opportunities ahead.

— David Moore, *Chairman, Xaxis; President, WPP Digital*

In the middle of the media industry's greatest crisis since Gutenberg put all the scribes out of business, Wharton's Jerry Wind and Catharine Hays have written the best marketing book of the decade, analyzing the serious problems of the ad business and, more impressively, explaining how to fix them.

— Kirk Cheyfitz, *Co-CEO & Chief Storyteller, Story Worldwide*

Change is happening all around us, and both the complexity and pace of change are accelerating. For those of us on this Advertising journey it is well worth getting the advice and guidance of a sage like Jerry, a strategist like Catharine, and from 200 thoughtful fellow travelers.

— Phil Cowdell, *CEO, Mediacom North America*

This book will force you to rethink the way you run your company, how you motivate and energize your work force to take risks and change process, and most importantly how to ensure that you are connecting with this new generation of consumers that are used to getting things when they want and the way they want.

— Steven Rosenblatt, *Chief Revenue Officer, Foursquare*

What a breath of fresh air! This book isn't a warning to advertisers to adapt or die, but rather a confident and optimistic overview of the growing opportunities and diversity within the industry.

— Cheryl Burgess, *CEO & CMO, Blue Focus Marketing*

With the rise of digital democracy the advertising industry has been lost. Fortunately, there's a new day dawning with Beyond Advertising. *It's a map for the future.*

— John Winsor, *CEO, Victors & Spoils*

Beyond Advertising *is a much overdue, clear-eyed look at how advertising is being disrupted and how our industry can avoid getting Ubered. The insights constitute a hard-nosed playbook for the new brand-customer relationship.*

— Kip Voytek, *CEO, Rumble Fox*

In Beyond Advertising, *authors Jerry Wind, Catharine Hays, and the rest of the Wharton team don't merely offer us a vision of the bright future awaiting us; they also lay out a clear and actionable path on how to get there.*

— Mark Burgess, *President, Blue Focus Marketing*

Advertising and marketing is in a state of chaos and everyone knows it. Beyond Advertising *lays out the primary obstacles to transforming organizations and marketing practices but more importantly, the book's prescription is visionary and yet practical.*

— Richard Smith, *VP Digital Agency Partnerships, Kitewheel*

Jerry Wind and Catharine Hays of the Wharton Future of Advertising Program have found the pathway to the future of marketing in their new book, Beyond Advertising: *find out what now are the secrets and the winning strategy when devising breakout marketing plans.*

— Scott Goodson, *CEO & Founder, StrawberryFrog*

Marketing as we know it comes to an end. But as always: the end is a new beginning as well. And this books is THE resource to understand how the future of Marketing, beyond advertising, will be and how we all can tackle it.

— Martin Nitsche, *Managing Partner, Solveta GmbH; President, DDV*

Building a brand that tells its story in every touchpoint authentically is a new art and science. This book provides a very good framework to go about it.

— Georgia Garinois-Melenikiotou, *SVP, Corporate Marketing, Estée Lauder*

'We've always done it that way' is the most dangerous phrase in any language. Jerry Wind and Catharine Hays provide a roadmap into the future to help marketers (and agencies) change from selling to serving and creating meaningful relationships with brands.

— Lisa Colantuono, *Co-President, AAR Partners*

No other moment in history has produced such remarkable times in a rapidly changing world. Whether you're charting a new course or growing what you have in the pages that unfold ideas are shared, objectives are set and future strategies are discovered that will get the reader excited around something new with many iterations.

— Dean Crutchfield, *Advisor, Amy J Wiener LLC*

This is the most profound and comprehensive book explaining how the role of an advertiser has fundamentally changed, and explaining in detail how to define a brand's purpose and relevancy, create content, engage with people, interact through all media, shifting from hard sell to shared values, to create bonding experiences and long-term relationship equity.

— Bill Harvey, *Co-Founder & Strategic Advisor, TRA*

In this important and timely book, Professor Jerry Wind and Executive Director Catharine Hays document why and how the future of advertising is beyond advertising to encompass all aspects of customers' interactions with companies.

— Earl Taylor, *CMO, Marketing Science Institute*

Jerry and Catharine provide a guide for dealing with turbulent market forces and a framework for how to take action.

— Brian Shin, *Founder & CEO, Visible Measures*

It is a must read, providing both valuable global context for the transformative changes challenging business today, while identifying specific actions to capitalize on new opportunities. Foremost among the abundant insights is the recognition that our industry has a huge opportunity to improve and change our world through inspiring purpose-driven initiatives.

— Gillian Graham, *CEO, Institute of Communication Agencies, Toronto*

What I love about Beyond Advertising *is the profoundly pragmatic and actionable nature of the findings. Technology has allowed the world to see all the fractures in a brand's construction. This text gives marketers a way to heal those fractures, not just photoshop the x-ray.*

— MT Carney, *CEO & Founding Partner, Untitled Worldwide*

Beyond Advertising *presents a compelling call to action for marketers to lead the way in identifying emerging dynamics and effectively engage the public in adaptive and innovative ways in order to create sustainable success.*

— Bob Kantor, *Chief Marketing & Business Development Officer, MDC Partners*

Part masterclass, part meditation, and all meaningful, Beyond Advertising *distills the collective wisdom from hundreds of marketing professionals comprising thousands of years of experience into clean and compelling action plans for the next generation of marketers.*

— Eric Porres, *CMO, Sailthru*

In a world where technology changes fast and provides even faster opportunities for disruption, advertising and brands have come full-circle, entering a new, more personal era that seeks to re-imagine, re-engage and re-envision intrinsic value to each person. This book demonstrates the fundamental need for every business to work cohesively across all functions in order to establish value at every touchpoint.

— Sandy Howe, *SVP of Marketing, ARRIS*

In clear and vivid form, and by relying on experts from each discipline, authors Wind and Hays provides a much needed contribution to facilitate not only understanding and insights in these times, but also what may be considered a much needed safe harbor and common reference for ongoing and future change in advertising and marketing.

— Thomas Ramsøy, *CEO & Founder, Neurons Inc.*

The simultaneous forces of increased globalization, localization, and personalization now buffet our business landscape. This book is about the need for dramatic new mindsets. This new approach must be required reading.

— Larry Light, *CEO, Arcature*

Finally a book that examines the true depth and breadth of change affecting all organizations through the lens of communications! Catharine and Jerry have beautifully articulated that reaching people now requires holistic thinking and elastic structures.

— Michael Lebowitz, *Founder & CEO, Big Spaceship*

This book is printed on acid-freepaper.♾

Published by John Wiley & Sons, Inc., Hoboken, New Jersey

Published simultaneously in Canada

For general information about our other products and services, please contact our Customer Care Department within the United States at (800) 762-2974, outside the United States at (317) 572-3993 or fax (317) 572-4002.

Wiley publishes in a variety of print and electronic formats and by print-on-demand. Some material included with standard print versionsofthisbookmaynotbeincludedine-booksorinprint-on-demand.If this book refers to media such as a CD or DVD that is not included in the version you purchased, you may download this material at http://booksupport.wiley.com. For more information about Wileyproducts, visitwww.wiley.com.

Library of Congress Cataloging-in-Publication Data

Names: Wind, Yoram, author. | Hays, Catharine, 1958- author.
Title: Beyond advertising : reaching customers through every touchpoint / Jerry Wind and Catharine Hays.
Description: Second edition. | Hoboken : Wiley, 2015. | Includes bibliographical references and index.
Identifiers: LCCN 2015036808 (print) | LCCN 2015043750 (ebook) | ISBN 9781119074229 (hardback : alk. paper) | ISBN 9781119074205 (pdf) | ISBN 9781119074090 (epub)
Subjects: LCSH: Advertising. | Communication in marketing. | Customer relations. | BISAC: BUSINESS & ECONOMICS / Customer Relations.
Classification: LCC HF5823 .W546 2015 (print) | LCC HF5823 (ebook) | DDC 659.1—dc23
LC record available at http://lccn.loc.gov/2015036808

Cover image: © iStock.com
Interior book design: Poulin + Morris

Printed in the United States of America

10987654321

For
John, Lee, Mark, Gavi, and Barbara

For
Olivia and Lizzy

And to our inspirational
collaborators, colleagues, friends, and loved ones

Contents

Acknowledgements

This book represents a milestone in a years-long collaborative process, both between us as co-founders of the Wharton Future of Advertising (WFoA) Program, as well as with all those who have helped develop, participate in, and contribute to the projects, initiatives, and gatherings reflected in these pages.

Focusing on the future of advertising was the brain child of Mark Morris, Joe Plummer, and Jerry, when they identified the revolution that was fomenting in the advertising world and the need to establish an independent, respected, academic endeavor to bring together forward-thinking practitioners, researchers, and academics to collectively chart the way forward. Since then, many individuals around the world have been inspired by our mission to become de facto members of the Wharton Future of Advertising Innovation Network – our co-authors. We are grateful for the opportunity to thank the many people and their organizations who have contributed and lent support of all kinds to make this profoundly collaborative book and initiative take shape.

For the actual book and ebook, we thank Richard Narramore at Wiley, with the wonderful team of Tiffany Colon, Peter Knox, and Suganya Babu, who provided the support, encouragement, feedback, and patience we needed to marshal the manuscript through production and to market.

We are grateful to those who took the time to provide early, honest and constructive feedback on the manuscript including Lisa Colantuono, Neal Davies, Vaasu Gavarasana, Tom Morton, George Musi, Joe Plummer, Jenny Rooney, Pierre Soued, and John Winsor.

We especially thank each of our brave Advertising 2020 Contributors *(listed in Appendix 2)* who took the time to craft their unique visions of the future. We'd also like to offer a special thanks to a few individuals who reached deep into their personal professional networks to expand and enrich the project scope. Kamini Banga interviewed eight industry luminaries to capture and reflect their insights. Neal Davies and Denise McDevitt curated their Effie Award-winning community to find relevant examples for the book and for subsequent, interactive material we'll be offering. Matthew Godfrey enlisted Jun Lee to tap the Z Apprentices in Y & R and Wunderman's Global Talent Program to ensure we heard from the next generation. Gillian Graham enlisted thought leaders from Canada's Institute of Communications Agencies. Bob Greenberg personally invited all of the tech innovators whom he and Greg Harper selected for the inaugural Advertising Week Experience in 2012. Bruce Crawford and Thomas Harrison brought us innovators from across their network. John Philip Jones reached out to his star alumni from the Newhouse School at Syracuse University. Mark Morris, who had tapped his Bates alumni network to ensure executive representation from each continent to form the original membership of our Global Advisory Board, then made sure that each of them contributed their points of view for the 2020 Project.

As much as this book has the content from the Advertising 2020 Project at its core, it is also very much informed and inspired by those who have been actively involved with furthering the mission of WFoA since its inception.

We have been privileged to co-host roundtable sessions with top practitioners and academics from around the world to exchange and discuss their initiatives, research, and insights and offer feedback on the emerging models we developed as a result. For these sessions we have been fortunate to work with first-rate collaborators and their colleagues: Byron Sharp, Elke Seretis, Jenni Romaniuk, and Karen Nelson-Field at the Ehrenberg-Bass Institute; Dan Feldstein and Mitchell Reichtgut at Jun Group; Rosemarie Ryan and Ty Montague at co-collective; Nick Primola and Bob Lidoce of the ANA; Bruce Rogers and Jenny Rooney at Forbes; Philip Thomas and Steve Latham and their teams at the Cannes Lions; Phil Cowdell while at Mindshare (and ever since); Rich Guest at Tribal Worldwide; Bob Kantor and the talented people throughout MDC Partners; Jae Goodman and Sylvia Friedel at CAA; Rishad Tobaccowala and Douglas Ryan at VivaKi and DigtasLBi; the late Bob Barocci, Gayle Fuguitt and the dedicated ARF staff; Nancy Hill and Mike Donahue at the 4A's; Randall Rothenberg and Susan Borst at the IAB; Peter Gatscha at the Austrian Trade Commission; Barbara Kahn and Denise Dahlhoff at Wharton's Baker Retail Center; Eric Bradlow and Pete Fader at the Wharton Customer Analytics Initiative; and Vaasu Gavarasana, who while at Bates 141, personally convened a powerhouse group of those at the forefront of advertising, marketing, and media in India for a 2011 roundtable session in New Delhi.

We have learned a tremendous amount through three major collaborations to bring research rigor to new practices just as they were emerging. Laurent Larguinat at Mars worked with us to understand more about the nuances of social media virality while the concept was still nascent in 2011. Vaasu Gavarasana, while at Yahoo! APAC, with leadership and research support from Yvonne Chang and Edwin Wong, led an effort to explore the topic of Native Advertising with agencies and client executives in Singapore in early 2013 when the term was just gaining traction. And in late 2014 we co-created a research project with Facebook to better understand personalization at scale. The core members of the team—Hamdan Azhar, Neha Bhargava, Gabrielle Gibbs, and Daniel Slotwiner—are collaborators of the highest caliber, as we work to understand not only the rigorous analytics, but the needed new collaborative alignment among clients, agencies, and platforms, to chart these uncharted waters.

Thanks to the efforts of Karl Ulrich and Brandon Lodriguss, Wharton launched Business Radio Powered by the Wharton School on Sirius XM Channel 111 in January 2014, and we became early collaborators to form the Marketing Matters show on Wednesday evenings. This has become a wonderful opportunity to hold live, on-air conversations with three or four astute executives during each two-hour show and we are extremely grateful for the time each of them has taken to share their insights. We also want to give a special shout-out to Jenny Rooney, editor at Forbes CMO Network, for co-creating the CMO Spotlight show once a month. We are thankful to all of the coaching and support provided by the unflappable and ever-positive Michelle Stucker, our producer, and to each of the student research assistants who provide us with first-rate background information on the guests and the topics to keep the conversations meaningful.

The foundation of our Program is the growing network of our active and generous Global Advisory Board members and other inspiring invited guests who have carved time out to participate in our annual meetings, to share with the WFoA and each other their successes, challenges, and insights over the years. At the very first session it became infinitely clear that it was valuable to both the Program and to the participants to take a step back, look ahead to the future, hear what others from across the ecosystem had to say about the most current approaches and findings as well as how to best prepare for the challenges and opportunities of the next 12 to 18 months, even while considering what we should be aiming for, and using our influence and resources to make happen, in 3–5 years.

Wharton and Penn have a host of impressive alumni who are now finding one another in this community of innovators who are redefining the landscape. Thanks so much to those of you who have connected with us. We encourage you to continue to reach out, reconnect, and leverage this community to make a positive impact on the field and on the world.

We also want to acknowledge the students and student organizations with whom we have partnered to create bridges and dialog between the WFoA Innovation Network Community and students across disciplines at Wharton, Penn and beyond, through the open, online courses we'll be creating. You make us all hopeful for the future. Be brave to strive for the triple wins for brands, people, and society in the work you do after graduation. We are just getting started and you are an essential driver for a better future.

All of this would not have been possible without Al West. Through his support of Wharton's SEI Center for Advanced Studies in Management, which he and Jerry founded in 1990 and where we have incubated the WFoA Program since 2008, Al has been our primary visionary and benefactor, continuing his investment is us and in our mission, year after year. Thank you, Al, for enabling what has become so widely and globally valued and appreciated.

We are also grateful to our other early stage funders who individually believed enough in the importance of our mission to champion corporate gifts when they were, and in some cases still are, at these companies: Sanjay Govil at Infinite; Sebastien Lion at Mars Petcare. Laurent Larguinat at Mars Marketing Lab; Andres Siefkin at Daymon; Christopher Lyons at Kodak; Alan Hallberg at Lenovo and at RFMD; Paul Bascobert at Bloomberg Media; and Graham Mudd at Facebook.

We want to give particular mention to the leaders of closely-held organizations who embrace the WFoA vision and have devoted a portion of their budgets to the Program, in addition to their time, over multiple years: Karsten Koed, Gorm Larsen and Zornig; Denise Larson and Gary Reisman, NewMediaMetrics; Kirk Cheyfitz, Story Worldwide; and Mitchell Reichgut and Dan Feldstein, Jun Group. Your personal commitment has been an inspiration and an engine.

Many in our community found other ways to support us along the way. Early on, Chuck Porter tapped the creativity of Mike del Marmol at CP+B to create our first logo and put us in touch with the people on his team and at Dominos to provide information and insights for our first "Insight Report" that we hope will become a model for future case studies. Cindy Goodrich and Sofia Buschmann at Google were the masterminds in co-creating our *Fast*. Forward Channel on YouTube in 2009 and we had a blast conceiving, launching, and scaling it together. Matt Scheckner and his indomitable, unflappable Advertising Week team welcomed us on very short notice beginning in 2009 to conduct roving interviews with the remarkable set of thought leaders he assembles each year. Scott Goodson, founder of StrawberryFrog, helped conceive and seed our first annual Super Bowl Tweet Meet in early 2011, which continues – thank you to all who have taken time away from the chips and guacamole to be part of this tradition. Celia Berk, our first GAB member from the HR world (how prescient was that!), offered to reach into her Y&R network many times to find hosts for our roundtables (Paris and Beijing), to bring research expertise, and to engage others from the executive ranks. Chris Yeh continues to generously provide us invaluable access to the PBWorks online collaboration platform to help us manage all aspects of the WFoA Program. How fortunate were we that the inimitable Phil Cowdell stepped up to become one of our trusted advisors. Barry Libert introduced us to our website co-creator/partner *par excellence*, Doug Ward (WatersWard), and underwrote the first year of development to make the WFoA Program, and the Advertising 2020 project in particular, accessible and interactive. Thank you, TED, whom we sought to emulate.

As WFoA was incubating in the SEI Center, we relied extensively on Katherine Rohan Grosh and Chu Hui Cha for their tremendous support in establishing the board, organizing meetings and conferences, and juggling Jerry's time and commitments. Megan Gillespie has taken over as close collaborator in that role while keeping the Center moving forward and developing new initiatives. Thank you for always being there for us.

Since the inception of the Program, and throughout the development of this book, we have been fueled by the intellect, energy, and dedication of the most wonderful team of Penn and Wharton undergraduate student research and administrative assistants. To all of you, we thank you for your contribution. In particular, there are a few who have really gone above and beyond to bring so much extra effort and value to this program and this manuscript including especially Elijah Cory, Imran Cronk, Raina Dhir, Zak Knudson, Carolyn Koh, Nicole Laczewski, Kaitlin Leung, Adam Rawot, Evan Rosenbaum, Hailey (Weiss) Suyumov, Jill Wang, Molly Wang, and Kelly Yao.

In addition, we are grateful to Sanjay Govil, who has supplied us with a wonderful group of high school and college students during the summers to provide research and administrative support while immersing themselves in the ongoing work of the Program.

In the last few years we have been incredibly fortunate to work with part time staff assistants who defy the term. Each came on to help with "administrative support" while pursuing advanced degrees, yet with their intellectual curiosity, creativity, professionalism, talent, and flexibility offered us so much more than we imagined. In succession we are grateful for Maisie Pascual, who helped us get our administrative house in order; Matt Wiegle, who shared his facility with words, graphics, and databases; and most recently, Alexis Rider who took on a tremendous amount of ownership in navigating so many critical aspects of the manuscript in its final stages and who distills the key insights from our live radio show into a highly readable blog. Thank goodness she is willing to stay with us through the rest of her PhD work in the History and Sociology of Science.

Alexa de los Reyes joined in 2010 in what was supposed to be a part-time administrative support role. But she soon emerged as a full-on co-creator and co-owner of the Program. She has been instrumental in expanding the involvement of the community, the student research assistants, the website content, the EG II Conference, the Advertising 2020 Project and pretty much everything else it took to build WFoA. Her sensibilities as an accomplished artist, her talent as a writer, her warmth as a person, and her healthy skepticism of advertising have graced all facets of WFoA. She has contributed so much to the heart and soul of WFoA and to the content development of this book with constancy, honesty, diligence, and laughter. As the book project began to heat up, she moved to focus her energies on helping to create chapters and marshal them to completion, and she still retains the role of resident historian, advisor, and confidant. Our love and thanks to Alexa, and in turn to Gastón, Inigo, and Eliam for their support of her throughout this endeavor.

We are so grateful that when Kelly Rhodes graduated from Penn with high honors in the spring of 2014, she chose to take a full-time position to help run the Program. And what an impact she has made. Her dedication and wisdom, positive, can-do attitude, unbounded enthusiasm, intelligence and resourcefulness has enabled us to more fully support and enable our growing WFoA network to innovate, inspire and learn. Kelly represents the best of what the next generation is bringing to our world. We treasure all that she has to offer and look forward to being part of her growth and life-long success.

We are thankful for the collaboration and friendship between us that began back on campus as we—Jerry as the founding Director and Catharine as a founding Fellow in Wharton's Lauder Institute for Management and International Studies—helped to shape that program as pioneers. And now these many years later, reconnecting to co-create and evolve this Wharton Future of Advertising mission, program, community, and content. We have grown together by working together and celebrate the yin and yang that our different yet complimentary backgrounds and personalities bring to this endeavor. We cherish the closeness that we share and the path that we have forged. And we look forward to continuing to find important and impactful ways, in collaboration with others, to make the future a better place in this particular and important space.

And finally, we thank our families and loved ones, who have been our rock and our inspiration throughout this project and especially as the book deadline loomed . . . and loomed. John, Lee, Mark, Gavi, and Barbara; Olivia, Lizzy, Stan, Terry, Bill, and David, your sincere understanding, support, encouragement, patience, constancy, and love sustained us through this entire journey, and throughout the personal circumstances we both faced along the way. To the extent that positive change happens as a result of this book, we dedicate it to you.

Preface

Who Should Read This Book?

This book is for those who recognize that tremendous and far-reaching changes continue unabated in the field of advertising and marketing. It is for those who are already feeling the effects as these fundamental shifts spill over into many, if not all, other disciplines of their organization. It is for those who no longer want to respond reactively or be blind-sided, and would like to get ahead of the curve. This book is for those who sense that the relationship between those with products or services to sell and the people they seek to influence is changing drastically. It is for those whose business models are supported in any significant measure by companies, organizations, and individuals who want to get people to consider, try, buy, or recommend their product, service, or idea—in other words, are supported by advertising. And it is by and for all those who are already pioneering new approaches, who bear the cuts and bruises of blazing trails for a more desirable future, and who are already sending news back from their forays into new territory—our collaborators in this book.

Based on the input from these hundreds of innovators and visionaries from around the world and across disciplines *(see Appendix 2)*, we have assembled a transformational set of concepts that all would benefit from considering, if not acting upon tomorrow morning. We quote our collaborators extensively throughout this book—we've italicized them to make them easily recognizable. The complete set of entries can be found on our website, and we encourage you to take advantage of the wealth of their additional thoughts, insights, and suggestions. You can find them all at wfoa.wharton.upenn.edu. Our observation is that the **impact and implications of five crucial and continuously evolving interrelated forces—which we unpack in Part I—have been felt first and foremost by marketing, media, and advertising professionals.** Therefore, the viewpoints of the most innovative and forward thinking among them offer a prescient guide to how to harness these forces of change in order to maximize opportunity and impact.

Why should our findings, drawn from the specific pool of advertising and marketing, be relevant to a broader audience? Because increasingly, the forces of change that have been buffeting these areas are reverberating across the executive ranks, throughout all reaches of organizations, and on to their stakeholders. The new concepts we present apply to large corporations and small enterprises alike, to anyone who has the desire to understand and harness the tremendous forces of change . . . or else risk being overtaken by those who do. They are relevant for those not yet in the workforce who can bring fresh thinking to their future endeavors.

Indeed, these concepts are for all of us who wish that advertising—and all interactions with potential and current providers of products and services—didn't have to be so intrusive, irrelevant, distasteful, clueless, or presumptuous.

Many executives remain dismissive of the significance of advertising, looking at it as if it were an afterthought—the final "gloss" added in order to sell stuff. It is clear that one of the main hurdles is gaining the attention of the business unit heads who see marketing as an expense item with unknown impact rather than an investment with measurable returns. Such is the persistent reputation of advertising. Deservedly so? Kevin Allen, founder and CEO of rekap Inc., examines this matter:

> *Advertising in 2020 will not be "buy me," it will be "join me." We will no longer be persuaders, rather advertising's role will be dedicated to promulgating the belief system of the brand citizenship, listening carefully to them, informing and entertaining them, taking active steps to support and nurture an ongoing dialogue, and in doing so the company and its brand will be made "buoyant" by this community because of their recognition of the genuine support for their interests. Products will become a living symbol and expression of the value system and will be seen as an ever-evolving pledge of service for the benefit of the citizenship. Brand Citizens will reward this authenticity and genuineness with their purchases. They will punish the selfish and predatory with their abandonment and the discussion in the hallways of advertising organizations must then elevate beyond the silliness of discussions surrounding ad integration or digital centricity. All disciplines will prove relevant but must be channeled toward the promulgation of a deep and abiding relationship with its citizens. (2012)*

Advertisers as valued listeners, informers, and entertainers in service of grateful citizens—this sounds appealing, and it is also within reach. **And yet, despite increasing evidence that this radical scenario is quickly becoming a reality, studies confirm that executives feel their organizations are not prepared to deal with the changing marketing environment.** In IBM's 2010 study of more than 1,500 CEOs worldwide, 8 out of 10 CEOs indicated that their primary challenge was increasing and accelerating complexity, but less than half felt prepared to handle it (IBM 2010). This pattern has persisted in every CXO survey IBM has conducted since then. In 2013, IBM research found that 82% of CMOs felt "underprepared for the data explosion" versus 71% of CMOs in 2011, highlighting the gap between what they need and what they have (IBM 2013).

The perceived lack of preparedness is not only in regards to so-called "Big Data" but all key marketing success factors. A 2014 survey by the Economist's Intelligence Unit found that more than 80 percent of marketing executives worldwide say they need to restructure marketing, and 29 percent say the need for change is urgent (The Economist Intelligence Unit 2014).

The insights of this book offer a roadmap for addressing these concerns, helping CMOs—and their entire organization—be prepared for the change that is happening and is likely to continue unabated for the foreseeable future.

Insights for the Entire Organization

As we look to the future that is already upon us, it is clear that the creation of a compelling, unifying brand theme and its delivery through *all touchpoints*—including every point of interaction a person has with a brand—affects the triple bottom line and cannot be relegated to advertising and marketing alone. It requires the engagement of all the organizational silos and top management, even those that are outside of the traditional purview of advertising and marketing, to include and coordinate product development to packaging and unboxing design, from offline to online retail experiences, from face-to-face sales to all aspects of customer service, from executive blogs to employee social media.

There are therefore five key reasons why all parts of an organization, and not just the leadership, will benefit from the insights of this book.

First, advertisers and marketers are situated to have the best insights into the changing consumer behavior and market dynamics that are key to the entire offering of a firm.

Second, our conclusion that effective advertising and any message should be delivered consistently across all touchpoints impacts all parts of the firm, as many touchpoints are outside the control of advertising and marketing.

Third, with the advent of digital, big data, predictive analytics, cognitive computing (e.g., IBM's Watson), and artificial intelligence (e.g., Google's DeepMind), all parts of the organization are in the position to collaborate to undertake innovative experiments that can benefit the entire firm.

Fourth, effective "advertising" at its best can offer a coherent and powerful vision of the firm to all its stakeholders (employees, suppliers, distributors, investors, partners, customers) that is relevant and inspirational both inside and outside the organization.

And finally, the speed, magnitude, and interrelated nature of change requires an agile and innovative organization which cannot be designed and implemented only within the realm of advertising and marketing. It requires collaboration among all organizational functions.

To be successful today and prepared for what's ahead tomorrow, everyone—from product development, sales, customer service, and HR, to the CIO, CFO, CEO, and presidents of the business units—must buy in, challenge the entrenched mindsets of what's possible, and start experimenting with new approaches. Already we are seeing a host of new titles to reflect a refined focus: Chief Experience Officer, Chief Insights Officer, Chief Customer Officer, Customer Journey Architect, to name but a few. Attracting and nurturing people with the competencies required to thrive in this changing environment is a challenge faced by all organizations today.

This kind of brand buy-in throughout the internal ranks of a company does more than improve external responses. A brand persona—based around an authentic message and genuine identity—is increasingly essential to retain employees and attract new talent. As John Costello, president, Global Marketing and Innovation at Dunkin' Brands Inc. explains, **"It's almost impossible for a brand to say one thing and then operate differently; the explosion of social media has seen to that. What is crucial to recognize is that marketing is not only targeting consumers, its targeting prospective—and current—employees"** (Marketing Matters June 2015). Building a brand that manifests itself in every touchpoint, and that everyone at a company understands, genuinely believes—and sincerely wants to advocate for—is an ongoing effort requiring collaboration far beyond the marketing department.

Inspiration and Insights for All

Do you think advertising could and should be far better? Do you believe you are seeing glimmers of some powerful new connections from and with brands? Do you recognize that social good is an increasingly crucial element of successful brand initiatives? Have you noticed that advertising is about so much more than television or billboards, with consumers—also known as people—taking increasing control? Given the pervasiveness of brands in everyone's lives today, you don't need to be in marketing to make these observations, just as you don't need to be in marketing to draw tremendous value from this book.

We hope to appeal to people across generations, disciplines, and geography who feel there are far greater possibilities for leveraging the bridges between brands, people, and society. The concepts in this book will especially appeal to those with curiosity, open minds, and a desire for a better future. **So, if you think advertising could and should be far better, if you are in a leadership position and want to know how to leverage what is possible and understand what is needed, or if you are determined to change and need inspiration and some language and frameworks to help engage your broader organization, read on.** We hope you are inspired by the rest of the book and look to the Advertising 2020 website for the complete set of entries from our insightful and aspirational contributors.

Our greater hope is that our findings enable you to take action toward co-creating a far more desirable future that aligns the interests of brands, their stewards, and people, creating a net-positive impact on society at every touchpoint.

Part I
The Motivation for Change

If you want to predict the future of advertising, imagine throwing a bottle into the ocean. . . . Many pundits point out singular 'futures' in marketing and advertising by watching waves and musing about where the bottle is headed. This is useful in the short run. If you have a long-term objective it's more useful to focus on recognizing forces beyond the waves that will intersect in unexpected ways to shape, if not predictably determine, the future. Many forces shaping the future of advertising are well known, just as it's well known that tides move the ocean. The question is whether we understand their effect in shaping the future.

— Christopher Kenton, *CEO and Founder, SocialRep (2012)*

Yes, the changes that you are feeling are real. There is something bearing down on traditional approaches to advertising and marketing with unprecedented headwinds—the first visible indicator of the size and scope and speed of change that is to come. As the saying goes, we ain't seen nothing yet. Understand these changes, heed their import, and there is still time to make a course correction and thrive. Others are already doing so by harnessing these new forces, finding the new North Star that we present in Part II, and creating the more nimble craft and crew that we outline in Part III.

Why do we need to bother changing? What is the motivation for change? How are the five forces of change speeding up our world, disrupting traditional approaches and mindsets, and yet providing unprecedented horsepower to enable needed new approaches?

In Chapter 1 we delve into the five dramatic worldwide transformations that are impacting everything we thought we knew about how businesses and organizations communicate and connect with their customers *(see Figure I.1)*. In brief, they are:

1. *Rapid, Breakthrough Advances in Science and Technology*
   What are these breakthroughs and how to harness their power?

2. *Exploding, Redefined, and Enhanced Media Landscape*
   How to allocate resources for the greatest return?

3. *Skeptical and Empowered People*
   How to attract and retain both connected and unconnected "talent" and "consumers"?

4. *Fundamental Cultural, Social, Environmental, and Geopolitical Challenges*
   What are the roles and responsibilities of brands as global challenges grow louder and more insistent, and what does this have to do with advertising?

5. *Disruptive and Compelling Business and Revenue Models*
   What are the means of survival when disruption is almost inevitable?

Equally important for a Beyond Advertising future, these forces of change represent not only the *source* of actionable insights to be monitored and tapped, but also the opportunity set for contributing a net positive impact from innovative and purposeful brand touchpoint initiatives. . . . And the Most Important Tool for Harnessing the Future

The industry clings steadfastly to conceptual frameworks that in many cases date back 50 years or more. And the fact is that many of these frameworks are not just wrong but seriously misleading, so much so that they often lead to suboptimal outcomes, outcomes that are the very opposite of what the marketing team both wants and needs.

— Mark Tomblin, *Chief Strategy Officer, TAXI (2013)*

If you think you already know what you need to do, or as may be the case, what everyone *else* needs to do, then you will either read the book searching for confirmation of that point of view and/or reject anything we offer that doesn't reinforce your point of view. Based on our conversations with even the most forward-thinking people, we realize that entrenched thinking, or expecting affirmation, is a danger. So, before we explain the model that will address these challenges, we have a favor to ask. Actually this will be a requirement, since the new model that we outline in Part II won't mean much if you are still holding on to some old ways of thinking. **Before you read the next part of this book, take a moment to suspend your current thinking, your mindsets, and those mental models that in all likelihood have worked so well for you for so many years.**

Figure I.1 The Five Forces of Change and Opportunity

Figure I.2 Challenge Entrenched Mental Models

II.
CHALLENGE ENTRENCHED MENTAL MODELS

What is the Best It Could / Should Be?

Across and Among ALL Titles, Roles and Expertise

	CURRENT	TOWARD
WHO?	Marketers and Agencies, through Media, at Target Demographics	Cross-Silo Collaborators
WHAT?	Ads	Orchestrated Value-Creation Touchpoints
WHEN?	Frequency	When Needed, Wanted, Appreciated
WHERE?	Reach	Where Needed, Wanted, Appreciated
WHY?	Push and Persuade For Sales	Multi-Win Outcomes
HOW?	Ad Campaigns	Initiatives in Holistic, Dynamic Ecosystem

Words Matter: Enlist a New Vocabulary

In Chapter 2, we walk you through this process of tackling what we have found to be the single greatest impediment to change and transformation: mental models that worked in the past but must be challenged, given new realities to meet the future (*see Figure I.2*).

For example: we should probably stop referring to "consumers," which implies a myopic mindset that defines "them" based on what and how much they consume. How would it change your mindset to think about "them" as "us" and about them as people whose lives we might enrich?

And that's just for starters.

Chapter 1

The Five Forces Driving the Need for Change

To prepare for [the] future, it is vital to understand that the greatest threat to progress is the inability to see around corners, the inability to respect our past and the unwillingness to realize that the way we succeeded is not the way we will succeed.

— Thomas Harrison, *Chairman Emeritus, DAS at Omnicom Group (2012)*

This Chapter Is about Inspiring You to Go Beyond Advertising. Why?
When we asked our Advertising 2020 contributors about what the future could and should hold—what was both necessary and possible—they scanned the horizon from their respective vantage points across disciplines and around the world and brought into focus an unprecedented convergence and interaction of extremely fast-moving trends, highly disruptive insights, and rapidly emerging capabilities that we will experience just a few years hence. A world that is becoming a reality in our daily lives, now.

As John M. Baker, CMO of Mirum Agency, notes, *"The challenge with predicting the future is something science fiction writers talk about all of the time. Aside from the difficulty of getting it right, the hard part is balancing the consistency of human experience with the pace of change in technology"* (2012). By asking what could and should advertising look like, we privileged aspiration over accuracy. By asking experts immersed in many different industries, we gathered together the viewpoints best suited to balance experience and change. The result: points of view that brought to life dramatic worldwide transformations that have occurred in recent years, impacting everything we once thought we knew about how enterprises communicate and connect with the customers they desire. **Initially identified as game-changers for the world of marketing and advertising, these forces are rapidly and irrevocably reverberating across all roles in the executive ranks—especially as they are being redefined and realigned—and throughout their organizations, challenging entrenched assumptions, mindsets, and methodologies.**

A power trio from Doremus—Evelyn Neill, executive creative director; Howard Sherman, president and CEO; and Mathew Don, chief innovation officer—paint an evocative image of where we're headed:

> *Technology is geography (it's one world)*
>
> *Sustainability is efficiency (greener is cheaper)*
>
> *Each person is empowered (freer to soar & freer to fall)*
>
> *These obvious points capture a snapshot of wonders—the ubiquity of Internet-facilitated revolutions, the rise of efficient technology, and the high cost of fuel that is inspiring it. The rise of the individual voice thanks to the technological amplification of that voice. The crumbling of the paternal employer and blue chip safety—replaced by the empowered, mobile, entrepreneurial, global, untethered, and unprotected individual finding his or her way in the world. It's a marvelous, dangerous, adventuresome world. A veritable plugged-in Dickens novel (2012).*

However, as we talk with executives in our Wharton Future of Advertising workshops and in Jerry's Wharton Fellows Programs, as well as with our students, there still seems to be an underestimation of just how these forces—and their interdependencies—will change established approaches. And, equally important, that they offer tremendous transformational capital to get at some of the most intractable issues facing business leaders today.

That's why the visionary thinking of our 200+ Advertising 2020 contributors is so essential. From them we distilled five key themes to help focus your thinking and spur you to take action *(see Figure 1.1).*

And just for good measure, add to the transformative nature of each of these forces the exponential rate of change, the magnitude of change, and the complexity and interdependencies among the forces. As Thomas Burkhardt, global brand builder, puts it, *"Following the mantra that 'the future is already out there, it's just not very evenly distributed' we are already seeing today what will be even more necessary and prevalent in at the beginning of the next decade"* (2013).

Figure 1.1 The Five Forces of Change to Motivate and Enable

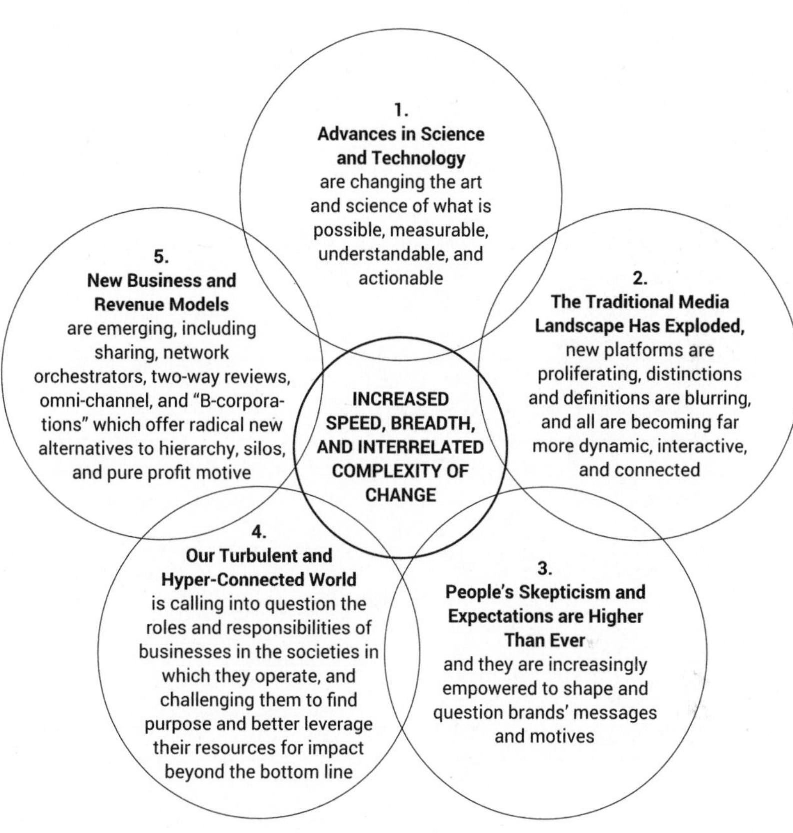

Bob Greenberg, executive director of Advertising Week Experience (AWE) brings these ideas to life in "Two Letters from 2020:"

THE FUTURE

To: Brands and their agencies

From: A customer

I was born in 2000. I'm 20 now. Just graduated college and starting my own life. Voting in my first presidential election this year—psyched!

I've grown up with mobile devices.

You used to call them "smart-phones"—quaint!

I have one in my pocket as intelligent as the Watson computer that humiliated Brad Rutter on Jeopardy 10 years ago.

And everything around me now tells its own story.

From buildings, to packages, to images, to products and more.

Like that car? Dog? Person? I just point my mobile device, click and learn all about them.

I carry my favorite companies in my pocket.

They're like having friends in the industry. They advise, consult, and propose, based on a deep understanding of . . . well, me. Not some cohort or quintile or special interest group.

And they'll stay my favorites as long as they anticipate my needs and provide services that make my life easier.

I don't own a TV. Not one like my Dad's, anyway.

Oh I have screens all right—big, thin, light, cheap, smart ones. And I have little screens, too. They're in my pocket, on my wrist, in my glasses, and in my car.

I never had a DVR.

Everything, and I mean everything, is waiting for me in the sky somewhere until I want it.

TV networks are a fading memory.

There are hundreds of "Networks" now and they don't "telecast" anymore, They "custom-cast".

I've completely personalized my content—24/7.

Now 360-degree imagery lets me control my point-of-view . . . not the networks', mine! Actually, they're not really "Networks" anymore, they're "Servers," in every sense of the word.

And now I've become the "Manufacturer."

I'm downloading "Product Access Keys." They let me "manufacture" stuff at home on my 3D printer—kind of like Grandma's fax machine, only it "prints" clothing, jewelry, appliances—whatever—right in my living room, and fast—so no waiting!

I don't use money anymore—not like my Mom does, anyway.

And I don't shop in stores anymore, unless it's exciting, fun, and a cool "hands-on" experience. I don't need to kick the tires . . . unless they kick something back to me.

Actually, lots of sites let you "feel" what's on the screen. Talk about "hands-on" experience!

These days my friends and I are saying; "Don't Hype me, Skype me."

We're dealing with humans now, face-to-face! Not always flesh-and-blood humans, but live people who get me. And some who just seem live, but they have all the answers, so what's the difference?

I don't go to "www" much anymore.

What you once called "apps" are now full-blown, interpretive "servicesites." For example, I have one for travel that "thinks "through my entire trip for me.

From wake-ups, to traffic, all the way to what's on the screens in my hotel room, taxi reservations, meals, shopping, siteseeing, nightlife—everything!

Are they "sponsored"? Of course—by service providers I choose! Privacy, schmivacy.

Back in the twenty-teens GPS was already telling you where I was located.

But you've always wanted to know more about me.

Stop guessing. I'll actually tell you what I'm wishing for, hoping for, and in the market for. But abuse that info at your own peril.

And it's gonna cost you: relevant information plus . . . points, awards, recognition, cash—make it exciting, I'm worth it!

So what's the difference between where you are and 2020? Attitude!

I suppose you're thinking that you have years to go before you get to 2020. But I guess the big question is—will you survive the trip?

Maybe loyally yours,

The Customer

To: All agencies and clients

From: One of your own

Guys, it's a different world out here! It's so . . . well . . . 2020! Supermarkets are connected to customer's refrigerators.

Doctors now track years-worth of patients' vital info—instantly!

Digital health, fitness, and well-being "connectivity" is off the charts. And there's remote "Help" diagnostics for everything. Our bodies, machines, appliances, cars, you name it!

Speaking of cars, they've become rolling, connected marketing platforms. They practically drive themselves, actually . . . nahhh—you wouldn't believe it!

Facial, Voice, and Gesture recognition and Haptics now enable people to interact with machines in incredible new ways!

And we now have a much clearer idea of each of our customer's multidimensional, changing-all-the-time lives.

We realized Big Data isn't about Big Brother, it's about Big Helper.

The killer point is we now have the capability to anticipate customers' needs and desires. And it's not like we had a choice—we had to!

Our big epiphany was that "caveat emptor" has made a 180-degree turn! Now it's truly "Caveat Venditor—Seller Beware."

2020 is a new era, where the customer is no longer king—now she's a goddess!

Brands are in her hands. She can make or break our reputation with a keystroke.

She's not only involved in driving the perception of our companies, but also in creating our goods and services.

Sounds scary? Not really. But we have to rethink ourselves. We're now service providers in the new service society.

But if we didn't learn to treat our customers this way, it would've been game over!

Brands were always about trust. Well, now we have the wherewithal and motivation to truly walk that talk. To interpret, align, advise, educate, service, and inspire. And provide unified services and solutions for all of our customers (2012).

How else are all of these forces converging and interacting? **Advances in technology and the power of mobile devices coupled with continuously emerging and evolving social media platforms have empowered people to gain a far more equal status with the companies and organizations who promote and deliver (or not) products and services and who take clear responsibility (or not) for their societal impact.** And yet this empowering technology sparks skepticism in this same individual: how is all this private data captured from my mobile device and my online activity being used and safeguarded (or not)? This caution, in turn, has yielded demands and standards of technology.

Alessandra Lariu, executive creative director at frog design and co-founder of SheSays, puts it this way: *"Things need to be fixed on many levels: transparency (users being able to see who knows what facts about them), access (users having a copy of the data themselves), and control (users owning the data or rights to their data exclusively)"*. She then points to the new business and revenue models emerging to address these demands:

> *The quest to give users more transparency, access, and control is on its way. A few companies have been working on giving individuals full control of their digital behavior that could hugely impact the dynamics of advertising. Projects like Tent, Kinetx, and Gluu allow other services to access data only when they can be trusted. These two-sided contracts mean users can then negotiate with Visa, Apple, and BestBuy and find terms that work for both parties. That's a power shift. (2012)*

Likewise, people are making less of a distinction between the tumultuous world in which they find themselves and what they expect their product and service providers to do about it. The trend will be a crucial pillar for future advertising and business strategy in general. As Yasir Dhannoon, product manager at HarperCollins Publishers, says, *"Occupy Wall Street, the Arab Spring, the #blacklivesmatter movement, and (who knows what may come) are simple proofs of the development of a digital-savvy civil society"* (2015).

The 2014 Edelman Trust Barometer found that now and into the future, one of the best ways for businesses to redefine how they create value is through social issues. Edelman notes that some of the key benefits are enhanced loyalty, a more engaged and inspired following of customers and employees, and an enlivened corporate and brand reputation. Clearly, this is what many people are demanding. And, as more do so, others from unexpected segments are taking note and adding this benchmark to what they expect of brands and the companies whose products and services they buy.

Edelman goes on to note that when considering the "how" aspect of delivering social impact, a standard or siloed approach is not enough; efforts must be expansive and orchestrated, addressing strategically selected issues (Cone 2014). Rather than purchase products from a cold and impersonal conglomeration that's donating a microscopic portion of proceeds to charity, empowered and skeptical individuals would rather spend their money with a brand that has a solid sense of responsibility and a track record to back it up. Kamini Banga, founder/director of Dimensions Consultancy, author, and columnist, states it simply:

> *It is becoming clear that brands need to go beyond just 'selling' the product to purpose based conversations. They need to have a point of view and a set of values and beliefs that they espouse. This calls for a shift from building a campaign to starting a movement such as Dove's "Real Beauty" or Mark & Spencer's "Look Behind the Label" campaign highlighting ethical sourcing and manufacturing of their products earning the company the distinction of being the most responsible retailer. (2012)*

A Nielsen survey of 28,000 online respondents in 56 countries found that 66 percent of people worldwide prefer to spend their money with companies who have programs and initiatives that benefit society at large, and 46 percent are willing to pay extra to support said companies. However, not all causes are created equal—most socially conscious people in the same Nielsen study thought that environmental sustainability, improving STEM education, and eradicating poverty and hunger were the top three imperatives for companies looking to do good (Nielsen 2012). As Maria Luisa Francoli Plaza, board member of ISP Digital Advisory Board states, *"Media and brands can no longer ignore consumers' calls for more socially responsible behavior—tomorrow's successful companies will put social responsibility and consumer well-being at the core of their media and marketing strategies while helping consumers play an active part in their community and/or cause"* (2012).

The Havas Media Group conducts an annual survey of 300,000 people on 1,000 brands in 12 industries across 34 countries to create its Meaningful Brands report, an index that measures the potential business benefits gained by a brand when it is seen to improve our well-being and quality of life. According to the 2015 report, "People want brands to improve their lives and the lives of the people they care about. Brands that focus on improving society and on making our lives easier and healthier, gain a greater share of our existence and receive higher levels of engagement and trust in return" (Meaningful Brands 2015).

The report found significant benefits of brands with the highest Meaningfulness, as defined by personal well-being, collective well-being, and marketplace.

> *Meaningful Brands see their marketing Key Performance Indicators (KPIs) perform 100 percent better overall compared with less Meaningful Brands. With every 10 percent improvement in meaningfulness performance, individual brand KPIs grow by 2.5 percent for Familiarity, 4.9 percent for Overall Impression, 6.6 percent for Purchase Intent, 3.2 percent Repurchase Intent, 4.8 percent for Advocacy, and 10.4 percent for Premium Pricing. Meaningful Brands gain, on average, 46 percent more share of wallet. Meaningful Brands outperform the stock market by 133 percent, with the top 25 brands delivering an annual share return of nearly 12 percent. (Meaningful Brands 2015)*

Just as the brands and their collaborators whom we admire take a compelling concept and bring it to life through a surprising story, here we feature a story from one of our Advertising 2020 contributors, Bruce Neve, former CEO Starcom Mediavest Group, to help us bring to life these concepts we have been discussing. Imagine the future scenario he describes in Vignette 1.

VIGNETTE 1: A DAY IN YOUR NOT-SO-FUTURE LIFE

As I walked into the bathroom, the body-scanning sensors could tell I had had a rough night. Sure enough, looking into the mirror, it displayed an ad for Tylenol (extra strength), which was dynamically inserted as sponsor of my morning sports video highlights. In addition, a coupon offer from Nabob coffee was presented along with my daily agenda, which I dropped into my mobile watch.

My automated home system had already connected with Google self-drive and ordered me a car. Since I had scored over 1,000 points last month based on my social sharing activity, I received an offer to try one of three new breakfast items from a sponsor, Tim Hortons, with the caveat to "please share your thoughts on the breakfast crab cake sandwich with your social network." I devoured the greasy delight that was delivered with my vehicle while riding in the back seat of my selfie-car as it drove toward the city.

The ads that rose from the ether as I looked out the window were personalized and obviously behaviorally driven with time and place considered. I somewhat regretted renting access to my personal data profile (purchases, preferences, geo location, content consumed, real-time body monitoring) but I needed the financial boost.

When I selected quiet, contemplative music for the drive, I wasn't surprised when the "brought to you by" sponsors were a spa and a yoga studio; both offered same week specials if booked within an hour and a voice link to testimonials from "friends" within my own social graph.

At the office I entered the Google collaboration holodeck with five others; we connected to the global team (another 12 members) and used voice, gesture, and touch-screen tech to share, move, grab, iterate on ideas, designs, models (which we 3D printed) for the proposed Olympic Stadium design for the Toronto 2028 games.

On the way home later I received several invitations to stop or to order dinner for home delivery all based on known preferences, what I ate yesterday, my bio read for today, with ratings from within my social sphere. I decided on delivery (noodles), and once home, decided I needed a good laugh, so asked my virtual video concierge for all Academy Award–winning comedies of the past decade, along with ratings by friends and also asked to see if anyone wanted to coview and connect this evening.

I caught up on sports headlines and when the downhill skiing results were shown, it gave me a reminder so I linked into the local ski store to book a sharpening/wax and read some testimonials on a new ski boot used by one of the competitors. Not surprisingly, the next ad served was for a last-minute deal at Mount Tremblant, with video links to live hill cams for ski conditions and a music video for a band playing at the resort that weekend. I booked immediately with my mobile phone/wallet and shared out my plan to see if I could get some friends to tag along (three booked that hour!).

While watching the comedy film, I was on Twitter and received sponsored Twitter amplified comedy shorts; both were out-takes from the movie I was watching and "best of" clips from the actor's other work.

I ended the day in bed with my e-book reading a few pages to me, along with sharing tomorrow's weather (brought to you by Chanook Winter Tires—must mean overnight snow), and any key meetings on my calendar (a reminder from Timex).

— Bruce Neve, Former CEO, Starcom Mediavest Group (2013).

What we find compelling about the "futuristic day in the life" Bruce paints is that the vast majority of what he describes is not only possible today, but is being put into practice, tested, and evaluated for new levels of effectiveness relative to traditional approaches by marketers across every category.

And equally compelling is how he helps us see the future from the perspective of a person, rather than a brand. Instead of describing all of the ways a brand is trying to talk at, to, and with its audience, he flips it around to force us to start with what is going on in this person's life, head, and heart. Importantly, this shift in focus is not merely narrative technique. As Don E. Schultz, professor emeritus of service, The Medill School, Northwestern University explains, *"By*

2020 . . . advertiser talking will be replaced by advertiser listening. Hearing what the customer is saying will be more important than trying to devise a break-through creative idea. Answering customer questions. Filling customer needs. Right now, not tomorrow" (2012). The core of Bruce's description reflects this: It is told from the perspective of the person who is "always on;" empowered to lead a life of value exchange or sharing with the brands he allows into his current and future endeavors as he determines their incremental value to what he needs, and where he is going.

Imagine what you and your brand could do to create value throughout an individual's day in all the ways that you interact with them. Let's deconstruct what Bruce describes in the vignette.

"As I walked into the bathroom, the body-scanning sensors could tell I had had a rough night" (Neve 2013).

In January 2015, The Next Web reported that "Mobile scanning software maker Itseez3D has released an update to its 3D-scanner app that can accommodate full-body 3D models. Designed to work with Occipital's Structure Sensor—a snap-on hardware device—ItSeez3D now allows the iPad to create realistic full-body models from 3D scans. Previously, it could only scan head and shoulders" (Dove 2015). The app itself is free in the iTunes store. By asking us,*"Imagine what your product or service could do with this technology,"* Erik du Plessis, non-executive chairman of Millward Brown South Africa, urges us to take this research even further.

"Sure enough, looking into the mirror, it displayed an ad for Tylenol (extra strength) which was dynamically inserted as sponsor of my morning sports video highlights" (Neve 2013).

Using increasingly refined artificial intelligence and cognitive computing tools, marketers are now able to deliver personalized content including video customized according to the device on which it is used and the geographic location of where the content is being viewed. They can also refine the content based on relevant environmental information about the weather, the news, cultural developments, and so forth. "Programmatic advertising has gotten a lot of hype in the past 12 to 24 months, but it's finally fair to say that today, holdouts on participation are proving the exception, not the norm," says Lauren Fisher, analyst for eMarketer (2014). "2014 has proven a pivotal year, and with the majority of infrastructure now laid and testing well in progress, we'll see programmatic ad spending explode from 2015 into 2016" (2014). It's still an evolving landscape, but now it's the Wild Midwest instead of the Wild, Wild West. East Coast establishment is just around the corner.

How far could you leverage the automation and the programmatic and artificial intelligence capability that can better connect with your customers and clients?

"In addition, a coupon offer from Nabob coffee was presented [in my bathroom mirror] along with my daily agenda which I dropped into my mobile watch" (Neve 2013).

With the release of Apple Watch, wearable technologies went mainstream. And while only just starting to take off, companies have been experimenting with wearables that provide real-time, contextualized information for years. Stop to wrap your mind around this benign phrase: contextualized information. Contextualized includes the wearer's biometrics (heart rate, mood), coupled with facial and voice recognition technologies, connected to social network and other publically available data, powered by affordable artificial intelligence to make sense of this, which then delivers relevant information via augmented reality and/or even triggers additional actions. And all this is doable now. Technology futurist Shelly Palmer, managing director digital media group at Landmark Ventures, imagines a future where there is a *"Kurzweilian split of our species into three new suborders: fully organic humans, exo-digitally enhanced humans, and endo-digitally enhanced humans"* (2013). Whether or not this reality comes to be, we do seem to be heading toward the possibility.

Interestingly, some of the strongest uses are on the B2B side. Though it halted its consumer offering in mid-2014, Google Glass continues on with its Glass at Work certified partners. As reported by Marketing Land, the first companies announced include:

- **APX:** APX Labs makes Skylight, the leading business software for Glass. It provides workers with hands-free, real-time access to enterprise data and the expertise they need to do their job. Skylight is used by Fortune 500 companies spanning multiple industries.

- **Augmedix:** Doctors spend over a third of their day pushing and pulling information to and from the Electronic Health Record. Augmedix provides a service for doctors that allows them to reclaim this time and refocus it on what matters most: patient care.

- **CrowdOptic:** CrowdOptic's software detects significant broadcast events from mobile and wearable devices, and provides breathtaking content for live broadcasts and context-aware applications for the sports, entertainment, building/security, and medical industries.

- **GuidiGO:** GuidiGO's mission is to inspire people to connect with art and culture through a compelling mobile storytelling experience. Glass brings us closer to that vision, and by partnering with museums and cultural institutions this becomes accessible to everyone.

- **Wearable Intelligence:** Wearable Intelligence creates Glassware for energy, manufacturing, healthcare, and more. Their workflow, communications, training, and data access products are in the field at some of the world's best known companies. (McGee 2014)

And as wearables move into mainstream with the advent of the Apple Watch, Hayley Ard, Stylus Media Group writes in *WIRED*:

> "Smartwatches shift existing technology to a new location—from the pocket to the wrist. More exciting are second-skin devices such as embeddables, ingestibles, and hearables. These will include flexible technologies that blend into our skin; devices that are controlled by eye-motion sensors; and earbuds that measure and respond to our heart rate. All are part of the ongoing journey to create technology that is so deeply interwoven with our lives that it becomes almost invisible." (Ard 2015)

What new value creation opportunities do wearables and other emerging technologies offer for your brand?

"My automated home system had already connected with Google self-drive and ordered me a car. . . . On the way home later I received several invitations along the way to stop or to order dinner for home delivery all based on known preferences, what I ate yesterday, my bio read for today, with ratings from within my social sphere" (Neve 2013).

On-demand vehicles to deliver you stress-free to your destination while you reduce your carbon footprint are the future. What do you need or want along this journey? A bit of entertainment? Updates for the day? Information to make decisions, be productive, support your loved ones?

In an article in *WIRED* from January 2015 titled, "Consumers Are in the Connected Car's Driver Seat in 2015," the author describes the increasing prominence of the "connected car":

> Car manufacturers and technology companies are racing to provide the best solution that will further usher in the Internet-of-Things with cars as a key part of the infrastructure. In fact, a recent report reveals that, by 2020, 90 percent of vehicles will have built in connectivity.
>
> This year alone, three giants—Microsoft, Google, and Apple—have announced their forthcoming "connected car" platforms . . . They all aim to bring the functionality of your mobile device right to your vehicles center consul and we'll soon find out who takes the cake.
>
> But it's more than mobile. It's a large growing market full of infotainment, apps designed for cars, digital diagnostics, monitoring services for new drivers, and enhanced navigation systems among other services, which is estimated to grow to nearly $270 billion by 2020. A giant leap from the $47 billion mark it's at today. It will be interesting to see what developments are in store for the coming year, but it can be safe to expect consumer needs to be at their center. (Kelly 2015)

Connected—from connected home to connected health to connected cities—opens up worlds of opportunities to deliver valuable communications and experiences at just the right moment. What are you doing to assess where your products and services fit into this connected future?

"Since I had scored over 1000 points last month based on my social sharing activity, I received an offer to try one of three new breakfast items from a sponsor, Tim Hortons, with the caveat to 'please share your thoughts on the breakfast crab cake sandwich with your social network'" (Neve 2013).

What is being described is gaming. As Mark Holden, worldwide strategy and planning director at PHD Media explains:

> *The concept of "gaming" will blur with the real world. Finally, the deeply connected social networks will allow for the emergence of what is being termed "gamification." Global research group, Gartner, predicts that 50 percent of companies that manage innovation and research will use some form of game-logic to motivate people's involvement and contribution. Early examples can be seen in companies such as The Extraordinaires—which reward people with points for contributing to causes set by external companies or organizations. One U.S. example was a game to encourage the photographing and geo-tagging of defibrillators so that the emergency services could direct people to their nearest one. In the UK, the Guardian used game mechanics to get people to trawl through hundreds of thousands of MPs expenses and categorize them.*
>
> *Game mechanics tap into something incredibly powerful and unleash rampant engagement way beyond most affordable financial incentives that could be offered. Game dynamics will be used for major tasks.In fact, the largest game-based system is still Wikipedia, which is built with all of the fundamental game mechanics. The front-end facias will be as much fun as playing Farmville, but the effect of our actions is offering real utility in the world.*
>
> *The Mark Zuckerberg of this "gamification" revolution is the twenty-year-old founder and CEO of a company called SCVNGR (pronounced Scavenger), Seth Priebatsch. SCVNGR wants to build a game layer on top of the world—and it is starting off by bringing "gamification" to the world of marketing. Its website and app enables small businesses to set challenges, such as tweeting or taking pictures whilst within the store in order to unlock complimentary products.*
>
> *Towards and beyond 2020, it is likely that a large percentage of us will be playing games; the resultant effect of which will be either greater corporate productivity, enhanced promotion for companies and brands (and free product for us), or contributions to significant human projects. (2012)*

How can gamification enhance your interactions with your current and potential customers?

"The ads that rose from the ether as I looked out the window were personalized and obviously behaviorally driven with time and place considered" (Neve 2013).

The desire for, and power of, personalization is one of the single biggest concepts mentioned by our Advertising 2020 contributors and a concept that Jerry has been promoting since 2001, with his seminal work on convergence marketing and the empowered consumer.

Russell Dubner, U.S. CEO, Edelman, asserts that customer service in particular will be subject to personalization and customization: *"A new generation of consumers has a new set of expectations for personalized, on-demand support from brands, which Helpouts by Google and the Mayday button of Amazon Kindle have taken to the next level. In 2020 live, immediate customer interaction will be the norm for brands and organizations and a centerpiece to their marketing strategy"* (2013).

Or as, Anneliese Rapp, corporate communications coordinator at 72andSunny phrases it:

> *The individual is increasingly the shaper of her own identity and its on- and offline presentation, thanks in large part to the proliferation of badge brands and ways to badge them.*
>
> - *She is a commentator with a voice in conversations that were once one-way monologues.*
> - *She is her own expert—and when she's not, she's as likely to ask another individual as a so-called authority.*
> - *She is a content programmer, choosing what she wants, when she wants it, and how she wants it.*
> - *She is a creator and distributor of her own content of all kinds, large and small—a micro-network with an utterly unique and wildly eclectic POV.*
>
> *In other words, she is no longer the consumer of media. She is the medium—the most trusted and most personal channel through which content is created, flows, finds shape, and gets presented to the world. (2012)*

Alok Lall, executive director at McCann Worldgroup, describes how "hyper-personalization of advertising will indeed further empower the consumer but it may also save advertising from its predicted doom:"

> *Today, Google has become a platform that has the answer to almost everything; Facebook has become a place where one can live out his or her alter ego. So in order to develop a future for advertising brands, there could come into existence: a Need Bar. The Need Bar would be personalized for every consumer, so as to give him the ability to look*

for anything he needs at any time. This would result in a brand not only being present in the life of a consumer, but also catering to his every need, from any brand. If Sanjay, sitting in his office, wants to order lunch from a restaurant close by on a limited budget, all he will have do is to enter this appeal in his Need Bar, and he will be provided with all the possibilities available (2012).

And how this personalization will be developed will itself evolve. As Walter McDowell, professor emeritus at University of Miami suggests, *"Inevitably, the future of advertising will incorporate more consumer knowledge derived from the hard sciences, such as biology, chemistry, and physics, to complement that acquired from the softer sciences of psychology and sociology"* (2012).

"When I selected quiet, contemplative music for the drive, I wasn't surprised when the 'brought to you by' sponsors were a spa and a yoga studio; both offered same week specials if booked within an hour and a voice link to testimonials from 'friends' within my own social graph" (Neve 2013).

This is the vision from the other side of disruption, evolution, and potential for integration across the media landscape. In this future vision, similar to the first television "soap operas," which were made possible by detergent companies, the advertisers are making desirable content available in exchange for the right to connect with an affluent individual. But in this case, the value exchange bar has been significantly raised to demand highly relevant and contextualized content, including extra value in the booking incentive and a highly frictionless way to share the goodness with others, thereby extending the reach and relevance and value of the message.

With the popularity of media that is less ad-dependent (everything from *The Economist* to Instagram to HBO), Tom Morton, director of strategy at co:collective, noted that the young and the wealthy are disappearing from the traditional paid media landscape. Why should other people be held hostage, simply because they don't have the technological or financial option to opt-out of bad, irrelevant, intrusive, and disrespectful messaging? Perhaps because studies show that a tiny percentage of them will succumb and as a result increase KPIs? In a world of what advertising could and should be, this arrogance and ecosystem pollution is doomed. As Lisa Colantuono, copresident at AAR Partners explains, *". . . most consumers exclaim, 'I don't want someone else dictating the media I get every day. I want to be in charge of what I see and when I see it.' Bottom line, consumers want to feel more in control—a basic human desire—and have a meaningful relationship with the brand"* (2013). Responding to this "basic human desire" in everyone, which is being brought to the fore through the intersection of advances in technology, the changing media landscape, and empowerment and skepticism in consumers, will enable a far more win-win equation.

"Once there and in the Google collaboration holodeck with five others; connected to the global team (another 12) we used voice, gesture, touch screen tech to share, move, grab, iterate on ideas, designs, models

(which we 3D printed) for the proposed Olympic Stadium design for the Toronto 2028 games" (Neve 2013).

Here Bruce alludes to another of the five forces of change: new and emerging business and revenue models, which in turn are "made possible by" new collaboration technologies, focused on an omnichannel product-service experience with high potential for transformative social good.

But let's just start with the ways in which new business and revenue models might be at play here. Imagine if he and the five others were meeting in a PeerSpace office (a sharing model) and the global team he describes was formed specifically for this client (a customer-driven/holistic model). What if they were from different companies (the network orchestration model), each of which meet rigorous standards of social and environmental performance, accountability, and transparency" (the B Corp certification). What if the global team was comprised of independent players from highly diverse disciplines secured through an expertise-sourcing platform (an open innovation model), Olympic athletes and fans (the co-creation model), and the real time interactive voice and visual display of a cognitive computing system they called "Florence" (perceptual computing). Add that they leveraged innovative approaches hatched in emerging markets (frugal innovation) and were compensated initially on the strength of the concept and over time based on post-game customer feedback and endorsement (a rewarding consumer model), the financial success of the stadium (performance-based model), and the social and cultural impact on Toronto before, during, and after the Olympics (impact-based model).

Depending on where you sit, your current approaches are either being disrupted by those employing these new and emerging business and revenue models, or you are the one using these new approaches to succeed where more traditional approaches are falling behind.

How are you learning about and leveraging new business and revenue models to try creative new approaches to the challenges that keep you awake at night and create more win-win and less zero-sum outcomes?

"I ended the day in bed with my e-book reading a few pages to me, along with sharing tomorrow's weather (brought to you by Chanook Winter Tires—must mean overnight snow), and any key meetings on my calendar (a reminder from Timex)" (Neve 2013).

As Bruce is tucked into bed, we find so much that is compelling and inspiring about his vision of the future. The reality is that brands need people and people need brands. Throughout his future day, Bruce's life is made better by companies who want him to purchase their products and services. There is an explicit and agreed-upon value exchange delivered through exceptional experiences with just the right information at just the right time in an easily actionable way. Though it does not pretend to be comprehensive in its future vision, it helps us to start to embrace the five forces of change that make a more desired future not only more desirable, but infinitely possible, with the requisite will. And the effects of these forces of change are, as Keith Blanchard, owner and CEO of Teamstream

Productions notes, are becoming more and more noticeable: *"... most advertisers by 2020 will have completed their natural evolution from adjacency ('stand next to the stuff people want!') to interruption ('stand in the way of the stuff people want!') to content marketing ('be the stuff people want!')"* (2012).

What if we were just able to make the relationship between people and brands not only a little better, but at least a net positive and what the heck, why not all the way to a decidedly and mutually acknowledged win-win? What's a revolution for if not for a far better future?

Bruce's entry brings to life so many of the concepts that our Advertising 2020 contributors mention as forces of change that have the potential to lift us out of our current way of thinking and planning and strategizing and executing. We also want to highlight another entry, beautifully visual, uniquely creative, and inspirationally brought to us by a NextGen team from Wunderman Z, Ruth Lim and Kai Hui Tan, from their vantage point in Singapore. They describe a future where advertising leverages advances in science and technology to invent a new medium that empowers the consumer to cope with the world using a new business model *(see Figure 1.2)*.

VIGNETTE II: INTRODUCING THE SUPER POD

In 2020, the effects of global warming and climate change can no longer be disregarded. Summer's heat so scorching it'll burn, blistering cold winters so icy it'll bite. Flooding, desertification, natural disasters ... it'll be unbearable to stay outside. It will be pertinent for humans to find a way to adapt to the harsh environment.

With the Super Pod, outdoor advertising will be highly personal and incentivized.

As the pod will be able to detect the user's brainwaves, advertising can be targeted not only to the consumer's demographic characteristics, but also to the consumer's current state of mind, his/her mood and needs, and so on.

As experiences are increasingly moving into the digital space over the years, energy that is used to power our digital devices will become, more than ever, a necessity to daily life. Thus, advertisements will make consumers come to them, with incentives such as free energy to recharge their pods: "Watch this ad on Coca-Cola's latest drink and get 10 percent more power for your Super Pod." (Lim and Tan 2012)

Lim and Tan go on to describe the many attributes that enable the Super Pod to interact with the environment of the future, including: augmented reality maps, digital fingers as credit cards, and an immersive outdoor advertising experience that lets people *"see, hear, smell, and even feel advertising messages, stimulated by the sensors in their super pods."*

The second part of the Super Pod vignette comes back to the present to answer, "What Do We Do Now?" Their recommendation captures the millennial sensibility, prioritizing the creation of "sustainable" advertising: *"Despite climate change being a global crisis, masses of natural resources are wasted every day because of advertising ... It is about time for advertisers to start learning to adapt to the reducing resources in the environment by producing more environmentally friendly and sustainable advertising."*

Figure 1.2 The Super Pod Envisioned by Ruth Lim and Kai Hui Tan

In addition to prioritizing the environment, Lim and Tan recommend enhancing the digital experience, integrating services into lifestyles, and closing the purchase loop: *"As consumers are becoming increasingly starved for time, advertisers need to think of ways to streamline the purchase process, and make the consumer journey from awareness to purchase as easy and convenient as possible."*

We highlight this entry for several reasons, not the least of which is the wonderful creativity and design elements it embodies (view it in its entirety at wfoa.wharton.upenn.edu). First, what Lim and Tan are proposing is strongly founded in some of the most compelling research about the power of "why" at the intersection of brands, their enterprises, and individuals. In short, people—your intended audience—are more time constrained than ever, and they have so much content they find meaningful to consume. Unless content, at each touchpoint, is at least as much or more meaningful, brands will not earn the right to get their attention.

Second, the proposal delivers content in such a way that multiple sources of value are created: for the creators, for the brand, for those who are working on behalf of the brand, for the consumer, and for the culture and society in which they all live their lives.

As much as these forces of change are disrupting the entire advertising landscape, they also bode well for society and for us individually. From a societal perspective, this suggests that businesses could take a page from the Wharton Social Impact Initiative, led by vice dean Katherine Klein, that declares, "Wharton is committed to being the best business school in the world and *for* the world" (Wharton Social Impact Initiative 2015). We are attracting and developing leaders who seek to achieve both. And from a brand perspective, it's time to recognize that, even if we could get more people to do what is good for the corporate bottom line but bad for humans, we need to stop and find a better way.

As challenging as this is, there have never been more forces providing the wherewithal—technological and psychological—than now. And we are hoping that by getting this point of view out broadly, we'll all have a lot of soulmates who are thinking similarly and working collaboratively to change what we don't like and what we don't want. As Cindy Gallop, founder and CEO of MakeLoveNotPorn, IfWeRanTheWorld, and Behance writes, *"We [need to] find a way to integrate social responsibility into the way we do business on a day-to-day basis, that makes it a key driver of future growth and profitability. I believe that the business model of the future is shared values, plus shared action, equals shared profit—social profit and financial profit"* (2012).

We have only begun to scratch the surface of the multitude of insights that our Advertising 2020 collaborators offer concerning these five forces of change. For Mark Holden, strategy and planning director, PHD UK:

> *Look[ing] at the different technological epochs . . . suggests that the evolutionary drive is that of liberating ourselves from physical and time-based constraints. If you project forward, this suggests that the ultimate end point will be a state of abundance—where you are able to be everywhere with*

everyone and everything in the moment. If we assume that this is the ultimate goal—any technology that ever works will, in some way, enable us to move one step forward to that state. (2012)

Doug Levy, CEO of TapGoods, CEO of MEplusYOU Agency, and chairman of the board at Conscious Capitalism, believes:

By 2020 we will have entered a new era in which I believe companies that do business using a Consumer Era "marketing as manipulation" mindset will become irrelevant and superseded by companies that demonstrate a Relationship Era mindset. As forces at play lead the Relationship Era to the tipping point of wide acceptance, I believe that marketers will be known not as the scoundrels who spin but rather people with the greatest expertise in crafting authentic relationships—and adding the most value to the business. (2013)

Figure 1.3 Beyond Advertising in Action: Five Forces of Change and Opportunity

Beyond Advertising in Action
FIVE FORCES OF CHANGE AND OPPORTUNITY

MISERABLE IN PUERTO RICO—PUERTO RICO TOURISM
Agency: J. Walter Thompson Puerto Rico
Cannes Lions: Gold—Promo & Activation 2015

OBJECTIVE/PROBLEM TO BE SOLVED

In March 2015, a man who had won a free trip to Puerto Rico but couldn't bring his family along documented his trip in a series of tongue-in-cheek photographs posted on Reddit called "Miserable in Puerto Rico." The post of the man making sad faces in various luxurious tropical settings gained viral popularity.

APPROACH

In order to become part of the viral response and not let these jokey photographs dominate the global image of Puerto Rico, JWT Puerto Rico, asked Puerto Rico Tourism to provide the man with an all-expenses paid do-over of the trip. The man returned with his wife and baby and retook all the photos, but this time showing them having fun. Within a few hours on Reddit, the post made it to the number one spot.

THE RESULTS

The post received 2 million views and significant press coverage. With an investment of $8000 and zero media buy, the 14 photos generated over 15 million dollars in earned media and recast the Puerto Rican tourism brand in a positive, light-hearted way.

LESSONS AND OBSERVATIONS

By paying attention to people's experiences in real time, opportunities to provide value can be quickly identified and acted upon. The global nature of the five forces of change and increased speed and complexity made possible this viral and potentially damaging social media post. Harnessing those same forces enabled a creative and memorable response.

CITATION: Cannes Lions Winners, 2015

And we'd be remiss not to include a perspective from the skeptical side, here again from Shelly Palmer:

> *Can a population of semi-connected exo-digitally enhanced humans possibly fend for themselves in a world where Fortune 500 marketing departments apply super-computer power to every aspect of business? It's an unfair fight – far more unfair than it is today. (2013)*

As Palmer reminds us, the five forces of change can bring opportunities for positive as well as negative outcomes. For now, we hope this chapter has convinced you, and those whom you think need convincing, that the world has changed so dramatically that we must go beyond advertising. What does this entail? What is the biggest impediment to "going beyond"? Entrenched mindsets that limit the art of the possible. In the next chapter we take a look at our mental models about what advertising is and has to be, instead of what it could/should be.

Key Takeaways

- **The only certainty today is change. We can't predict the future, nor can we control it, but we can imagine and aspire for a certain type of future. Change can, and should be, guided.**
- **Technological advancements are impacting our social fabric, but equally society's expectations guide technology: this is a powerful feedback loop.**
- **Ethics and utility are increasingly valued equally: the newest technology will mean little without an authentic identity.**
- **Connectivity is key: between platforms, within organizations, across fields. Crucially, these connections must be technical and emotional. We can make the world more, not less, humane *(see Figure 1.3)*.**

Chapter 2

Challenging Entrenched Mindsets about "Advertising"

The future of advertising is not about new technological platforms or killer apps. It is about a change in the industry mindset. That is, it is about opening our collective mind.

— Yaakov Kimelfeld, *Chief Research Officer, Merkle (2012)*

If you ask most people around the world what they think about advertising, the responses are pretty dismal. "Manipulative, interruptive, annoying, lowest common denominator." Not pretty. And pretty understandable given much of what we are exposed to.

Let's just take the banner ad that pops up and won't go away. How about the video ad that starts to play, loudly, without your even clicking it. Or being forced to watch the same ad over and over before being allowed to navigate to where you want to go online. The ad for something you already bought that continues to follow you. The offensive ad during sports you really wish your kids didn't see. The late-night mattress-warehouse dealer who still insists on having the owner scream at you. The junk mail that you deliver straight to the recycle bin. The unavoidable message on hold, during an interminable customer service call that chirps how great they are. What is your worst story about advertising? Why do advertisers think it is acceptable to create experiences that degenerate into intrusive and annoying clutter? Why don't they/we care? Why can they/we get away with this waste of everyone's time and energy? Brian d'Allesandro, senior vice president of digital intelligence at Dstillery, writes:

> *To elaborate on this point, let's quickly review the state of things today. We don't have pop-ups anymore (thankfully), but we still have loud commercials, full-screen takeovers, disturbingly persistent (and creepy) retargeting, and mobile ads that manage to trick my fat thumbs into clicking on them. There is no doubt that advertisers are embracing the latest technologies in delivery, targeting and measurement, but it mostly feels like this is all for their own ROI benefit, and not exactly for creating a better experience for the consumer. (2012)*

Marketers and their constituents have traditionally had an equally negative reaction. As Chris Arnold, creative director and cofounder of Creative Orchestra puts it,

> *Generation after generation comes into the ad industry and just accepts the status quo rules. And those of us, few in number, who challenge the status quo win over few supporters. Human nature, being what it is, most people prefer the way things are to the way they could be (2013).*

And media and other content providers are in the same boat, often viewing advertising as a necessary evil that enables what they really want to offer, which is desirable content and a great experience, which in turn attracts valuable audiences and users. Arthur Tauder, founding partner at Thunderhouse captures the issue concisely, writing:

> *For a hundred years, advertising has been mostly a one-way street dominated by a single mindset: "pushing" messages to audiences. Great efforts and great strides have been made on inferring the target audiences for advertising delivery. The industry has achieved new heights in technology-driven sophistication for targeting push messages to the point where many believe that advertisers and media have the crossed the line in violating consumer privacy.*
>
> *Today the customer audience is still considered a passive recipient of advertising—never asked directly for input on what products and what messages are of interest. One result: advertising is viewed as disruptive by many consumers and to be avoided when given the option. Time and again, the consumer has reacted positively to technology-driven empowerment. By 2020, customers will have a voice in both what advertising will be seen and in what medium. The balance will swing to favor "pull" rather than "push." (2012)*

All these negative impressions alone should be enough for us to create better advertising. What if people loved and welcomed all advertising because it was just so darned good?

Even with all these negative impressions of advertising, what happens when you ask people about their favorite ad? Most light up. They show you something they just shared because it was so great and so meaningful. They tell you that they now follow a brand because of the great value they get from what the brand says *and* does. And they look forward to what else this brand will deliver. They remember it because it is memorable. It sticks. And then, they want to learn more. And that is either easy or burdensome. They want to purchase, and the purchase experience does or doesn't measure up. They try the product or service and it either does or doesn't. They contact the firm and what happens next does or doesn't match the promise of the ads.

What if marketers and their organizations saw their marketing and advertising budget as an investment and a value creation engine rather than as an expense to be squeezed? What if the brands were seen as bringing not only advertising dollars but valued content to the media properties and channels they use?

What if the creative, analytic, and strategic genius that lies within the sum total of the world's advertising, media, digital, creative, etc. agencies, research firms, ad tech companies, sponsorship, brand placement—and all the other players who feed off "advertising"—were given a more inspired brief: increase sales *and* leave the world a better place in the process. Come in on budget *and* be proud to tell your family about what you helped create. Help us, all of us, be in thought, word, and deed, something truly exceptional.

What if this community were expanded to *all* those whose actions impacted the brand and how it actually came to life for its audience? Not only the traditional stakeholders, but also others who could potentially describe the broader value of the brand and the brand experience in even more creative and impactful ways.

What if all the ways that brands were brought to life with their potential and current customers were thought of holistically, and resources were allocated accordingly?

What if every bit of the $500 billion paid, earned, and owned advertising expenditure around the globe not only resulted in sales and profit, but also resulted in a net positive impact on society and culture? What if, in addition to impacting sales and profit, it made a positive impact on the lives of all those who were involved in it and who were influenced by it?

Why not?

With all this potential for good, why is most advertising stuck in an adversarial, zero-sum game among its key players? If the combined and interrelated five forces of change outlined in the last chapter are providing both the compelling need to change and the tools to transform to a new, more desirable future, what is holding us back?

The number-one answer from our Advertising 2020 Community: entrenched mindsets, anchored by entrenched business and revenue models. Sally Williams, global president of business development and client relations, DAS for Omnicom Group, explains, *"Modern Marketing is different—that's clear. But what do we need to do differently as we approach 2020? First is to accept that it's not business as usual. The speed of change means we need a completely different mindset"* (2012).

With this acknowledgment, we tapped into Jerry's years of work on the crucial role of mental models for transformational leadership and found the critical first step in fully benefiting from this pivotal time in advertising. His research and work with senior executives suggests that the primary obstacle keeping us back from fully embracing the potential of change is the current way we *think* about advertising.

As Albert Einstein famously asserted, "Without changing our pattern of thought, we will not be able to solve the problems we created with our current pattern of thought."

Without changing our mental models, we find ourselves in a reactive mode, scrambling to understand the changes and struggling to assess where the new fits in with the old.

The Power and Potential of Mental Models

What are mental models, why are they important, and why must they be challenged?

In the words of Peter Senge, director of the Center for Organizational Learning at the MIT Sloan School of Management, "Mental models are deeply held internal images of how the world works, images that limit us to familiar ways of thinking and acting. Very often, we are not consciously aware of our mental models or the effects they have on our behavior" (1990). **Put another way, mental models are ways in which we explain, simplify and make predictions about the world to ourselves.**

If we lived in a static environment, our mental models would serve us well. However, in an environment under transformation, such as the one we described in the last chapter and live in today, current mental models may prevent us from seeing and responding to changes, capitalizing on opportunities offered by the changing business environment, and be blinding us to potential threats to our business and current way of thinking. Most of our mental models about advertising were established back in the Mad Men era. Williams describes:

> *Advertising was born in a different time—and in a different media world. It was about mass communication to mass markets for mass manufactured products. Advertising worked because it was one of the only ways consumers could get information. In a world where information is limited, "content" has a special authority. Advertising wasn't just a form of communication—it was a substitute for essential inputs about culture, society, and the way the world works. (2012)*

Are we still thinking about the mass communication of limited information? How might that be limiting our grasp of new media?

Although fixed representations of the world can keep our minds from becoming overwhelmed, we can miss important details and trends that don't align with our expectations and assumptions. In Jerry's book, *The Power of Impossible*

Thinking, he explores the notion of the inner city. Imagine if someone asked us whether we'd like to invest in the inner city. Most of us would probably say "no" because of associations with endemic crime, poverty, and drugs. However, what if someone suggested investing in an "emerging domestic market?" **"Emerging domestic market" captures a sense of possibility and opportunity associated with emerging markets, but of course it's referring to the same reality as "inner city."** Nothing has changed, just our perception. (Wind and Crook, 2005)

For another example, think of a great accomplishment such as Roger Bannister's four-minute mile in 1954. Before he broke that barrier, the four-minute mile was considered the human physical limit. As soon as Bannister broke it, it was broken again within 46 days and several times over that same year by other runners. Nothing had changed in the human physiology, of course—the mental model about what was possible had changed.

And for some, this example resonates the best. You are walking down a dark city street toward your car parked several blocks away, when you hear footsteps behind you. You don't turn around, but you quicken your pace. You remember a news story from a few weeks ago about a robbery at knifepoint in the neighborhood. Your pace quickens. But the footsteps behind you are also moving very quickly. The person is catching up to you. At the end of the block, under the streetlight, the steps are immediately behind you. You turn suddenly. You recognize the familiar face of one of your colleagues, heading to the same parking lot. With a sigh of relief, you say hello, and you and he continue on your way together.

What happened in these examples? Reality didn't change; the only change is what was happening in the story inside our minds. Our mental models help us make sense of the world, but they also can negatively impact our ability to see the true picture.

These mental models are tied closely to the Five Forces of Change we outlined in the previous chapter. Change is happening, pushing us to hold our mental models up to the light, to question the shadows they cast—once so absolute—on the wall of the proverbial cave. And when we step outside our mental models, magic really can happen. In his seminal book, *Flourish*, Marty Seligman upends the traditional goal of psychology to relieve human suffering and instead, through his Positive Psychology movement, focuses on exploring personal attitudes and aims with the goal of raising the bar for the human condition (Seligman, 2011). Indeed, his work has influenced the tone and aspirations of this Beyond Advertising project.

From a brand perspective, take, for example, a recent development by R/GA for McCormick—the spice company. Such a mundane and practical product might seem immune from the advances in technology our contributors identified as game-changers. Chris Stutzman, managing director of business transformation at R/GA puts it this way: "McCormick is a brand that dominates the spice category, but how can it engage in the connected age?" (Marketing Matters Blog, February 2015). R/GA came up with an answer: FlavorPrint, a digital service that essentially works out what flavors you—and each of your family members—like. The system suggests hundreds of recipes based on your preferences, helping a cook get out of a recipe rut, encouraging consumers to try new McCormick spices, and, of course, creating connected taste buds. Bringing an old-school product into the digital age was as simple as challenging the mental model of what falls under the "connected" umbrella.

Take a Moment: Your Current Mental Model of Advertising

To change our models we must first recognize them for what they are. A good place to start is with what you might consider as "givens" or that which is "self-evident." Take a moment to jot some notes, or draw some images, or select a song title, or pick a metaphor, or find any other way to express how you currently think about advertising *(see Figure 2.1a)*.

Now what if none of these descriptors had to be true? Or you could just pick the parts of them you like most? Considering the potential for change described in the last chapter and your own insights about the future, what could/should advertising be if it represented the best of what you could personally hope for *(see Figure 2.1b)*? Given that we all are affected by advertising, whether we are in the advertising industry or not, we all have a right to say what it could and should be—at any level, with any title, simply as people who experience advertising and interact with brands throughout our lives.

Figure 2.1a Advertising Is

ADVERTISING IS

WHO:

WHAT:

WHEN:

WHERE:

WHY:

HOW:

Figure 2.1b What could/should they be?

ADVERTISING COULD/SHOULD BE
WHO:
WHAT:
WHEN:
WHERE:
WHY:
HOW:

The Foundations of Mental Models "Beyond Advertising"

> *"Digital advertising has demonstrated the concept of punctuated equilibrium, a theory that originated in evolutionary biology. Punctuated equilibrium posits that evolution is a slow process except when major environmental events precipitate swift biological change. Like an asteroid igniting the evolution of new life forms, the Internet has transformed the organization and methods of the once staid advertising industry."*
>
> — Robert Morais, *Principal, Weinman Schnee Morais (2012)*

As we are experiencing unprecedented change, a "punctuated equilibrium," what are the "givens" of advertising that might be holding us back, and what are the new models that will prepare us for success in a more desirable future?"

Looking across our Advertising 2020 collaborators' collective visions of what advertising could and should be, we thought it would be helpful to contrast the foundational building blocks of the current/former mental models with those that represent the future that we collectively desire, that we envision, and that, together, we have the capacity to co-create. We enlisted the journalistic construct of "who/what/where/when/why/how" to create these building blocks *(see Figure 2.2)*. For each, we simplify the "givens" about what advertising is and we collectively

Figure 2.2 Challenge Entrenched Mental Models

II.
CHALLENGE ENTRENCHED MENTAL MODELS

What is the Best It Could / Should Be?

Across and Among ALL Titles, Roles and Expertise

	CURRENT	TOWARD
WHO?	Marketers and Agencies, through Media, at Target Demographics	Cross-Silo Collaborators
WHAT?	Ads	Orchestrated Value-Creation Touchpoints
WHEN?	Frequency	When Needed, Wanted, Appreciated
WHERE?	Reach	Where Needed, Wanted, Appreciated
WHY?	Push and Persuade For Sales	Multi-Win Outcomes
HOW?	Ad Campaigns	Initiatives in Holistic, Dynamic Ecosystem

Words Matter: Enlist a New Vocabulary

propose new mental models that effectively pose the challenges "What if?" and "Why not?"

It is important to note that not all current mental models are wrong nor need to be changed. Some may continue to prove valuable and may coexist well with new mental models. The main point is to be mindful to

ensure that the mindsets we have are by choice and based on new and future realities. In the sections that follow, we contrast the traditional and the new as stark differences, but in reality, these are better thought of as a spectrum, along which we move and evolve over time.

Mental Model 1

Why: *From Push and Persuade for Sales* toward *Multi-win Outcomes*

The old model of advertising was about making a sale, but the new model recognizes the greater potential for an ongoing relationship with triple-win outcomes—benefits for the brand, people, and society.

Why does advertising exist? If we ask someone on the street, they might say something along the lines of, "To make us want something we don't need and buy something we can't afford." Oof. Neither particularly savory nor inspiring. Not something to be proud of. And not what we envision it could and should be.

Granted, sales must happen for organizations to exist. But does the bar have to be set so low and the focus be so narrow? Given the reach and impact of advertising and brands in our lives and world, more is now expected and demanded. It is beyond dispute that advertising has to deliver results. But if advertising is a value exchange entered into willingly by all parties, a concept we discuss more below, we can re-conceptualize the purpose of advertising. **The new model requires rethinking the singular notion that the purpose of advertising is only to sell as much as possible to as many as possible as soon as possible—a very short-term, narrow view—and not one grounded in research.** The five forces of change are converging to make the new "why" of advertising win/win/win rather than a zero sum game. Cheryl Burgess, CEO and CMO at Blue Focus Marketing, explains: *"The one-way street model of advertising has never been ideal, but today it's poised for a precipitous collapse. Advertising—as it is already becoming today—will be much more about relationship building through transparent, authentic interactions"* (2012).

The relic of the "why" of advertising seems to still persist: Since I, as the advertiser, am paying, you have to put up with whatever I dish out. But think of it this way: just because my date pays for my ticket or dinner, does that give them license to do anything they want? No.

The goals, needs, and desires of brands and people can be in alignment, and be accountable to one another. The new model is non-adversarial—given the turbulent times and the cultural, societal, and economic challenges we face, we have the opportunity to find mutually beneficial opportunities, and find common ground to be on the same side. Advertising could and should achieve the triple bottom line: positive returns for the brand—and all those who build it, the people they hope to serve, and society. As Gillian Graham, CEO of the Institute of Communication Agencies puts it, *"The future of advertising could/should be leading innovation, culture, and social responsibility"* (2014).

Our work in the Wharton Future of Advertising Program has given us the strong sense that we are indeed at the proverbial tipping point. Rumblings have been going on for a while, but there seems to be a confluence of significant initiatives that suggest that a broader notion of "why" is driving the key players in a "beyond advertising" world. And maybe this is the point where those in the traditional area of advertising and marketing take the opportunity to leverage their powerful talents and proven optimism for far more meaningful impact.

Here are three examples from three different camps within the ecosystem: brand executives, advertising agency innovators, and the next generation.

Corporate Leadership

EY's Beacon Institute launched at Davos in 2015 with the goal of "transforming business through the science of purpose." Through events, thought leadership, and community building, they aim to support and facilitate corporate innovation that is "attuned to the changing expectations of customers, employees, and other stakeholders." This community of diverse business leaders agree that "[t]he most effective executive teams are harnessing purpose to innovate and transform all elements of their business—across their strategy and structure, culture and leadership, tools and technologies" (EY 2015).

Agency Innovators

Jonathan Wise, former planner at J. Walter Thompson and Red Bee Media, and anthropologist Ella Saltmarshe launched Comms Labs in London in June 2015 to "help ad agencies do good." As Saltmarshe explains:

> Agencies need to define the positive impact they want to have on the world. Moral neutrality might have served agencies really well in the past, but that is kind of coming close to its sell-by-date. What we are seeing now is that agencies operate in a different world. (Swift 2015)

The Next Generation

In a recent MediaPost op/ed, Melanie Schreffler, editorial director of the Cassandra Report, explains the phenomenon for the rising generation of teens:

> Teens demand to be recognized as the grown-ups they are fast becoming, and it's critical for brands to treat them in a respectful manner that acknowledges their maturity. They see through marketing ploys and don't like companies that merely want to sell to them. Instead, they want brands' help as they progress in life and work to gain new skills that they'll need when they enter the adult world.
>
> From sponsoring contests to establishing a summer workshop program to hiring a lucky fan, brands can be highly influential in teens' seasonal prospects and dreams for the years ahead. And for their young fans, there is nothing as rewarding as recognition of their efforts and work from the brands they love. It shows them that companies value the same things they do and confirms their connections with brands that understand the importance they place on preparing for their futures. (2015)

Easy? No. Quick? Hardly. Ripe for skeptics and doubters? Undoubtedly. But what if it was done right? Could the full upside potential be built into what motivates and incentivizes people to come together to make it happen?

Mental Model 2

What: *From Ads and Campaigns* toward *Orchestrated Value Creation at Every Touchpoint*

The old model involved one-way communication, with advertisers and agencies crafting a message and pushing it out to an audience with the attempt to "convert" as many as possible. The new model acknowledges and invites two-way interactions that create value for brands and all those they impact at every point of interaction. Tara Walpert Levy, managing director of global ad development at Google, describes it this way:

> *Advertising in 2020 should look like a gift. People should seek it out the way they do the best media or apps today because it will be simple and heavily programmed to draw you in with strong human interest, emotion, and/or utility. (2014)*

Is advertising a gift? Is it something people seek out? Perhaps this mental model has not yet caught on widely, but our contributors have been starting to think that the "what" of advertising should be an exchange of value that transpires at every touchpoint. **Each point of interaction between a brand and a person can be an opportunity to collaborate or to serve, and there can be a true value exchange: Your attention in exchange for entertainment, your time in exchange for an offer, your feedback in exchange for a better product, your data in exchange for more personalization.** If we reconfigure our thinking to the consumer point of view, we start to see unlimited new areas of potential value exchange and creation.

When all parties benefit from an exchange, it will be entered into willingly. When we change our mental model of advertising as a positive, value-adding experience, we change the whole idea of an ad from something furtive and unpleasant to something valuable and desired. Isabelle Quevilly, director of brand services at Brilliant Noise (UK), explains, *"Advertising used to be pollution. Today, it's conversation"* (2013). We don't have to calculate how to reach, convince, manipulate, or capture attention and dollars from consumers; we could and should be thinking about what we can offer of value to people so they willingly enter into a relationship with a brand, whether it be temporary or long-lasting. Mark Burgess, president at Blue Focus Marketing, imagines it this way:

> *In 2020, consumers and advertisers will form a collaboration of brands. This model moves beyond traditional advertising and past today's trendy inbound marketing approach as brands assume their new roles as trusted advisors. Brands will have mastered the art of earning consumer trust through the co-creation of valuable content. (2012)*

How can advertisers create interesting and useful experiences in which consumers choose to participate? One example from the past year involved Art Series Hotels in Australia, which found that guests did not appreciate the standard 11 A.M. checkout time. The hotel wondered what would happen if they were to allow guests to check out only when the room was needed for the next guest. The unusual approach, which challenged a long-held industry standard, translated into real value for both travelers and the hotel: an $80,000 budget yielded a 359 percent return from increased bookings and additional services used during the extra hours and days spent in the hotel before check-out (Ferrier and Hall 2013). The communication succeeded on the strength of a game-changing, customer-centric idea.

Another example of mutual value creation comes from IKEA. In 2012, the home-furnishing giant offered to "rent" the space that their catalog would take up in people's homes. Participants were encouraged to keep the catalog at home year-round in exchange for monthly rent checks that could be spent in IKEA stores. The initiative cost $1.3 million in the first eight weeks and yielded a $39.5 million boost in sales during the same period—a return of more than 3,000 percent. The cross-platform campaign used attention-grabbing creative ("Give a catalogue a home and get paid for it") to attract new customers to spend time with the brand. People signed up to receive a catalog—critical opt-in from consumers (Warc 2012).

In general, people don't trust advertising today. Why? Because we've been taught to think of advertising as a zero-sum game where advertisers will say anything to make us buy what they are selling; that the interruption of our media experience is the price we pay for "free content." **We are taught that the purpose of advertising is to increase the company's bottom line at our expense, that we are targets of campaigns, whose military resonance does not inspire confidence. But does this have to be the case?** When advertising is offering a genuine value exchange, individuals can determine for themselves whether they choose to participate in it and brands must *earn* this engagement.

That is why it is especially essential for advertising to be transparent. It is no longer acceptable to practice deception, peddle unsubstantiated statements, or broadcast disrespectful messaging crafted for a cheap attention grab. And it's not just a question of ethics; that type of advertising no longer has a place in the digital information age. As Seth Godin, author and entrepreneur, explains:

> *Now we [consumers] are going to get the truth, whether you want us to or not. So the question is for the companies, are you going to bet on secrets, or you going to bet on open? The companies that are able to bet on open will always do better in a world that is leading to open. (2012)*

Our position is that brand communications and connections with people should be so entertaining, inspiring and/or useful that the brands behind them will want the credit.

Indeed, in an idealized world, brands would work hard to ensure that they are credited with all that they say and do, collaborating to "get it right" and create value, in order to garner the positive results. And this leads us to the next question, the "who" of what advertising could and should be by 2020.

Mental Model 3

Who: *From Siloed Advertising and Marketing* toward *Cross-Silo Collaborators with and for People*

All those involved in creating and distributing and receiving an advertising message used to be limited, sequenced, and siloed. The future, beyond advertising, will involve cross-silo collaborations with and for people.

Who should we be including as players in the solution set of the future? If we set our sights high enough *(see "Why" above)*, maybe the question is who *shouldn't* we include? We are no longer thinking about advertisers as a small unit of people within a greater organization with a specific and limited set of goals and tasks. For the idealized "beyond advertising" future, those involved could and should include a greatly expanded set of potential participants throughout the organization and beyond, as collaborators instead of adversaries; this includes current and potential consumers—fellow individuals who deserve respect and consideration. As David Ogilvy quipped, "The consumer isn't a moron; she's your wife" (1963). By expanding our mental model of the role of players we can start to dismantle limited thinking of who contributes what to the process of value creation. The new model of the "who" beyond advertising involves personalizing all the players and participants rather than treating them as simply a means to an end. Engaging consumers as partners—co-producers, co-designers, co-distributors, and co-marketers—is not easy for those of us who are accustomed to polishing a message to perfection before letting it see the light of day. But as we can see, that is the reality of today and the future. As Mel Exon, managing director at BBH London and cofounder at BBH Labs, writes:

> *Everyone is a Producer. By 2020, a generation who can read and write code will be hitting their stride. Whilst this won't have redefined what we mean by literacy, tools will exist to make information (music, news, fiction, sound, video, design) electronically ubiquitous, manipulatable like clay and yes, probably 3-D printable. And we'll be doing it together. (2012)*

One place to start is to rethink entrenched titles such as "creatives." **For beyond advertising, we will thrive more by recognizing that creative ideas and initiatives can and should come from anywhere, and that teams of creative people from across disciplines are essential given the forces of change.** Thomas Hong-Tack Kim, former executive creative director at Cheil Worldwide Korea, observes:

> *Creative directors must be renewed as creative technologists. The original pair system that consists of a copywriter and an art director must be switched so that everyone is a storyteller, media creator, and a curator all at once. (2012)*

In a conversation on our radio show with Nick Law, global chief creative officer at R/GA and one of the minds behind the Nike Plus campaign, he explained that, "At the highest level, R/GA is divided into two creative hemispheres: the story-telling side, and the systematic side." These two sides of the "R/GA brain" are not isolated: they work closely together, bringing temporal and spatial thinkers together to "create a wonderful symbiosis" (Marketing Matters February 2015).

Recognizing and re-evaluating entrenched mental models that hold us back also requires some serious self-reflection. What are the names we give departments? How do they create silos? What happens if we think outside the titles? In recent years an alphabet soup of new positions have emerged in an attempt to recognize and capitalize on these new roles and potentials: Chief Agility Officer, Chief Content Officer, Chief Experience Officer, Chief Innovation Officer, Chief Growth Officer, Creator of Opportunities, Chief Customer Officer. But even the advent of new titles does not necessarily challenge the mental model adequately.

As Frederik Andersen, chief operations officer, strategy and operations at Vice Media Group + VIRTUE Worldwide, writes:

> *When agencies absorb new creative disciplines, such as storytelling, content creation, brand building, digital innovation, product and packaging design, they fit these into the organizational structure and business model of the so-called traditional agency, a model based on smaller teams distributed across a pyramid structure. But this is not how the new creative disciplines operate. At all.*
>
> *The agencies that will succeed in 2020 are the ones that understand the difference between advertising and innovation—or content creation, or any of these new creative disciplines—and actively address the heterogeneity between them. Since the creative process and organization of one creative discipline is different from another, we must abandon the one-size-fits-all organization of our agencies. This is not limited to how creative teams work together, of course, but impacts the entire agency organization, including its business model. (2012)*

Hayes Roth, former chief marketing officer at Landor and now principal at HA Roth Consulting LLC, takes the same point one level higher, challenging the very notion of an "ad agency" as the basic unit for the industry. He explains:

> *If Ad Agencies intend to maintain a leadership role in the marketing services industry of the future—and if they don't, they will most certainly be trailing behind it—they may want to start by reconsidering now what they plan to call themselves. "Ad Agency" as a term may be fond and familiar, but it implies a one-trick-pony, for whom the solution to virtually every marketing communications challenge ultimately resides in a piece of advertising copy. Sadly, this too often remains the mindset of many of today's ad agency professionals. (2013)*

Thus, new marketing job titles, new mental models for the "who" of advertising encourage us to rethink the labels of everyone involved in the larger ecosystem that advertising encompasses. **The traditional communications model no longer exists, and "advertiser," "agency," "media," and "consumer" are no longer very useful terms.** While the advertiser was once the creator of all messaging, today and in the future "advertising" ideas and content come from all sides and head in multiple directions. As John Winsor, CEO of Victors and Spoils, puts it, *"Now one person with a wireless connection can be an agency, a media company, or even a manufacturer with the help of a 3D printer"* (2012).

If a single person can replace the traditional communications model, what does this mean for the new role of the brand? Agencies? Media companies? The supporting organizations? **When our product development teams include a gamer, an expert in payment technologies, a social anthropologist, and a data scientist, how different will our end products and touchpoints be?**

The titles and designations that have served for decades may no longer be significant, and in fact are preventing us from taking advantage of our innovative potential.

Mental Model 4

Where: *From Reach* toward *Where Needed, Wanted, and Appreciated*

"Where" used to mean reaching as many people as possible through a limited set of channels. "Where" has been completely transformed so that brands have the opportunity to be exactly where needed, wanted, and, at last, appreciated.

The "where" of beyond advertising means the many diverse opportunities for net positive or net negative experiences people can have with a brand. There are numerous touchpoints that can be involved in the beyond advertising construct, far beyond the basic media mix: consider packaging design, call centers, sales floors, and the product itself.

In the new mental model, we can positively impact the consumer in all the many different ways they come into contact with us with consideration of place. **Paid advertising should not be considered in isolation; for starters—whether something is paid, owned, or earned, it should be considered as a cohesive whole.** As Mark Burgess explains, *"By 2020, the term 'advertising' will be redefined from today's definition of 'paid media only' to the true integration of all relevant paid, owned, and earned media. The distinction between these three elements will blur as each ingredient blends into a new brand formula for success"* (2012). We need to open our minds to myriad ways that the consumer's perception of a brand and their relationship can be impacted.

Crucially, in our interconnected and mobile world, "where" is no longer a static notion. As Jason Hill, global head of media at BlackRock, explains it, *"To be ready for 2020, brands must commit to global, they must think and act in borderless ways—from their strategic insights, to their creative campaigns, to how they plan and buy media"* (2014). We take this one step further and apply this sense of borderless-ness to the customer, too. "Where" needs to take into consideration the ways that the customer journey is rapidly evolving, and will continue to evolve. This means that the orchestration across and among touchpoints must be consistent and create synergies regardless of where the audience has been and where they are going. How does one touchpoint lead to the next or logically and seamlessly follow from the last?

Advances in technology transform the "where" of advertising. The notion of "mobile" helped us to think beyond a person on the couch in front of the television to consider ways to be with an individual as they went about their lives. For much of the world, this means increasingly omnipresent, increasingly smart, devices. But to get ahead of the present and be open to technology evolution into the future, we have to leave the mental model of "mobile" behind and conceptualize "where" broadly.

Recent research by AOL revealed the tendency of marketers to think of "mobile advertising" as connecting with people who are on the go, walking down the street, traveling. However, AOL's study found that 68 percent of all mobile minutes are at home, and 46 percent of the time people are on their mobile devices is for "me time" when we are in our homes or places of work (AOL and BBDO 2013). **Are we "mobile" when we check our devices just as we go to bed and as soon as we wake? That is "where" we are, and it is extremely telling about what might be needed, wanted, and appreciated.** The "where" of beyond advertising will be less about "mobile" and more about a nuanced understanding of real-time location together with the multifaceted surroundings—made even more nuanced by an understanding of previous and likely future location and surroundings. Where did they come from and where are they going? And why? What else is going on in the "where"?

Mental Model 5

When: *From Frequency* toward *When Needed, Wanted, and/or Appreciated*

"When" used to mean frequency: bombarding people long enough until you finally got through to some, the science of which focused on the results of the advertiser but in most cases neglected to take into account any negative fallout effect on the impacted population. Akihiko Kubo, chairman, group representative at Ogilvy & Mather Japan, explains: *"Consumers these days are getting better at sniffing out a commercial campaign disguised as something organic or homegrown. These can have the opposite effect and actually alienate consumers"* (2012). A very narrow lens on something with very much broader impact.

Now, the "when" of advertising acknowledges that timing is everything. Timing has always been everything in relationships. But given on-demand technologies and the computing horsepower behind them that can deliver, and can anticipate the right time, the stakes for making this happen at each touchpoint will only continue to rise. And it works everywhere. In those parts of the world where we have come to expect instant gratification, this is the bar that must be met. In other parts of the world, finding ways to create value exactly at the moment when it is most needed generates appreciation and gratitude. Delivered consistently over time, good mutual value can be fostered.

As in the "where" of advertising, the "when" requires a thorough understanding of people's preferences and tendencies in order to provide messages and experiences at the "right time," as needed and wanted. Models that follow the old advertiser-in-control mentality include the idea of advertising as intrusive and interruptive. In the old model, the advertiser is pushing something on people that they don't want, so they have to either trick them or force them into seeing it. As Arthur Fleischmann, president/partner at john st. advertising, writes:

> *Advertising was built on an interrupt and repeat model. Frequency and reach were the deities to which we prayed. Like a petulant child, marketers hoped that if they spoke sufficiently loud and often, they would get noticed.*
>
> *Today, the consumer has as much control over the success of a marketing campaign as the CMO. Maybe more. With an ability to comment, create and share, the consumer takes the brand's message and makes it jump the tracks from one medium to another—from TV to YouTube; YouTube to Twitter or a text—morphing, enhancing, or denigrating it as spreads.* (2013)

Mental Model 6

How: *From Ad Campaigns* toward *Holistic, Dynamic Ecosystems for Value Creation*

If ad campaigns with narrow objectives and short-lived impact will be replaced with infrastructures that create, enable, deliver, and build value across network collaborators over time, how will it happen? In short: more intentionally. Starting with a lot more EQ and then doubling down on the IQ. We have lots of both at our disposal. We just don't seem to expect or enlist or reward them.

The old "how" is simplistically characterized by a campaign managed by marketing with creative from an agency and media buys through a media agency. **The new "how" is an infrastructure that captures information from each of the touchpoints both in real time and over time, to provide a comprehensive picture of how the touchpoints are working both independently as well as interactively, multi-directionally (with consumers and brand stewards), and virally (earned and social media).** Ideally it is continuously informed with levels of contextual relevance: cultural, socio-political, regional, local, hyperlocal, individual. It has both automated elements based on continuously refined algorithms as well as non-automated innovations, initiatives, and collaborations. Mark Stewart of Townsquare Media writes that *"In 2020 advertising has evolved from an "interruption" to a "service" as the consumer's smart phone aggregates all individual user media, social, location, payment activity and privacy preferences, informing the intelligent ad serving of highly relevant commercial messages and perceived high-value incentives across all linked devices"* (2012).

With this technology-enabled decision-support and action-making/taking infrastructure, orchestration is not achieved by an individual (command and control model), but by a community aligned around a compelling brand purpose, empowered with real-time feedback and parameters to ensure cohesiveness and value from the standpoint of consumers. As Eshwar Belani from Rocket Fuel explains, *"Every consumer interaction will be driven by real-time intelligence to spark innate interest and a desire for action; the resulting two-way dialogue will be continuously improved throughout the customer's cross-channel journey with the brand"* (2015).

The final, crucial, "how" is **creative throughout the entire process.** Not as a standalone discipline or title, but as a culture that infuses all players to leverage data and analytics to inform, inspire, and transcend. As John Costello, president of global marketing and innovation at Dunkin' Brands Inc. explains, "We've tried to make innovation part of everyone's job, to create an environment beyond the innovation lab [where new flavors are developed and tested] where people are encouraged to take risks and push the envelope" (Marketing Matters June 2015).

Creative and data are partners not adversaries, and every member of a company can create.

Advances in technology and science are providing us with new insights into human behavior and the importance of aligned objectives. **It is important for advertising to design and curate platforms for co-creation based on these integrated insights; to cultivate and identify creativity and innovation wherever they appear.** We will be addressing this more in the chapters ahead. Most importantly, we have to accept that the traditional communication model, which is based on many of the outdated mentalities challenged above, is in all likelihood not the one to ride into the future.

Toward a New Vocabulary: A New Talk and a New Walk

Of course, the greatest power of mental models does not come from them sitting dormant in our heads, it comes from how they influence the choices we make about what we say and what we do. So consider this, or your own modified and improved version, as a new vocabulary that guides what you say and do, and begins to shape what others think and consider *(see Figure 2.3).*

And as you begin to move toward new approaches, work with your current and potential collaborators to "take a moment" and assess both current mental models and what a more desirable future could and should look like. Start your collaborations by bringing to the fore, discussing, and debating, the mental models that we hold and may just need to reconsider.

The capacity to adapt to and capitalize on the rapidly evolving challenges and opportunities requires that we reconceptualize advertising from top to bottom. When our many different mental models of the who, what, where, when, why, and how of advertising are challenged and reimagined, together we can begin to visualize and create the new idealized future of advertising today. Cue Part II.

Figure 2.3 Toward a New "Beyond Advertising" Vocabulary

TOWARD A NEW "BEYOND ADVERTISING" VOCABULARY

FROM	TO
Campaign	Initiative
Content	Substance
Persuading	Inspiring and enabling
Selling	Serving
Seeking loyalty	Earning trust
Disruption	Better/alternate solutions
Features and benefits	Brand role in people's lives
Brand differentiation	Brand distinctiveness
Employees	Brand ambassadors
Talent	Brand stewards
Consumers (myopic)	People (with lives)
Advertising campaigns	Value creation initiatives
Direct response	Actionable communications
Big data	Actionable insights
Success/Failure	Learning

Key Takeaways

- **Mental models help us understand the world—we couldn't live without them. But mental models can also hold us back, limit our exploration, and restrict our daring.**
- **The world is fluid, not static, and our mental models must adapt. Of course "change" is not implicitly good, but resisting change without realizing we are doing so is dangerous.**
- **The traditional mental models of advertising have reached a tipping point: the world—technologically and socially—has outgrown them. To hold onto them is to hold ourselves back.**

Figure 2.4 Beyond Advertising in Action: Challenge Your Mental Models

Beyond Advertising in Action
CHALLENGE YOUR MENTAL MODELS

CLEVER BUOY—OPTUS
Agency: M&C Saatchi
Cannes Lions: Gold—Creative Use of Technology 2015

OBJECTIVE/PROBLEM TO BE SOLVED

Optus has Australia's second largest telecommunications network. To improve consumer awareness and brand perception, Optus wanted to showcase the amazing things the network could do.

APPROACH

Australia has the largest number of fatal shark attacks in the world: four times as many as any other country. Prevention depends on detection, but established methods were ineffective. Optus created Clever Buoy, a shark detection system relying on their technology and satellite system. When a buoy detects a shark, lifeguards are notified through the Optus network. The data is also shared with scientists and other researchers.

THE RESULTS

The initiative had 84 percent positive sentiment, was featured in over 800 global news stories, and generated PR and social media impressions totalling 40 million. If implemented widely it has the potential to save many lives.

LESSONS AND OBSERVATIONS

Optus challenged their mental model of what advertising could be. Using their skills and products to create something impressive and useful became a living advertisement for the brand with triple win outcomes.

CITATION: Cannes Lions Winners, 2015

- **To challenge mental models, we must self-reflect and aspire: we have to forget "givens" and think of possibilities. Imagine the future where advertising is collaborative, respectful, appreciated, valuable, and inspiring.**

- **The who, what, where, when, and why of challenging mental models—laid out in this chapter—help uncover entrenched thinking. But mental models are ours alone—it's up to each of us as individuals to push beyond them *(see Figure 2.4)*.**

Part II
Toward a New Model Beyond Advertising

By 2020, advertising will shift from being an additive element to being an invisible, inspirational, and indispensable part of product and service experiences.

— Karl Isaac, *Head of Brand Strategy and Innovation, Adobe (2014)*

Given the increasing rate, magnitude, and impact of change, advertisers, marketers, and their colleagues throughout their organizations and across their external collaborators outlined in Part I are looking for a way out of the reactive mode. Importantly, instead of focusing on what is wrong with the current approaches and players, our approach has been to engage our Wharton Future of Advertising Innovation Network in an exercise of "idealized design." Simply put, we asked executives, academics, next gen, and others, **"Given what you know about what is transpiring, what could/should advertising look like in 2020?"**

Collectively, we propose a future with radically new mindsets and approaches that could enable far more effective and more desirable outcomes for advertisers, their organizations, their collaborators, and their audiences. We've termed this vision the **All Touchpoint Value Creation Model**, summarized as: **The ongoing, synergistic orchestration and optimization of all touchpoint value creation among an enterprise, the people in its network, the people**

it seeks to reach and serve, and the societies and cultures in which it exists and has responsibility.

The All Touchpoint Value Creation Model has four key elements as shown in Figure II.1 and which we explain in the subsequent four chapters.

Chapter 3: Aligning for Win-Win-Win Impact.

The objective of orchestrating across all touchpoints is to **gain maximum value for all parties to result in multi-win outcomes.** It bears emphasizing that this is *not* philanthropy in the traditional sense of giving away a portion of profits, though such a move may still be part of a strategy mix. Nor does it ignore how sales, revenue, and profit are important indicators of success. It's just that it turns out, in this new world, you'll do better for yourself, your fellow brand stewards, and your current and potential customers if you broaden your definition of success to include more than the bottom line or increased sales. Instead, success means the creation of value for all at the intersection of a given touchpoint as well as along the journey from one touchpoint to the next.

Chapter 4: Orchestrating Value Creation across All Touchpoints

In order to be fully effective, brands should coordinate and allocate resources across *all* touchpoints: every point of interaction a person has with a brand, including those that are outside the control of advertising and marketing. *All* touchpoints must create a symphony, and importantly allow and encourage improvisation as a component. This requires alignment of objectives throughout the entire organization. Nike, Apple, and Warby Parker are still the most lesson-rich pioneers of this model to date, though we offer up interesting examples of several other brands that are blazing trails for learning and insight.

The interactive nature of touchpoints means that information is flowing and data is being thrown off to be captured, leveraged, and protected. Touchpoints are rarely unidirectional and are increasingly less so with the desire to learn and adapt based on what happens at each touchpoint interaction and along the touchpoint journey.

Chapter 5: New Guidelines for Desired Content - R.A.V.E.S.

The five forces of change described in Chapter 1 make it worthwhile for all involved to ensure the content offered through each touchpoint is wanted and welcomed. What kind of content will people choose to watch, listen to, or experience? Distilling the responses from our Advertising 2020 collaborators, we created the *R.A.V.E.S.* guidelines for the content and substance of each touchpoint: Each interaction a brand has with people could and should be relevant and respectful, actionable, valuable and value-generating, and provide an exceptional experience and a share-worthy story *(see Figure II.2)*.

Chapter 6: The Expanded Power of Context - M.A.D.E.^{S}

The digital transformation and redefinition of media, the broad reach of mobile and connected devices, the increasing functionality of platforms, and the

Figure II.1 The All Touchpoint Value Creation Model

III.
ALL TOUCHPOINT VALUE CREATION MODEL

An ongoing, synergistic orchestration and optimization of all touchpoint value creation among an enterprise, the people in its network, the people it seeks to reach and serve, and the societies and cultures in which it exists and has responsibility.

1. Aligned Objectives for Multi-Win Outcomes with Short Term and Long Term Impact

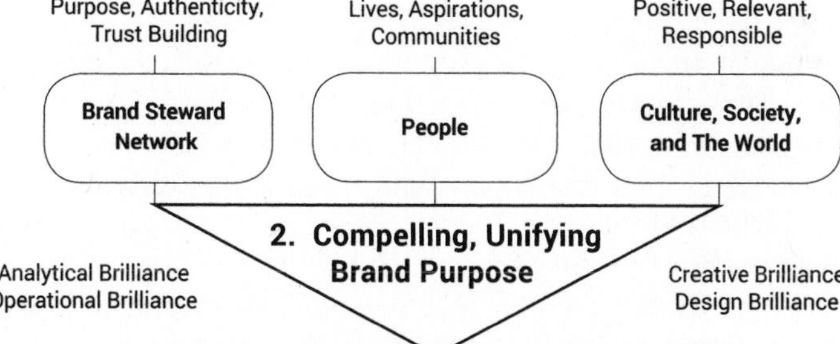

3. Orchestrated Across ALL Touchpoints

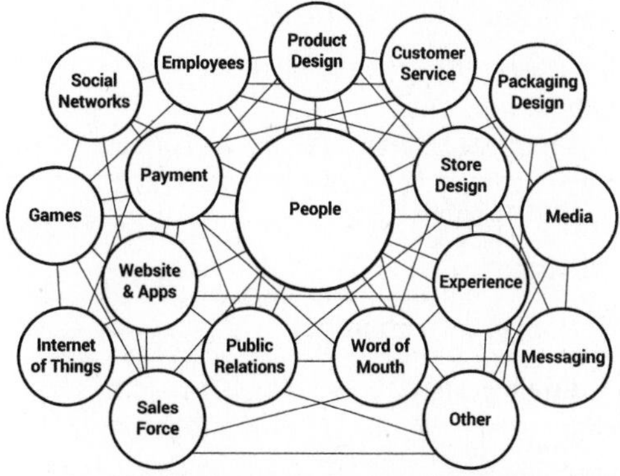

4. Touchpoint Value Creation

Maximized Context +	Maximized Substance
M.A.D.E.[S]	R.A.V.E.S.
✓ **M** ultisensory	✓ **R** elevant & Respectful
✓ **A** udience	✓ **A** ctionable
✓ **D** elivery Mechanism	✓ **V** aluable & Value-Generating
✓ **E** nvironment	✓ **E** xceptional Experience
✓ **S** ynergy	✓ **S** hareworthy Stories

Figure II.2 The R.A.V.E.S. Content Guidelines

	MAXIMIZED SUBSTANCE R.A.V.E.S.
R	Relevant and Respectful
A	Actionable
V	Valuable and Value-Generating
E	Exceptional Experience
S	Shareworthy Story

opportunities for enhanced experiences now enables each touchpoint to be designed and leveraged in full consideration of a richer set of contextual elements. This approach results in the M.A.D.E.^{s} guidelines we developed to reflect the guidance of our contributor community *(see Figure II.3)*. Each touchpoint has the opportunity to engage all of our senses, resonate with the mood, mode, and circumstances of its audience, suit the features and uses of its delivery platform, fit in or stand out relative to the dynamic and continuously evolving environment, and synergistically enhance its role and connection in relation to other touchpoints.

Figure II.3 The M.A.D.E.^{s} Guidelines for Advertising of the Future

	MAXIMIZED CONTEXT M.A.D.E.^{S}
M	Multisensory
A	Audience
D	Delivery Mechanism
E	Environment
S	Synergy

A vision of the future of advertising from Mark Earls, writer, strategist and consultant at Herd Consultancy and John Willshire, founder of Smithery, exemplifies this thinking and is presented in Figure II.4.

In the following chapters we examine each of these components of the All Touchpoint Value Creation Model. Even as we describe and promote this future vision, each reader must customize these concepts to their own idiosyncratic situation and objectives and ideally start experimenting with innovative approaches that are guided by the various elements of the model.

Figure II.4 Make Things People Want > Make People Want Things

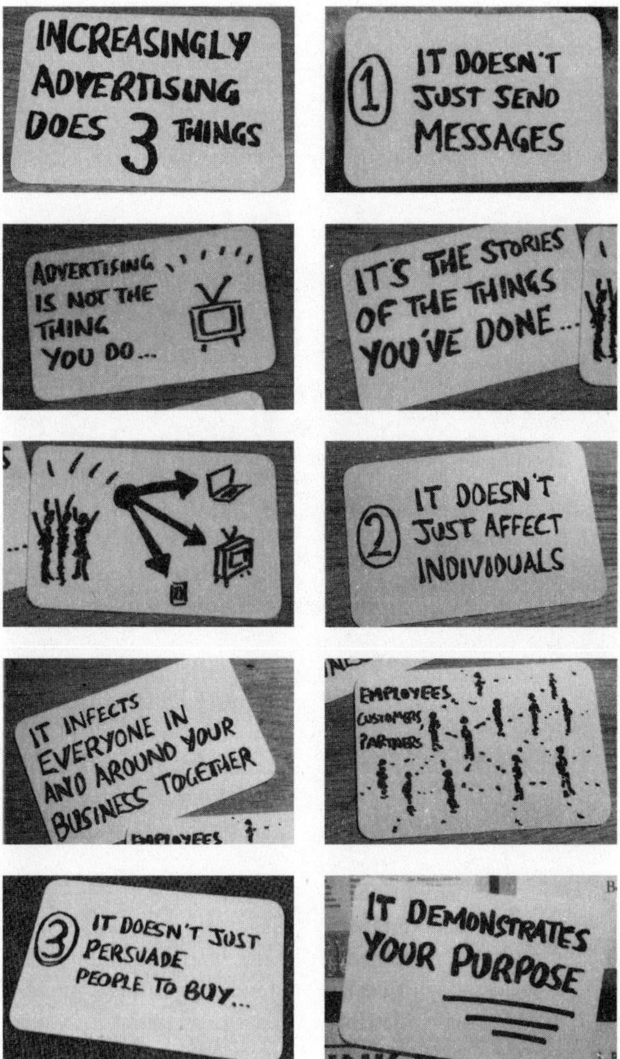

Figure II.4 Make Things People Want > Make People Want Things (*continued*)

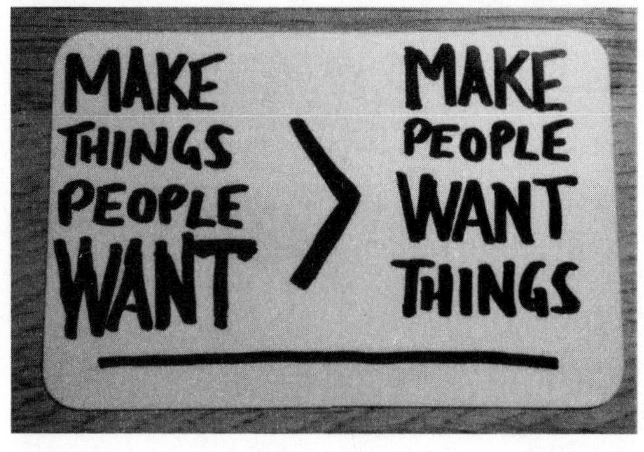

Chapter 3

Aligning for Win-Win-Win Impact

The days of creating something that people don't need (or that hurts people) and yelling at them about it from the rooftops so that they buy it are waning. These businesses will soon be space junk.

— Mark Pollard, *EVP, Director of NY Planning, Edelman (2012)*

In this part of the book we offer a model that represents the best of what advertising could/should be five or so years into the future. We asked our collaborators to suspend the tyranny of the moment and get out of the current maelstrom, but not so science-fiction that it would seem completely unattainable.

What we gleaned from their insights is a very radical change from most of what is currently practiced. We are seeing many who are making pioneering moves and major investments in this direction, and we are hearing from many others who are working to share and spread this vision. Here, for example, is what Faris Yakob, founder and principal of Genius Steals, writes regarding what advertising could and should be:

1. *A much broader definition of advertising*

2. *As the creative solution to business problems*

3. *Or the commercial leverage of creativity*

4. *At its broadest*

5. *Not just the development and distribution of pre-determined commercial units*

6. *Different kinds of thinkers able to concept, articulate, and execute ideas that lie far outside the units of the past*

7. *An embrace of strategic experimentation*

8. *An understanding that technology is a medium*

9. *That art and copy are not the only creative elements*

10. *Since Arduinos and code can also solve problems and earn attention*

11. *A willingness to help people not just sell them things*

12. *Respect for everyone: clients, customers, interns, each other*

13. *The desire to add value to companies and culture at the same time*

14. *Niceness, empathy, intelligence, enthusiasm, curiosity, manners*

15. *And lots and lots of good ideas. (2012)*

We were struck by how many of our collaborators emphasize a new, higher purpose role for brand advertising for brands in people's lives and in the world. **Collectively, they describe the importance, if not the imperative, of finding more alignment among brand objectives, the objectives of the people they seek to influence, and the culture, society, and world in which they all exist.** The relationship they imagine is one with far more alignment among all those in the world beyond advertising, especially when all touchpoints are brought into the equation *(see Figure 3.1)*.

To be clear, this isn't some pie-in-the-sky notion believed in by a few altruistic souls. This is an undeniable, fundamental theme that a large community sees as being fueled by the forces of change outlined in Part I and is supported by compelling arguments for how an innovative approach will address many daunting contemporary challenges. It comes down to a better understanding, appreciation, and respect for people. Of us, as humans. Not just as "consumers" and not just as "talent" or "employees." **If we can find common ground that is meaningful and compelling, are putting something better into the world,**

Figure 3.1 Aligned Objectives for Multi-win Outcomes

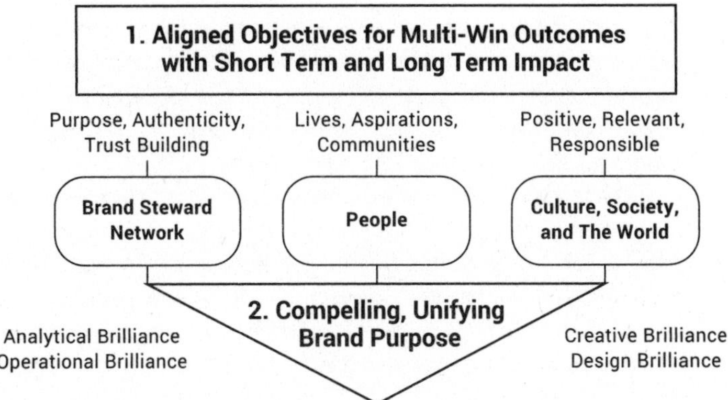

and can get aligned around it, outcomes will be better for us individually and collectively. "Outcomes" meaning people being better off and building good businesses.

Mel Exon, managing director at BBH London and cofounder at BBH Labs sets the stage:

> *Win-win-win platforms are a simple shorthand to describe when a brand, its users, and a third party or cause are connected by a campaign and everyone wins. In the future, these "three-way" campaigns like Amex Small Business Saturdays and Google's It Gets Better will become more frequent. The web accelerates virtuous circles like these and is already taking things further: into collaborative consumption and the championing of access over ownership. Witness Spotify, Netflix, LivingSocial, Airbnb, and Zipcar. For sure, the sharing economy will break business and marketing models, or at least offer credible alternatives.*
>
> *One thing to do now: reimagine brand partnerships and product lifecycles. Is there a cause our brand and its users are naturally aligned with? Could we offer a (paid-for) service that eschews selling the product for a moment and helps users share or loan effectively instead? (2012)*

The need for this alignment is also born of the emergence of the empowered and skeptical individual described in Chapter 1. Kelly O'Keefe, professor and chair of Creative Brand Management at VCU Brandcenter, explains,

> *In 2020, the advertising field will be more respectful, more trustworthy, and more focused on brand touch than on brand voice.*
>
> *Today the brand world is more challenged than ever by the inattention of cynical consumers who believe the field of advertising is unethical and*

the work we do is untrustworthy. In the advertising field we tend to write of the embarrassingly low scores for ethics that our industry gets, but enlightened marketers are not content to stand witness to the humiliation of our profession. By 2020 we will see a growing trend toward straightforward and truthful communications. We will see more and more brands moving to tell honest stories and deliver meaningful experiences. And we'll see more and more agencies move toward ethical practices.

The so-called Millennial generation will go from an interesting segment to the dominant segment. (Which arguably has already happened.) Their patronage comes at a price. They trust Airbnb more than Hilton, Uber more than Hertz, and Kickstarter more than Citi Bank. And even Baby Boomers are following Millennials as they eat more organic food, ride more bikes, and move back to urban areas when they become empty nesters. (2015)

As Brian d'Alessandro, SVP of Digital Intelligence at Dstillery, points out, we live in the same ecosystem, and we all breathe the same air, which has the positive by-product of discouraging the production of pollution: *"As a grad student, I studied the mathematics of dynamic ecosystems. A common result was that the more aligned the objectives of the various components of the system were, the healthier the system. In 2020, the best advertising system will be one where the incentives of the demand and supply sides are aligned with those of the consumer. People like to have a good time—the ad ecosystem should offer that"* (2012).

Brand Steward Network

This new Aligned Objectives component of the model begins with a more holistic view of the brand, the organization behind it (company, government, nonprofit, etc.) and its stewards. We chose the term stewards to represent all those who are in the service of the brand, both inside the organization, including all employees as well as those in agencies, media companies, ad tech firms, research and insight providers, and any others whose efforts work to further the brand's purpose.

Malcolm Roberts, founding partner of Corktown Seed Co., describes it from an agency perspective:

In the end, the most successful communications agencies will be brand stewards. They will create work that forges relationships with all stakeholders–both internal and external–that are profound and lasting. They will marry science and art to uncover insights and connect deeply and personally with the target. In addition to informing, entertaining, surprising, and provoking they will set the bar higher. Tomorrow's increasingly conscientious consumer will demand this. The best communications agencies will recognize the inevitably interconnected system of which brands form a part. And they will mobilize the power of brands to go beyond one-dimensional self-interest and embrace benefits that ladder up to society at large. (2013)

What our collaborators describe are four foundational elements for brands and all who are in the business of building and delivering the brand's promise (employees, agencies, collaborators):

1. A Clear and Consistent Purpose in the World

   How does the company serve humanity?
   — Mark Pollard, *EVP, Director of NY Planning, Edelman (2012)*

2. Authenticity and Authority

   Authenticity of a brand will be demonstrated by the ability of the employees to attract new consumers and impact existing customer loyalty via every channel of contact. Both small and large organizations, nonprofit and private and public organizations, will benefit (or not) from their employees who spread the brand message in their own words and creative expression.
   — Julia Gometz, *Founder and Author, The Brandful Workforce (2012)*

3. Build Trust in Thought, Word, and Deed

   Trust Will Be Everything. Advertising is—and always was—about trust. It is likely the behaviors of marketers and advertisers that has driven low admiration of those professions. Regardless, the stakes are rising. Social media and our real-time connections have prompted a new age of transparency and consciousness around values, motivations, behaviors and outcomes of institutions. Doing good marketing and advertising means embracing responsibility and accountability throughout your organization's entire value chain, and respecting their communities.
   — Max Kalehoff, *CMO, SocialCode (2012)*

4. In Concert with Fellow Brand Stewards

   A brand would no longer be a "thing" that we "pushed," but rather communities of people bound by a shared value system. I asserted that our job in coming years would be as custodians of these value systems and our job as advertisers would be to nurture a relationship with these communities on behalf of our clients.
   — Kevin Allen, *Founder and CEO, rekap Inc. (2012)*

Know Thyself: A Clear and Consistent Purpose in the World

It is essential to be very clear about what the brand and its company stand for. As Doug Levy, chief executive officer of MePlusYou, puts it, "a little soul-searching is required."

What is your company's purpose? This isn't a quick answer, and it's no snappy slogan. To discover a brand's purpose, brand stewards must delve into what motivates them, and what role they see for the goods they put out in the world. For example, the furniture giant IKEA states its purpose is to "create a better everyday life for the many." (2013)

Mike Doherty, president of Cole & Weber United describes it as follows:

... in a fragmented, constantly streaming world, brands will need to be very clear and focused about who they are and what they stand for. Marketers and their agencies are in the business of fame creation and in a streaming world, how and where they bring their brand to life will continue to become increasingly fragmented. Without a clear and concise focus on what the brand stands for, its meaning could be lost. This is incredibility evident in the music business even today. The difference between how Madonna and her manager built her brand three decades ago and how Lady Gaga and her manager drive her brand today is staggering. They not only manage her music, videos, books, tours, TV appearances and specials, and movies, but they also direct her Born This Way Foundation, branded products, Haus of Gaga, collaborations (Polaroid, Nicola Formichetti, Barneys, Monster Cable Products), websites, Facebook pages, Twitter, and all the content they distribute daily to a myriad of fan sites like gaganews.com all with a laserlike focus on what the Lady Gaga brand is about.

Lady Gaga is also a good example of what won't change and that's the currency of a great idea. To be a successful marketer, it will still take a smart person with vision, a big idea, and the brashness to make it a reality. That can't be crowd sourced. (2012)

Michael Pollard VP, Brand Strategy, Big Spaceship, continues,

Purpose—How does the company serve humanity? Behavioral economists have repeatedly proven that businesses with purpose outperform businesses that focus exclusively on "maximizing shareholder value." Brand essences and single-minded propositions aren't useful in a world where a company's beliefs and the behaviors that such beliefs lead to are so transparent. (2012)

The KIND company exemplifies the power of a clear and conscious purpose in the world. There is one simple belief that underpins the company: "There is more to business than just profit." Kindness is promoted in multiple ways—from being kind to your body by eating well to acting kindly to others. Likewise, their marketing reflects this ethos. We spoke with Lisa Mann, executive vice president at KIND on a recent episode of our radio show Marketing Matters. Mann described a KIND field marketing event in San Francisco, where the team set up a flower wall in the central business district. "We gave people two KIND bars and a flower," she said. "They kept one bar, and then did a kindness for someone else, giving the bar and flower away" (Marketing Matters March 2015). **Respecting the generosity of people reflected the brand's core values, as did the style and size of the initiative: they interacted face-to-face in an honest, humanistic manner.** This method, far more than a banner ad insisting their consumers "do a kindness," reflected what the company is really about.

We see more and more companies embracing these concepts and building them into the fabric of their everyday relations with both customers and employees. Take for example the B Corps, the increasingly valued third-party certification given by the nonprofit B Lab to for-profit businesses with proven track records of social and environmental accountability and transparency.

To Thine Own Self Be True: Authenticity and Authority

Old mental models position advertising as something completely separate and distinct from the company that paid for it. Public relations used to be about deflection and spinning a story rather than opening the proverbial kimono. What really happened in the hallways, meetings, conferences, and on phone conversations may or may not have borne any resemblance to the image created for public consumption.

Conversely, our new model is pretty straightforward for what the future could/should be. Don't try to pretend to be what you are not, or at least really trying earnestly to become. Don't use advertising to whitewash what you are actually doing and who you actually are. **Ensure that what you say, do, support, and pay for can be easily traced back to you, and that you have the credentials to be taken authoritatively.** In fact, be so proud of who you are, what you are, and what you are offering that your involvement is clear—without being intrusive, boastful, or distracting.

Here's more from our Advertising 2020 contributors:

> *"Authenticity" is a key tenet of social media generally, and online crowds quickly sniff out anything that's fake.*
>
> — John M. Jordan, *Clinical Professor, Department of Supply Chain and Information Systems, Smeal College of Business, Pennsylvania State University (2012)*

> *There are of course vested interests on both sides but Storysharing truly works at its best when there is an authentic connection between the two sides.*
>
> — Simon Dolsten, *Copywriter, Momentum Worldwide (2012)*

> *[People today] want to own the brand and to use it as an authentic expression of their identity. Image advertising is spoiling such authenticity.*
>
> — Ron Shachar, *Professor, Duke and Arison School of Business, IDC Herzliya (2012)*

Authenticity as a value in business is gaining traction, and will continue to do so. In a June 2015 edition of Marketing Matters, WFoA's monthly radio show, we talked with Jeff Diskin, EVP, Commercial Services at Hilton Worldwide; John Costello, president, Global Marketing and Innovation at Dunkin' Brands, Inc.; and

Denise Karkos, CMO, TD Ameritrade about recruiting and retaining talented people. Throughout the conversation, brand authenticity was front and center: each CMO saw it as absolutely crucial to their brand. And not simply in terms of building a relationship with customers, but in terms of recruiting: people want to believe in what they buy and where they work.

Likewise, business authenticity is a growing area of academic study, as brought to life in the title of this 2012 UPenn PhD thesis by Pamela Teagarden: *The Authentic Organization (TAO): The Tao of Positive Business in an Authentic Culture.* What Teagarden finds is that "By reframing engagement to the side of the employee, promoting an authentic culture and creating a fair and balanced way of measuring the outcomes at work, businesses may flourish for the impact of their flourishing employees" (Teagarden 2012).

The necessary companion of authenticity is authority: do you have a leg to stand on? Are you holding forth on what is within the sphere of what your brand likely has knowledge, experience and expertise? The IAB (Internet Advertising Bureau) in both the UK and US conducted research in the realm of native advertising that determined that "authority" was a critical element of what audiences expect from content marketing and native advertising. Many B2B brands are paving the way by showcasing their fascinating advances and the expertise of their associates in editorially curated and managed content for audiences that include client audiences as well as potential employees and collaborators. GE, IBM and SAP are just a few of these recent success stories.

Do Unto Others: Trust-Building

Let's be clear: authenticity doesn't mean perfection. Who among us isn't without faults and warts and failed attempts and set-backs? And yes, that goes for people as well as organizations. That's why trust-building is so important. **It's what we do over time that matters; not what we say we are going to do, but the choices day in and day out, in good times and in bad times—especially under pressure and duress—that builds trust.** One choice, one action, one building block at a time. Clearly this is a mindset and a culture that is instilled at the most fundamental level, for all who are the stewards of the brand and the lives of those who the brand seeks to serve.

Many of our Advertising 2020 contributors shared thoughts about trust:

> *My argument is that sustainable economic relationships are built on trust in the exchange of value. We've gone off the rails in trying to make economic relationships more efficient by controlling every detail of the process, and focusing only on the aggregate value of short-term transactions. That transactionalism has reached the point of terminal efficiency, and the pendulum is swinging back toward the process of developing trust as the basis for exchanging value—human engagement.*
>
> — Chris Kenton, *CEO and founder, SocialRep (2012)*

> *Companies still stuck in the mire of the Consumer Era often make the critical mistake of thinking of trust as just another mechanism for influencing transactions. They view it as a means to an end, and many squander it as quickly as it accumulates.*
>
> *According to a Nielsen survey, 92 percent of people trust personal recommendations, but only 29 to 47 percent trust advertising. Customers trust personal recommendations because they are founded on relationships. By operating in the Relationship Era, companies develop deeper relationships with their customers, relationships that result in high levels of trust—and transactions.*
>
> — Doug Levy, *CEO, MEplusYOU (2013)*

> *For one thing, as companies become more transparent, their behavior will be compared critically to their messaging: what they do will be as important as what they say. And the "what they do" part will become more and more encompassing. How does a company treat its employees (Apple, Nike)? How does it treat the environment (Monsanto, BP)? Are its products safe (Mattel, Toyota)? Where does it stand on social issues that have nothing to do with its business (Chick-fil-A)? Is it a good citizen, or is it just out for itself (Wall Street)?*
>
> *In a world where every corporation is a glass factory, building a brand isn't just a function of advertising. Everything a company says and does adds a piece to its brand edifice. And to succeed in this new world, companies must not just accept this reality, they must welcome it.*
>
> *Does that mean advertising will turn into a checklist of corporate good deeds? Not a chance. For one thing, consumers care, but they're too busy to care much. The average attention span has gotten even shorter. Plus, if once there were 57 channels and nothing on, now it's getting closer to 57,000. If people are not interested or entertained by your message, buh-bye.*
>
> *Moreover, two-way interactions between consumers and companies will become the norm. People will speak (or shout) through those open factory windows, and the wise company will listen and respond (as Starbucks did, with MyStarbucksIdea.com). Not just glass factories. Glass houses.*
>
> — Lynda Resnick, *vice chair and co-owner, The Wonderful Company, and* Ken Youngleib, *Associate Creative Director, Apple (2012)*

If this desired future is not motivation enough, let's turn to our friends at McKinsey to add a little research-based gravitas.

> *Become the trustees of the consumer. Already, we're seeing significant demand for—and profits from—being relevant and trustworthy. A recent McKinsey survey showed that 35 percent of online buyers are willing to share personal information in return for targeted offers (e.g., promotional coupons). Another study showed that among the 30 percent of customers interested*

in active co-creation, the bulk will only participate with brands they trust. Customers are already very concerned about their privacy. Imagine those concerns in 2020, with the unprecedented levels of interaction and personal data collected. Despite whatever regulations are enacted to address that tension, the 2020 digital world will demand something similar to an implicit contract between the brand and customer, based on trust. Marketers will need to run their business in a way that never disappoints and always delights the customer. If not, the mobile and vocal consumer will refuse to cooperate, abandon them and call on their social networks to leave as well.

—Jacques Bughin, *Director, McKinsey & Company, Brussels;* David Edelman, *Global Co-leader, Digital and Marketing and Sales, McKinsey & Company, Boston (2012)*

In Concert with Fellow Brand Stewards

Done right, creating a purpose for anyone who is involved in influencing and bettering the brand can be inspiring and motivating. Why is this important? Michelle Cerwin, principal at mCerwin Consulting, puts it this way:

Brands, too, must not only make a commitment to developing female leaders internally, but must also wield their influence to impress upon the leadership in their agencies. It is undeniable that the industry will pay attention to behemoths such as Unilever who recently announced a corporate diversity program that aims for gender-balanced management by 2015. Brand decision-makers naturally retain the right to understand whether their agency team has the appropriate blend of talent required to think and work effectively on their behalf. Brian Morrissey, Editor-in-Chief of Digiday, puts it poignantly: "After all, it's hard to see how agencies can hope to create work that drives their clients' businesses if they pretty much do it without the input and sensibilities of more than half the world's population." (2012)

People, Not Consumers

In a more desirable future of advertising people are front and center, as humans worthy of respect. They are presented with what is truly worthy of people's time and attention. As Ryan Ku, managing director of Redscout, puts it:

If I were to look ahead to 2020, I would hope advertising would be focused more on authentic engagement through human insight rather than relentless stalking through data mining. (2014)

Imagine your own life. What if all of your messages from a brand made a net positive impact, helped you achieve your best goals and aspirations, and/or furthered your role in your social and community circles? **The new model of advertising asks advertisers to spend the time and energy to avoid the pitfall of projecting your biases onto your intended audience, to instead take the**

time and energy to understand their world, their lives, their aspirations and their communities. Sam Hanna, international director of Athenaeum Worldwide states:

> *Advertising will be a cooperative partnership between consumer and brand. In 2020 the role of brand manager will be shared by the consumer. . . . Because the consumer is part of the dialog, and chooses to surround themself with connectivity, advertising becomes non-invasive. This is the elaborate human ecosystem that advertising could not have imagined just 25 years earlier. (2013)*

Ayal Levin, strategy associate at McCann Tel-Aviv, and David Fogel, head of Strategic Research and Business Consulting Department at McCann Tel-Aviv suggest a very simple way to begin: *"The solution, as we see it, consists of a change in our mindset and approach to the consumer-brand relationship and a transition from a one to a two way relationship. We should start by looking at consumers as partners"* (2013).

Their Lives

Several Advertising 2020 collaborators used the concept of "service" to describe this notion of aligning with people. What can we say and do to be of service to people? **How does it make their lives better, even if in some small way? How does it make them smile, inspire them, help them cope, energize, get done more easily what they need to get done?** What if they felt grateful for all the ways that brands made their lives better? What if it is less about the product to be sold and more about how the brand helps someone get through their day?

> *The idea of "advertising as service" is nothing new. Some of the wisest, gray-haired advertising luminaries I know have told me this as far back as I can remember. However, if you look around, it seems that few advertisers live up to this ideal. It seems most are interested in serving only themselves. With daily messaging exposures continuing to rise to stratospheric heights, avoidance and intolerance will only increase as a matter of survival. As a result, there will be a growing premium and receptiveness to marketers and messages that actually serve and deliver value. Of course, this would mean that customer service be aligned with advertising.*
>
> — Max Kalehoff, *CMO, SocialCode (2012)*

> *I see advertising in 2020 as more and more of a service to consumers and customers to help them enjoy life, learn about things/events/ideas, to live a healthier life longer, and to take better care of our planet.*
>
> — Joe Plummer, *President, Sunstar Americas Foundation (2014)*

All brands can make moves towards inspiring a greater respect. Being true to the viewers, creating or being associated to content they like and with which they share common values, conveying messages only to viewers willing to receive them are some of the ways to gain respect. . . .

— Timothy Duquesne, *Screenwriter/Consultant, We Support Creators (2013)*

Their Aspirations

Again, this is not about appealing to and preying upon people's dreams and aspirations to manipulate them. **It's about seeking to understand in order to determine how to be of service, how to collaborate and enable that better future *while* achieving the brand's objectives.** What are they hoping, trying to achieve, what do they have ahead of them, and how does what I have, or can access, help to make that happen in a real and positive way? David Sable, global chief executive officer of Y&R, reminds us that his firm's concept of the "Whole Egg" was hatched precisely to see people as organic wholes and be approached as such. (Y&R.com) The service industry and B2B salespeople know this well. They get it, that it is all about where people are going and how to help them get there. And how to make that journey authentic with both short- and long-term value.

Many of our contributors addressed these concepts:

Understand the consumer to fulfill their aspirations. . . . Consumer understanding and insight generation can no longer sit in isolation in the office down the hall, acting as the lone voice of the consumer. Consumer insights must be seen as everyone's responsibility. We all must be consumer-inspired, from our thinking through to our execution. To better engage and build loyalty with the consumer, the entire working team must seek to understand on a deeper level in order to demonstrate we've heard them and we know what matters most to them.

— Lori Billey, *CEO and Founding Partner, RED the Agency (2013)*

Immerse ourselves deeply in the lives of those we serve and always remember that the office desk is a dangerous place from which to view the world. A few minutes' encounter with the consumer doesn't yield genuine understanding of the people we serve. We need to go back to the basics and remember even digital needs a human touch for it to be soulful. Soulful advertising comes from those who interrogate their souls and that of the people they serve in order to be able to tell the truth in a way that affirms, alters, and enhances people's lives while making money or profit.

— Mzamo Masito, *Managing Executive, Brand and Comms Africa Group, Vodacom (2013)*

Know your consumers to the finest details, from their dreams to their fears and social habits to their family rituals. Only then might we be able to empower them to own our communication and advertising in a positive manner. And then... maybe... as we hand over to consumers our most cherished jewels to own, they will handle them with care—almost as much as we do.

— Michelle Taite, *Senior Global Brand Manager, Unilever (2012)*

Their Communities

This is a significant shift in how we think about aligning with, instead of exploiting, people's fundamental need to connect and belong. Advances in the social sciences help us, and, along with an ongoing analysis of the continuously evolving realm of online and offline social connections, give us tremendous insight into the nature of how we connect with, are influenced by, and influence others, and the resultant constructive role brands can play.

Communities, or "tribes," suggests a far more nuanced way of understanding commonalities among like-minded and like-motivated people. We first came across the notion of "tribes" from John Zogby, Founder of the "Zogby Poll." His Tribal Analytics are described as "how people naturally self-organize into 'tribes' based on shared values, interests, preferences, and behaviors that transcend categories and is built on the premise that people aren't fixed nodes. They evolve within a larger social ecosystem. Their values, preferences, and behaviors shift as social and cultural norms do" (2013).

Russell Dubner, U.S. CEO, Edelman, agrees, saying *"Marketers are increasingly moving away from channel planning based on reach numbers and generalized demographic data in favor of new planning methods based on identifying the right consumer "tribes" with niche cultures and passion points that align perfectly with their brands"* (2013). We have to get beyond demographics, as many contributors explain.

Traditionally, marketers have used quantitative and qualitative data to find consumer-marketing opportunities through a targeted media approach. Terms like "African-American 18 to 34-year-olds," "Second Generation Hispanics," and "General Market Women" are utilized to define specific messaging approaches and appeal strategies designed to connect with affinity to these groups, but mainly as a method of media investment.

By 2020, however, exactly who the target is will be more elusive than ever. While these groups will no longer fail to exist, omniculturalism will drive marketers to think about connecting to consumers beyond ethnic categorization. For example, we already see that in many cases, an African-American earning $75,000 a year has more in common with a Caucasian earning $75,000 a year than an African-American in a higher income bracket and an African-American in a lower income bracket. Thus, brands will have to become more defined by the values that they wish to connect to consumers regardless of race and become far more invested in connecting to cultures of people–not races of people. In short, mental complexions will become the new epicenter of brand engagement.

— Steve Stoute, *Founder and CEO, Translation (2012)*

J. Walker Smith, executive chairman of The Futures Company talks about community way beyond the potentially narrow notions of what is "social," in a way that will take us beyond social media to a more nuanced way of thinking about our social selves.

> *Technology intensifies social influence. The more new media grow, the more social our lives will become. Our networks will get bigger. More information will be shared. The scale of information we share will swell exponentially. Confronted with more, we will be ever more aware of our connections with others and of their influences on us. We will spend more time monitoring our connections. Indeed, we will depend more and more on the guidance of others to help us sort through the ever-growing deluge of data flooding our lives.*

He continues,

> *. . . advertisers will have to accept that brands will not be at the center of any conversation. Instead, brands will have to deliver opportunities for people to have the kinds of conversations they want—with other people. The imperative for advertisers is to avoid butting into conversations and instead to facilitate the kinds of interpersonal conversations people want to have. Interactions per se must be a key brand benefit. Only that will make a brand relevant and valuable. (2012)*

Culture, Society, and the World

> *Advertising will shift from communicating a brand's functional and emotional benefits to co-creating brands with clients that are both functional for the planet and emotionally positive for humanity. It's not about the best brands on the planet, rather the best brands for the planet.*
>
> — Marco Vega, *Co-founder, We Believers (2014)*

Our Advertising 2020 community is especially passionate about aligning their resources and creativity with what could and should be accomplished in this world. They understand that given the billions spent promoting our brands, products, and services across all traditional and new and emerging media channels, we have an outsized influence: $500 billion a year in traditional messaging through traditional media channels. What if all of those monies were held to a standard of having a net positive impact on society?

The standard should be simple, straightforward and compelling:

- Have a net positive impact in all communications and at each touchpoint
- Align with a relevant purpose as a "north star"
- Be responsible for the repercussions of choices and actions

Isabelle Quevilly, director of brand services at Brilliant Noise (UK) imagines this for the future:

> *Now that advertising is made in real-time, people realize that brands actually care. It's good to know that brands we love won't let us down anymore. Advertising used to be pollution. Today, it's conversation. Thanks to data, it actually feels good to come across an ad. (2013)*

Chris Arnold, creative director and cofounder of Creative Orchestra suggests another bar: be so entertaining that people would actually pay to engage.

> *I believe that with so many other changes going on within the industry, now is a great time to stop at the crossroads and look in a new direction. To look at the outcomes—to create work that is as clever and creative as the best entertainment—in fact, so good we could even charge people to watch them....*
>
> *Today's ads now compete not just with other ads but millions of moments of entertainment from professionally made work to home videos....*
>
> ***How differently would we approach advertising if we actually had to sell it?*** *It's a brief I often set students, to produce an ad, using any medium, that the public will pay for. Which means they have to like it—there's a novel concept! Forget "intrusive" or "disruptive" techniques, try entertainment. (2013)*

And Scott Goodson, CEO and founder at StrawberryFrog suggests an even higher bar, advertising that makes a difference in the world, and attracts those who see value-creating advertising as worthy of their creative, analytical, and tech-savvy talents and capabilities. He offers the following headlines:

> ***New York Times, January 1, 2020***
> *GLOBAL WARMING ENDED. ICE CAPS RETURN. AIDS AND CANCER CURES SHARE NOBEL PRIZE. WAR? WHAT'S THAT?*
>
> *Sound too good to be true? Okay, here's two more from the industry trade magazine Advertising Age:*
>
> *CMO OF GOLDMAN SACHS RECEIVES BIGGER BONUS THAN BANKERS. CMO WINS NOBEL PEACE PRIZE*
> *Well, here is my view of the future and . . . what I believe it will hold. Not only do I think that this represents a realistic view of where our industry could be in 2020—I think that our being there today could actually have a bearing on the 2020 world news headlines I've put up.*
>
> *What better way to contribute to a new world model then by ensuring that the power of ideas can be channeled, harnessed and endorsed by*

the involvement of businesses—businesses who have a responsibility to contribute ideas that will enable them to operate as productive, profitable, socially responsible entities? And what better way than to use what we DO, to develop ideas in a way that always ensures that we are defining or redefining culture in a social and business context, that in however small a way we are doing it, we are doing together with our clients, to benefit the community, society and the world? (2012)

Many brands today are already engaging in advertising that goes beyond sales to social impact. LifeBuoy, for example, is a global soap company that has worked to spread awareness of how handwashing can prevent the spread of serious diseases, especially in children. In 2013 they created a video capturing a father's celebration for the first child he had raised who reached five years of age. For each share of the video, "Help a Child Reach 5," LifeBuoy donated a unit of the local currency. Within a year more than 350 thousand children were reached through donations. Moreover, there was a 13% raise in the perception that "LifeBuoy is a company that cares about society" (Warc 2013).

Aligning objectives between the brand, its audience, and society and culture shines a light on what we have known for decades but have not taken responsibility for: advertising has a tremendous influence on people and how they think about themselves relative to others, therefore influencing culture and societal norms. A new model of advertising names this inter-relationship and calls upon those who analyze and create to seek alignment of objectives and outcomes, rather than some notion of hunter and hunted, societal casualties be damned.

Words and labels matter. Here in Figure 3.2 are just a few that reframe the relationship between brand/firm, person, and society and culture.

Figure 3.2 New Roles to Frame a New Future

**EMERGING ROLES
FOR BRANDS REFLECT NEW MINDSETS**

- **Brand Citizenship (Allen)**
- **Trustees of the Consumer (Bughin and Edelman)**
- **Trust Advisors (Burgess)**
- **Customer Stewards Inspiring Great Respect (Duquesne)**
- **Demonstrate Character (Earls & Willshire)**
- **Very clear about who they are and what they stand for (Doherty)**
- **The engine for innovation and value for businesses, people, and society (Hays)**

To return to Scott Goodson:

Let's go back to those headlines I put up from early January 2020. I believe, based on the future I envisage . . . that these are entirely possible.
And if we all work together to generate ideas that create more involved, more meaningful cultural connections, which drive business decisions that create more involved meaningful consumer relationships which feed back into companies as a virtual circle of interactivity that can leverage the company's position to identify and effect relevant . . . social, environmental, world change—well who wouldn't want to be a part of that? (2012)

For Short- and Long-Term Impact

Measure the journey. The model of the consumer journey has evolved but the way it's measured hasn't changed much since the 1970s. Marketers in North America spend nearly $12 billion on tracking consumers' awareness and intentions. Over the next decade we'll have more integrated real-time tools that track the behavioural journey from awareness to engagement to evangelism. Agencies will need to get on board to be thought leaders or suffer the consequences of being followers.

— Arthur Fleischmann, *President/Partner, john st. advertising (2013)*

By 2020, lines of code bundled as software, doing things that customers value but don't "see," and with shelf-lives of years instead of quarters, will be recognized as powerful and efficient brand drivers.

— Kip Voytek, *CEO, Rumble Fox; SVP, Director of Digital Innovation, MDC Partners (2012)*

For every marketing team, and every organization, balancing the need for short-term sales improvement with long-term brand prosperity is essential. Like the perceived binary of analytics and creative, the short term and long term are often in tension: should a brand aim to increase sales now by focusing on the quick sell, or should a brand play the long game, patiently waiting for their numbers to climb? Each strategy has different pros, different cons, and requires very different marketing strategies. In their 2013 book, *The Long and the Short of It*, Les Binet and Peter Field present their research comparing the two approaches. The pair analyzed 996 case studies from the IPA Databank, which spans 700 brands, 83 categories, and over 30 years of marketing effectiveness data.

Their solid approach and practicable findings inform this book's point of view: long-term strategies, where you treat 'consumers' like the individuals they are and appeal to them as important, emotional beings, leads to bigger returns. Field says, **" . . . if you measure success over the short term, as big data will push you to do, you will select marketing and communication strategies that deliver the best results in the short term: unfortunately these will not deliver the**

best long-term results and in many important ways will undermine long-term success." Short-term strategies, focused on "rational" approaches (a "real bargain," for example) are not memorable, and do not appeal to the emotional response of the individual—something we have argued is essential. Binet writes, "emotions affect the prices people are willing to pay as much as they affect the volume that gets sold. And [the effects] last much longer. In the long run, emotion is where the really big profits lie" (Binet and Field, 2013).

We have two clear take-aways: while Big Data is a revolutionary force, short-term metrics—to which it leans—do not predict long-term effects. And emotional, creative campaigns—which focus on the long term—will benefit an organization far more than a quick spike in sales does. The two must work together: investment in long-term brand- and trust- building combined with short term "brand activations" to reap the sales benefits of those investments.

Bringing Analytic, Creative, Design and Operational Brilliance together to Bring a Compelling, Unifying Brand Purpose to Life

Brands as business strategies brought to life.
— Jez Frampton, *Global CEO, Interbrand (2012)*

Battle lines used to be drawn, with creative factions of brilliant designers and storytellers on one side and quantitative and analytic geniuses on the other. There was a sense that somehow numbers could kill a great idea, or that numbers never really got at what was really important. We were first introduced to the collaboration among these seemingly disparate titles by Scott Prindle, former vice president, executive creative technology director at CP+B, when he discussed the collaborative approach that resulted in a series of breakthrough winners that continue to this day. Witness the 2015 Cannes Lion-winning pizza emoji.

And now, with the growing importance of interface and utility, we are reminded of the importance of design and how it unleashes exceptional experiences. Making all touchpoints come together seamlessly for an audience, while packaging, presenting and delivering upon actionable data requires nothing short of operational brilliance.

In the future, analytics and creatives will be a match made in heaven. Designers and operational experts will work hand in glove. Ok, we do admit to a fair amount of idealism, but that is the whole point. What if the new collaboration yields an even more compelling and unifying brand purpose that goes beyond "the big idea" of the traditional ad campaign to something more lasting, more connected to the aligned objectives that draws heavily on all of these disciplines? Something that articulates what all those in the service of and serviced by the brand can relate to, as it is how the brand betters their lives.

Brands need to focus on their reason for being and what emotional benefits they provide to the consumer and society.
— Anne Rivers, *Managing Director, Global Brand Strategy, BAV Consulting (2014)*

One of the things you need to think about is the idea of having a Chief Futurist or a Chief Innovation Officer. I need to constantly be looking at what's happening out there. This is no longer a comfort zone where I can behave a certain way for 20 years and it won't change. Just before you know it there's a this and there's a that and they're all over the place. So part of really embracing the future is putting some of your resources on the cutting edge because the cutting edge becomes mainstream so fast. You might look back and realize that you really are missing this whole opportunity.

— Allen Debevoise, *Chairman, Machinima (2012)*

If you have a truly big idea the wrong technique won't kill it and if you don't have a big idea, the right technique won't help you.

— Alan Schulman, *National Director, Creative Experience and Content Marketing, Deloitte Digital (2013)*

Take a moment to consider what Gareth Kay, cofounder at Chapter SF, calls taking the small path. Behind this "small stuff" lies a really great, compelling brand notion. Consider this:

So, if we accept the argument that thinking and acting small can drive business better than thinking or acting big, we need to rethink some of the assumptions that have become the false laws of advertising. Small ideas are different than big ideas and, as a result, they tend to have different characteristics:

1. They tend to be in the service of people

Sounds like rule one of marketing, but too often we forget this (probably calling people "consumers" doesn't help). Far too often we get narcissistic about the brand (people must be interested in what we make) rather than be humble, empathetic, and interested in their lives.

The great brands today understand what people are interested in and work back from there. Great communication ideas act as a bridge. A bridge between what people are interested in and what you make/sell. A bridge between your world and theirs; real life/culture and commerce.

2. They reduce friction

Brands today seem to be learning from design and thinking about how they can remove friction between themselves and people; between what people do now and what they want them to do. Ogilvy created a great example of this for Hellman's mayonnaise in Brazil. If your shopping cart had a jar of Hellman's in it, it would print on the back of your receipt a number of recipe suggestions using mayonnaise and the other ingredients in your cart. An elegant solution to the need to get people using mayonnaise as more than a sandwich spread.

3. They're one of many

Brands today need to do lots of things, not one big thing. It ties back to the point about placing little bets and is about managing portfolios rather than playing roulette. Google is a great example of this type of prodigious brand—search to Google 411 to Chrome (the list goes on).

Creating brands built around a coherent stream of small ideas makes them stickier (the velcro analogy of lots of little hooks that Russell Davies has used that I still think is an incredibly helpful metaphor) and more powerful—being the brand of new news and seen as having momentum and energy is the best leading indicator of future preference and usage. It also means you are more likely to thrive in a world where 95 percent of things die.

4. They do rather than say

Actions speak louder than words. We need to make communication products, not just communicate a product. Create actions and things, not ads. (2013)

Infrastructure to Enable Brands to Listen, Process, Deliver, Learn, and Repeat

> *The secret of how to thrive in this changed advertising landscape is curiosity. Without an inherent sense of cultural and technological curiosity embedded into advertising's DNA then our industry is doomed to irrelevance. We don't have to have all the answers, but we do need to be asking all the questions because our future will be built by the curious.*
>
> — Amelia Torode, *Chief Strategy Officer, TBWA London (2012)*

Having "curious" organizations is a key piece of the alignment for win-win outcomes. A technology infrastructure that is fully integrated into the organization, not as a separate division, enables the kind of relevant two-way communication that is essential for innovation and effectiveness. The infrastructure should provide organizations with ways to listen to people, process their input, deliver on their requests, learn what works and what didn't, and continue to improve for future communications. Many of our contributors refer to the importance of developing such an infrastructure:

> *With the fierce urgency of now coursing through the veins of marketers, they are loath to invest marketing dollars in emerging platforms or products that deliver a sub-par user experience. Getting ready for the future of*

advertising means innovating advertising products that foster creativity, support flawless brand experiences, and keep up with changing consumer behavior.

— Nikao Yang, *SVP, Global Marketing and Business Development, Opera Mediaworks (2013)*

Brands will immerse themselves into daily reality, become dynamic, and responsive. They need to dialogue, and be "active social listeners." Brands should leverage trending topics, cultural triggers, and plan for scenarios. Create content calendars around topics and insights relevant to the target. Marketers should plan the predictable, create creative templates, identify moments where these can be used. Exceptional marketers leverage the unpredictable, moving the brand into the spotlight in real time.

— Robbert Rietbroek, *Managing Director and CEO, Kimberly-Clark Australia and New Zealand (2014)*

Marketers should begin to organize themselves around their data now or it remains useless. They can position themselves for success by reorganizing their business to analyze and capitalize on the newly available data through nimble, strategic communication plans. Companies should acquire talent now who can not only mine and analyze the multitude of data pouring in, but who can also apply it to more effectively reach individuals. Key specialty divisions will likely emerge to ensure that all other parts of the organization, including sales, marketing and retail, receive the applicable insights to improve strategic direction. It will be important to build operational infrastructures that minimize low value tasks so that strategic leads can focus on the biggest opportunities.

— Laurent Larguinat, *Director, Mars Marketing Lab;* Judy Yeh, *Global Media and Integrated Marketing Executive Director, SC Johnson (2012)*

Figure 3.3 Beyond Advertising in Action: Seek Triple Win Outcomes

Beyond Advertising in Action
SEEK TRIPLE WIN OUTCOMES

LIKE A GIRL—ALWAYS
Agency: Leo Burnett Toronto, London, Chicago
Cannes Lions: PR Grand Prix 2015

OBJECTIVE/PROBLEM TO BE SOLVED

Girls experience a large drop in confidence during puberty. Always, a feminine protection brand, wanted to address this issue.

APPROACH

Always created a video where boys and girls were asked to perform certain tasks, such as run, "like a girl." This led to stereotypical weak or silly behavior. But when younger girls were asked to perform "like a girl" they showed strength, grace, and determination.

THE RESULTS

The video was viewed 85 million times globally and the hashtag #likeagirl made 4.58 billion media impressions. The description "like a girl" no longer has the same negative connotations.

LESSONS AND OBSERVATIONS

Every brand has the opportunity to align their success with higher goals and purposes. Feminine protection products might not have obviously been linked with girl empowerment in most people's minds, but once Always launched this initiative it became clear that there was a natural fit and clear opportunity for mutual benefit.

CITATION: Cannes Lions Winners, 2015

Key Takeaways

- **We may not personally know each individual we communicate with, but there is no doubt that they are as informed, conscientious, and astute as our nearest and dearest. It's time to treat them as such. Indeed, "they" are "we."**
- **A meaningful purpose adds depth and authenticity to any brand: a trait that is essential in the information age. Connect with people's values and perspectives, and you create a community.**
- **This community is not a dictatorship—a one-way flow of messaging from advertiser to all who happen upon it. It's an ecosystem: each interconnected member strengthens and contributes to a dynamic, adaptable, whole.**
- **This ecosystem is made up of people outside and inside your company. Finding ways to break down the timeless creative/analytic divide, or the design/operational divide, and developing a working space where a shared vision permeates, is crucial *(see Figure 3.3).***

Chapter 4

Orchestrating Value Creation across *All* Touchpoints

We believe that great brands are "business strategy brought to life" and deliver a seamless experience across product and service, physical spaces and places, internal culture and communications. Companies like Apple have already set customer expectations and it doesn't matter if you are a bank, a business consultancy, a retailer, or a hotel chain, the message is simple: join up!

— Jez Frampton, *Global CEO, Interbrand (2012)*

We begin this chapter with perhaps the second-most organizationally challenging change (see the previous chapter for the most challenging): moving beyond a narrow focus on media mix to a more holistic orchestration of *every single* touchpoint of a brand including, but by no means limited to, what is traditionally known as "advertising."

The forces of change described in Part I suggest that a continued focus on a narrow notion of what is currently within the purview of advertising and marketing will threaten the life of a brand and its company. Brands need to provide the seamless experience that people are taught to expect by each day's new technology-enabled and insight-inspired pacesetters. Even the notion of "omnichannel," which is currently limited to the realm of retail, will work within a larger ecosystem as retail and advertising undergo a fusion.

More and More Ways to Connect

In order to reach, serve, and stay connected with people in comprehensive and effective ways, advertising's scope must go beyond its traditional reach to encompass the entire firm. The boundaries between external and internal touchpoints are blurring and will continue to do so. As Nigel Morris, chief executive officer of Dentsu Aegis Americas and EMEA, muses:

> *The point of convergence is the empowerment of people and the dynamics of convergence are enabling people to take control over their relationship with businesses and with media.*
>
> *In a convergent world, no person and no touchpoint exists in isolation. Everything is interconnected.*
>
> *In a convergent world, every action can potentially have an effect on everything else. Everything is interdependent.*
>
> *In a convergent world, it is impossible to keep things separate, or to control the way that a consumer interacts with a company. Everything is transparent.*
>
> *The future of advertising and communications will move from channeling brand messages to designing and creating valuable consumer-brand interactions. But they will only be valuable to brands if the brand delivers relevant utility or enjoyment at the right time, place, and social or physical context to the right people. (2012)*

Just for starters, think about this from a fairly traditional purchase perspective. Faith Popcorn, chief executive officer at Faith Popcorn's BrainReserve, imagines how the notion of purchase will disseminate, challenging today's static conception of point of purchase: *"Every media—from billboards and print to TV, radio, and social networking—will incorporate purchase options that enable us to buy on the spot without traveling to a separate retail location . . . . Virtually every point in space and time will be a point of purchase"* (2012).

Consider the many different ways that we now encounter brands on a daily basis—tv, radio, print; online searches; mobile apps; websites; billboards and digital out-of-home ads; branded social media posts; offline and online conversations; personal interactions; web browsing; store design and displays; package design and packaging; conversations with sales people; in-store promotions. And that is all just the "before purchase" exposure, followed by interactions with customer service, online help features, surveys, loyalty programs, etc.

This list is by no means exhaustive: it's today's bare minimum. J. Walker Smith, executive chairman of The Futures Company, captures an important element of these encounters:

> *[A]dvertisers must target conversations, not individuals. It is less common for people to encounter advertising head-on. Conversations have become the pathways by which people encounter advertising. People talk about it, solicit*

opinions about it, watch parodies of it, hear stories about it, do research on it, compare and contrast it with other advertising, and even add their own personal touches. Advertising that makes for good conversation is what works these days." (2012)

Smart brands today are starting these conversations through increasingly unexpected channels. For example:

- In August 2014, IKEA partnered with international accommodations site Airbnb to offer three groups of guests, selected by submitted essays, the opportunity to sleep overnight at an IKEA in New South Wales, Australia, in **actual display rooms**. Guests were promised special activities and surprises as well as the take-home gift of the sheets they slept on and advice from Airbnb hosts on how to prepare their homes for guests.

- In 2012, a Russian website dedicated to local news, Ura.Ru, painted caricatures of local politicians directly over **neglected potholes** in dire need of repair; the global media coverage spurred the shamed politicians to act.

- In 2013, the UK Department of Transport shocked pub-goers in London with a stunt where a mannequin suddenly smashed through the back of a **bathroom mirror**, accompanied by car crash sounds, simulating a pedestrian going through a wind shield in a car crash (presumably caused by a drunk driver). The "Pub Loo Shocker" was part of a larger campaign for driving safety and was connected with online, television, social, and print campaigns.

This is not to say that potholes and bathroom mirrors should be added to every brand's touchpoint matrix, **but these examples begin to demonstrate the breadth of ways to connect with people and the creative and analytical opportunity this presents.** Amy-Willard Cross, founder and editor of The BUY UP Index (NB: an app that helps you make purchasing decisions based on a company's demonstrated commitment to gender equality), cites the example of Levis Curve ID: *"The company retooled its jean sizing and production after discovering that most women had to try on nine pairs of jeans before finding a pair that fit"* (2013). Jeans sizing that is engineered to solve a problem is an effective touchpoint.

Recent research by Wharton marketing professor David Bell confirms that location and word of mouth play a strong role in brand preference (Bell 2015). One recommendation based on his research is to make packaging that stands out—then when someone is carrying around an eye-catching shopping bag, there's a new touchpoint. If a fabulously designed package is opened at the office, you've just expanded the audience of your touchpoint. We will delve

Figure 4.1 A Sampling of Touchpoints

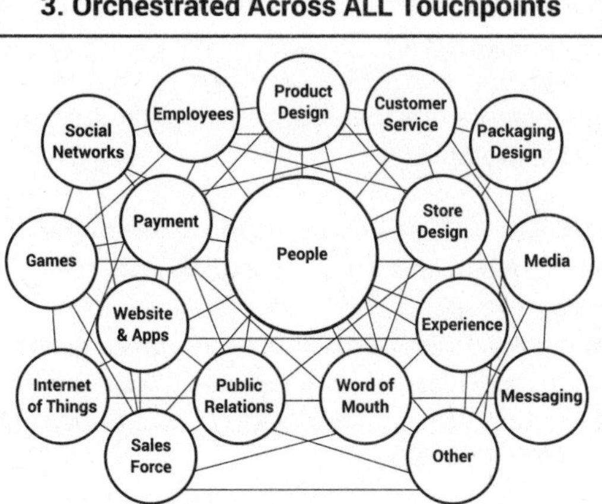

more deeply into leveraging touchpoint context in Chapter 6, but consider the many different ways we interact with brands. Figure 4.1 offers a starting point for thinking far more broadly about all touchpoints.

Thought of in this way, brands and the people who find ways to make them meaningful have never had more ways to reach and engage people. Importantly, touchpoints will continue to multiply as we enter an era where every object has the potential to become connected and interactive. Technology is evolving so rapidly that we hesitate to define it lest we do so too narrowly: the Internet of Things, of people, of needs, of concepts, of service . . . of solutions? We are entering, as Tom Goodwin—senior vice president of strategy and innovation at Havas Media and founder of Tomorrow Group—calls it, the era of "the ambient Internet:"

> *The ad world of 2020 will be anchored in the new consumer landscape, a new world where words like TV or radio mean nothing, where everything is digital, and where we endlessly record, share, process, and act upon data that has become an ambient layer around us. Our TVs become large screens to access this ambient Internet and content in an at-home, entertainment context. Smartphones become our portable, personal gateways, and smart watches record data while providing the simplest access points to this Internet. Meanwhile refrigerators, thermostats, cars, and ever more devices become connected through seamless background transfer of data between them. The Internet won't be a deep experience of search and browsing like it is now, but it will mainly form a thin layer that will assist us in our daily lives. (2014)*

Just to be clear, "ambient" means we don't have to do anything to be connected. The environment will connect us. Sensors will be placed in public and private places to capture multisensory information about us. Our face will be matched with online images, our expression matched with facial recognition technology that can connect to our most current social media activity. Our facial expressions can further be analyzed to predict what our mood is at any given point in time, enabling a continuously optimized algorithm to give us just what we want, when we want it. Or it can capture our voice, and within a few words, assess our mental and emotional state and then connect with us in the ways that work best for us, and for what the brand wants to accomplish. All this can be instantaneously connected with other data and then processed using the artificial intelligence of IBM, Google, Amazon, Facebook, and myriad emerging tech-intelligence companies that continuously optimize these touchpoints.

Connected transportation, homes, appliances, health, pets, gardens, education, waste, clothes, leisure . . . all potential touchpoints. Now, imagine each of these in the most diverse locations in your community, your country, and in the diversity of locations around the world. They come to life differently, don't they? But in each case, with tremendous potential for impact.

And of course, connectivity is not a replacement for reality. As Matthew Godfrey, president of Y&R Asia notes:

> *Digital does not mean we will stay glued to our devices. We all still crave real experiences, parties, concerts, sports, meetings, dates, comedy clubs, and more. It's just that we will want technology to be blended with those real-world experiences. Digital will not be a silo, or a medium. It will be a facilitator and an enhancer to our lifestyles. (2012)*

This vision of the near future brings into focus the limitations of the concept of "media mix." Vinicius Reis, partner and chief operating officer at CP+B Brasil, captures this contemporary inadequacy:

> *This decade will put in check what today we call "channels." The new world won't present mediums. Anything will be able to deliver a message. . . . Content will flow through everything. Especially if by then holography becomes something anyone can have on a device in his pocket. We will truly have to be able to create formats for whatever exists. (2012)*

Goodwin shares Reis's radical channel-free vision: *"Media channels of today are irrelevant in the future; we will instead see media buys for contexts, the act of being near a mall, watching a movie, or listening to happy music"* (2014).

Unfortunately, many organizations are not prepared for these scenarios. **Can your organization "buy for contexts"? Will you be able to "deliver a message" when content is "flowing through everything?"**

The image of "content flowing through everything" is captivating, and we debated using the term "experience" instead of touchpoint. Yes, it is critically important that the experience with a brand be as rich as possible, as we point out in Chapters 5 and 6. But the current discussion of experience tends to focus on existing customers, as in those who have already engaged with a brand by some kind of connection, be it as benign as search or as definitive as a purchase. We need to take this increasing standard for experience all the way through what has traditionally been known as advertising and hold it to the same standards.

The practical challenge is that in many, if not most, firms, people who create the television ads do not communicate with the team who designs the product package; loyalty programs are designed and managed by a team with no connection to the branding experts who throw the product launch party; social media messages are created without input from the salespeople who interact with live or online customers. Siloed organizations like those will not survive in the 2020 era. As Frederic Bonn, chief creative officer, North America, at the Mirum Agency puts it:

> *To be ready for that future, we need to start thinking beyond campaigns, beyond media buys or social tactics. Beyond mobile apps or CRM, beyond advertising or e-commerce. The ways people interact with brands will expand exponentially through digital channels. It is time to think about brands' ecosystems—the brand's multiple touchpoints and how they interact with each other, from a digital out-of-home experience to a tablet, from mobile to the store. (2012)*

We talk more about the plague of silos in Part III.

The notion of all touchpoint value creation is that all interactions with a brand, from the first time you become aware that it exists to every touchpoint that you encounter along the way of your daily life, there is a net-positive impact. As Anne Rivers from BAV Consulting writes, *"Brands will be measured on people's experiences with the brand across and regardless of all channels"* (2015).

Touchpoint connotes a sense of neutrality, of opportunity. Anything could happen at that point of interaction for all parties involved. What could/should that be? At that point of intersection, data and information is potentially flowing, being captured and acted upon in multiple ways – including what was the last touchpoint and what could/should/is the next for that particular individual along their particular (very likely non-linear) journey. **Not only are we and the brand impacted, but at that point of intersection, action, information exchange, a lot of valuable data is being thrown off for those who are facilitating the touchpoint.** Channels, media, ad tech companies, metrics trackers, researchers, friends, communities . . . everyone with his or her finger on the pulse who seeks to glean insights and create value is affected. In the future, we have a lot of company at these touchpoints.

To be clear, it's not only brands that create touchpoints. However, they need to be able to have sensing systems in place to know and react, if not anticipate, where and how these touchpoints are happening. A touchpoint is an opportunity. An encounter. What happens at that moment either paves the way for the next moment of truth or chips away at the value built to date.

Empirical Evidence of the Influence of All Touchpoints

Research conducted by word-of-mouth market research and consulting firm Keller Fay Group strongly supports the power of an all touchpoint approach to marketing. The Group's research study, TalkTrack®, "measures over 350,000 conversations about brands annually, allowing for finely-grained time series tracking, plus detailed analyses for niche markets, across hundreds of brands in dozens of categories" (TalkTrack® 2015). The survey encompasses both the digital and non-digital world, as 90 percent of brand-related conversations take place offline.

Particularly relevant is that a diversity of touchpoints drive word of mouth—people talk about a lot more than just traditional media. In the results for May/June of 2015 *(see Figure 4.2)* the research shows that consumers discuss

Figure 4.2 Findings from Keller Fay Group's TalkTrack – Average Across All Categories

NET MEDIA/MARKETING REFERENCES	AVERAGE ACROSS ALL CATEGORIES
Any Media/Marketing	**56.7%**
Television Ad	9.2%
Something in a Store	4.9%
Television Program	2.9%
Brand Website	8.4%
Coupon/Circular	3.0%
Online Social Media	4.8%
Digital Ad	3.9%
Product Package	3.4%
Other Website	5.6%
Online Customer Reviews	7.6%
A Sales Person	6.9%
Product Sample	2.7%
Newspaper Ad	3.4%
Billboard Ad	2.9%
Customer Service by Phone/Online	3.3%
Magazine Ad	4.2%
Something in a Stadium Theater, Convention Center, Or Other Event	2.8%
An Ad Or App On a Mobile Device	2.3%
Newspaper Article	2.2%
Magazine Article	3.5%
Direct Mail	1.8%
Email Or Text From A Business	2.6%
Radio Ad	2.0%
Radio Program	1.9%
Any Other Type Of Advertisement	1.0%
BASE SIZES (Branded Category Discussions	*1749*

Source: Findings are from Keller Fay Group's TalkTrack®, the most comprehensive ongoing study of word of mouth. The results in this table were collected in May & June 2015; during this time, 5746 respondents aged 13-69 were interviewed. The question text reads: "Did anyone in the conversation refer to something about the brand/company from any of these sources?"

non-media touchpoints, such as the product packaging, product samples, physical object, sales people, coupons, customer service, and more (Keller Fay Group, 2015).

Furthermore, different touchpoints have more resonance in different product categories. When asked "Did anyone in the conversation refer to something about the brand/company from any of these sources?" responses showed that sales people were most often referred to in relation to cars, the home, and technology; customer service was most often referred to in relation to finance, telecommunication, and healthcare; and product packaging was most referred to in relation to beverages, personal care/beauty, and household products.

Figures 4.3 and 4.4 are extracted from the Keller Fay Group's findings and offer insights on the importance of touchpoints beyond traditional media.

A Seamless Experience

From the customer perspective, touchpoints with a brand or product are not differentiated: it is the seamless experience that matters. When we buy a product on Amazon, we may not care whether the product is mailed from a warehouse or any number of retail shops. We expect an easy and secure shopping experience, prompt, reliable delivery, and exceptional customer service. The same is true for all interactions we have with brands: we want the information/product/service at our convenience, and it may not matter who is responsible for making it happen. What brands today are working toward providing this kind of seamless experience?

Iconic retail brand Macy's is one. Recognizing that customers use a multitude of media to shop—from stores to websites, from in-person to mobile—the company developed a thorough omnichannel retail strategy. (Wharton's Jay H. Baker Retailing Center is a reliable resource for cutting-edge insights on retail.) By converting and amalgamating back-office operations, including establishing a chief omnichannel officer, customer orders anywhere could be met—should something be out of stock at their local store, another store would fill the order, no matter how the request was made. Their mobile platform is sleek, includes point of sale, and offers endless aisle technology—more is available online than in store. **Macy's effectively removed silos between e-commerce and in-store retail.** As a leader in embracing omnichannel initiatives, Macy's will be one of the first retailers to support Apple Pay, ensuring that customers can research, buy, and collect their purchases when they want, where they want.

If Macy's offers a well-recognized in-house seamless experience, the future of "seamlessness" is already upon us. Consider the newly launched service GoButler, that makes Internet search functions, the most intuitive online ordering services, and even apps seem clunky and time-consuming. As TechCrunch reported, "you simply send a text message to GoButler and the service's 'butlers'—who act as virtual assistants—process your request, keeping you informed along the way. So, for example, you could have GoButler book a movie or order your favorite pizza." (O'Hear 2015)

Figure 4.3 Findings from Keller Fay Group's TalkTrack by Category – Part 1

NET MEDIA/ MARKETING REF.	AUTOMOTIVE	FINANCIAL SERVICES	HEALTH/ HEALTHCARE	FOOD/ DINING	BEVERAGES	TECHNOLOGY	TELECOM	TRAVEL SERVICES
Any Media/Marketing	**56.7%**	**60.2%**	**55.1%**	**55.2%**	**57.3%**	**66.8%**	**62.8%**	**62.4%**
Television Ad	9.2%	7.8%	5.9%	10.0%	8.4%	9.5%	11.5%	6.5%
Something in a Store	4.9%	3.9%	8.4%	11.7%	14.9%	7.6%	6.0%	3.2%
Television Program	2.9%	3.2%	3.3%	2.0%	3.1%	3.3%	4.3%	2.3%
Brand Website	8.4%	12.3%	7.0%	3.8%	3.1%	8.0%	8.2%	20.2%
Coupon/Circular	3.0%	3.2%	4.4%	10.3%	6.6%	2.4%	2.4%	2.8%
Online Social Media	4.8%	4.8%	2.8%	4.1%	4.0%	8.9%	4.5%	6.5%
Digital Ad	3.9%	6.2%	2.8%	3.9%	3.8%	9.2%	5.7%	7.3%
Product Package	3.4%	3.2%	5.9%	7.1%	9.6%	4.9%	3.4%	2.4%
Other Website	5.6%	3.4%	4.1%	2.7%	3.0%	6.5%	4.5%	6.7%
Online Customer Reviews	7.6%	3.9%	4.2%	3.0%	2.7%	8.2%	5.8%	5.6%
A Sales Person	6.9%	4.9%	4.4%	2.6%	3.2%	5.1%	4.5%	2.6%
Product Sample	2.7%	3.0%	4.1%	4.1%	6.0%	3.1%	2.8%	1.6%
Newspaper Ad	3.4%	3.1%	2.1%	3.3%	3.0%	2.6%	2.7%	2.2%
Billboard Ad	2.9%	5.9%	2.9%	2.2%	2.2%	3.9%	3.5%	7.6%
Customer Service by Phone/Online	3.3%	9.3%	6.2%	1.9%	1.8%	3.9%	7.0%	4.0%
Magazine Ad	4.2%	2.7%	4.6%	2.4%	2.6%	2.4%	3.2%	2.9%
Something in a Stadium Theater, Convention Center, Or Other Event	2.8%	5.6%	5.9%	1.7%	2.2%	2.7%	4.7%	3.6%
An Ad Or App On a Mobile Device	2.3%	2.1%	2.3%	1.9%	2.1%	5.3%	3.2%	2.7%
Newspaper Article	2.2%	2.7%	3.0%	1.5%	2.2%	2.5%	2.2%	1.5%
Magazine Article	3.5%	2.3%	2.6%	1.8%	2.2%	3.3%	2.3%	2.3%
Direct Mail	1.8%	1.7%	1.0%	1.8%	2.4%	1.8%	3.3%	1.7%
Email Or Text From A Business	2.6%	1.7%	1.0%	1.8%	2.4%	1.8%	3.3%	1.7%
Radio Ad	2.0%	2.2%	2.3%	1.9%	2.1%	2.4%	2.9%	1.8%
Radio Program	1.9%	2.1%	1.2%	1.3%	1.6%	1.9%	2.1%	1.6%
Any Other Type Of Advertisement	1.0%	1.1%	1.8%	2.0%	1.4%	0.9%	1.4%	1.2%
BASE SIZES (Branded Category Discussions	*1749*	*1244*	*1278*	*3909*	*3019*	*2432*	*1535*	*1166*

You can also have your GoButler reserve plane tickets, pick up dry cleaning, or even bring you an iPhone charger—all free of charge (barring delivery fees). What kind of service will brands have to offer in the future to keep people directly engaged? Or will the notion of engagement change?

If people do not get the seamless experience they expect, they leave. Or if we are fortunate enough that they care to take the time, they make it clear on social media that a brand does not have a consistent, holistic message, or worse, the message is at odds with their practices.

Figure 4.4 Findings from Keller Fay Group's TalkTrack by Category – Part 2

NET MEDIA/ MARKETING REF.	PERSONAL CARE/BEAUTY	HOUSEHOLD PRODUCTS	THE HOME	CHILDREN'S PRODUCTS	RETAIL/ APPAREL	MEDIA ENTERTAINMENT	SPORTS/RECREATION HOBBIES
Any Media/Marketing	**71.6%**	**60.3%**	**66.5%**	**73.3%**	**68.7%**	**65.3%**	**66.6%**
Television Ad	12.3%	9.5%	7.2%	6.6%	5.7%	14.8%	7.6%
Something in a Store	12.9%	12.7%	14.3%	16.9%	17.4%	2.7%	3.6%
Television Program	3.3%	3.4%	5.5%	5.9%	2.7%	21.9%	19.4%
Brand Website	4.8%	4.9%	7.5%	6.1%	8.3%	3.2%	3.4%
Coupon/Circular	11.0%	9.1%	5.6%	9.8%	10.9%	1.4%	2.1%
Online Social Media	3.3%	2.7%	3.5%	4.4%	3.8%	9.0%	8.4%
Digital Ad	7.4%	5.2%	6.0%	6.3%	5.3%	5.1%	3.6%
Product Package	9.7%	8.1%	6.2%	6.8%	3.7%	2.0%	2.6%
Other Website	3.6%	2.9%	5.2%	3.9%	4.7%	4.7%	5.9%
Online Customer Reviews	4.2%	3.5%	6.2%	5.7%	4.2%	2.5%	2.8%
A Sales Person	4.3%	3.6%	6.0%	4.4%	5.4%	1.3%	1.7%
Product Sample	9.8%	5.0%	3.9%	5.9%	3.1%	1.4%	1.6%
Newspaper Ad	3.4%	4.3%	3.8%	3.1%	5.8%	1.9%	2.6%
Billboard Ad	2.8%	2.8%	2.8%	6.4%	3.8%	1.6%	2.8%
Customer Service by Phone/Online	3.2%	1.9%	3.2%	2.8%	2.7%	1.4%	1.5%
Magazine Ad	5.1%	2.0%	3.6%	4.1%	3.2%	2.3%	2.9%
Something in a Stadium Theater, Convention Center, Or Other Event	2.9%	3.1%	4.7%	4.2%	3.5%	1.7%	1.8%
An Ad Or App On a Mobile Device	2.7%	2.4%	2.9%	3.1%	2.4%	3.1%	1.9%
Newspaper Article	2.5%	2.9%	3.2%	2.1%	2.9%	2.1%	6.1%
Magazine Article	4.0%	2.9%	3.2%	2.6%	1.8%	2.8%	2.9%
Direct Mail	1.9%	1.5%	1.7%	2.0%	1.2%	4.0%	9.3%
Email Or Text From A Business	1.7%	2.3%	1.9%	3.7%	2.9%	1.7%	2.1%
Radio Ad	1.8%	2.3%	2.1%	2.4%	2.1%	1.8%	1.5%
Radio Program	2.0%	2.8%	0.9%	2.9%	1.9%	1.7%	4.3%
Any Other Type Of Advertisement	1.0%	1.2%	1.5%	1.7%	1.2%	1.8%	1.5%
BASE SIZES (Branded Category Discussions	*1309*	*1041*	*1079*	*620*	*2706*	*4104*	*2535*

Paul Worthington, president of Invencion, Inc., and Karl Heiselman, senior director of Apple, capture these ideas in their description of "total experience management":

> *Today's brand experiences are highly fragmented and as a result are a significant source of competitive weakness (as any trawl of social media will demonstrate). By 2020, this will have changed considerably. Instead of focusing on individual touchpoints, brands will instead be considering the rich*

ecosystem of experiences they create. They will look at the integration of their brand ecosystem under a common "operating system" as a means of enhancing customer value. By thinking of the total experience, and usefulness, of the brand from the customer's point of view, brands will create superior experiences across not just a single touchpoint but across the entirety of the branded experience. (2012)

The concept of all touchpoint orchestration is compelling . . . but granted, it's not easy. In the following chapters we look more closely at what it takes to enable these "superior experiences across the entirety of the branded experience," or all touchpoint value creation.

What would it look like and feel like if all of your current and potential touchpoints were orchestrated in a way that yielded maximum value to all involved?

Figure 4.5 Beyond Advertising in Action: Orchestrate All Touchpoints

Beyond Advertising in Action
ORCHESTRATE ALL TOUCHPOINTS

KAN KHAJURA TESAN STATION—HINDUSTAN UNILEVER
Agency: Lowe Lintas & Partners
Warc 100: #1, 2014

OBJECTIVE/PROBLEM TO BE SOLVED
Bihar and Jharkhand are two of India's most media-dark regions, but they make up a lucrative demographic for Unilever, who wanted to find a way to market to this audience in a place where traditional channels were unavailable.

APPROACH
In 2014 Unilever created a free-of-charge phone service that people could call for 20 minutes of entertainment and branded content: effectively a replacement radio or T.V. There was no limit to the number of times people could call in, and content was customized for each region.

THE RESULTS
During the first weeks of the service, the station was receiving 150 thousand calls a day. Within six months, the station had clocked 24 million calls and 8 million unique users, meaning Unilever had achieved reach in 25.5 percent of the population. The entire initiative was conducted for a cost of less than four U.S. cents per person.

LESSONS AND OBSERVATIONS
Understanding local needs and customs leads to valuable insights into the touchpoints and delivery mechanisms that will resonate best with a given group of people. Innovative touchpoints, such as a call-in phone service, can have a dramatic impact.

CITATION: Warc 100, 2014

Key Takeaways

- **The days of a simplistic division between—and limitation to—paid, earned, and owned advertising are gone. The five forces of change demand diversification beyond the traditional definitions.**

- **Touchpoints are everywhere, and of course some work better for one brand than others. But don't stay mired in the familiar, be it platform, content, or medium. Seemingly unconventional channels may be the most powerful, especially when considered in concert with others.**

- **To reach savvy and unique individuals today, we need to take a holistic approach to communication. New technology and modes of communication have made such an approach possible and necessary: and will continue to evolve.**

- **Connectivity is already virtually everywhere, and is only going to expand. How brands choose to embrace and utilize the connected world defines our exciting and challenging future.**

- **Touchpoints are not a theory—they have proven impact. As the Keller Fey research shows, people respond to brands in myriad ways: anything can spark a connection – far beyond the traditional realm of advertising and marketing – though still very much inclusive of them *(see Figure 4.5).***

Chapter 5

New Guidelines for Desired Content: R.A.V.E.S.

"I want advertising to be useful to people. I want it to be something we want in our lives when we need it. I want it to contribute to how we live and understand our culture and society. Is this a marketing utopia that will never happen? There are a few signs to the contrary."

— Calle Sjoenell, *CEO, Lowe Brindfors (2012)*

On May 12, 2015, *Business Insider* published a story titled "Soon you can order a pizza by tweeting the pizza emoji at Domino's." It read:

> Domino's is introducing a "tweet to order" system that will allow customers to place direct orders for pizza via Twitter.
>
> Frequent customers will barely have to type; just tweet a pizza emoji at the brand and a hot, fresh pie will be on its way . . .
>
> "Domino's has become something closer to a tech company that sells pizza," Doyle says.
>
> The pizza company is not the first to experiment with Twitter as an ordering platform. Both Starbucks and the Miami Dolphins have tested similar promotions. Starbucks offered consumers the chance to "tweet to send a coffee to a friend" and the Miami Dolphins allowed fans to tweet for a beer to be delivered to their seat. (Lorenz 2015)

Commonly held notions of how advertising is defined and why advertising works have been challenged and upended by rigorous analyses of studies conducted across multiple channels; now we know more than ever about what reaches people and motivates them to act. Cleverly adapting to these results is clearly a mark of talent: Domino's Emoji Ordering campaign won the Titanium Grand Prix award at Cannes Lions 2015, the highest award for *both* creativity and effectiveness.

Most people today think of advertising as an interruption, a distraction, a nuisance, a waste of time. If we could skip or ignore it all, we would. Most of the time, that is; there are exceptions. And in the future, the exception must be the rule. As Michael Jacobs, managing partner and executive creative director at Our True North and chief creative officer at iRGONOMIC writes, *"Advertising as an interruptive act will be gone, replaced by narrative content that is informative, entertaining and on brand in a much more relevant way"* (2012).

What are these exceptions? Videos that we share with friends because they are funny, moving, or provide useful information, that inspire us or engage our creativity or teach us something we didn't know. Touchpoints and brand experiences that make us talk, think, and reflect.

As we have been advocating, "beyond advertising" needs to earn people's attention. To do this, it could and should be *relevant, respectful, actionable, valuable and value-generating;* and provide an *exceptional experience* and a *shareworthy story* delivered through all touchpoints. It could and should be R.A.V.E.S. *(see Figure 5.1).*

Why R.A.V.E.S.?

As we have discussed, effective advertising and marketing in 2020 could and should be something we all embrace. With the R.A.V.E.S. content standards, advertising could and should be **relevant and respectful**—custom-fitted to the individual yet

Figure 5.1 R.A.V.E.S. Content Guidelines

	R.A.V.E.S. CONTENT GUIDELINES
R	RELEVANT AND RESPECTFUL To Individuals and Of Individuals
A	ACTIONABLE Intuitive and Frictionless
V	VALUABLE AND VALUE-GENERATING Wanted, Needed, Effective
E	EXCEPTIONAL EXPERIENCE Delight and Inspire
S	SHAREWORTHY STORY Authentic and Authoratative

not overstepping the line of privacy. It should be **actionable**—create a dialogue, enable people to interact, share, or co-create. It must **provide value**—monetary, cognitive, or emotional—as well as **cultivate the value** of the brand. It should provide an **exceptional experience** for the individual and incorporate a share-worthy story to stand out amongst the media melee. And most important, all R.A.V.E.S. communications should be delivered through every point of contact that people have with a brand before, during, and after a purchase. To quote Akihiko Kubo, chairman, Group Representative at Ogilvy & Mather Japan, *"People are no longer happy to sit back and be easily influenced. They want engagement. They want to better understand how products and services are relevant to their lives. And if they are happy, impressed, or satisfied (and we hope they are), you can bet that they will let their friends and family know it"* (2012).

Michael Maslansky, CEO of Maslansky + Partners, paints a compelling picture of our intended audience of the future:

> *As Alex prepares for bed, she surveys her apartment. She is very conscious of what she buys and why. Her purchases are deliberate. She doesn't buy things, she buys things with meaning. Though she sees less traditional advertising than she used to, she is more engaged with the ads that she views. She can connect her purchases to strong creative content created by brands, or co-created by brand fans. Though she is exposed to lots of targeted ads, she feels that she is one who controls the content she sees. She accepts new brands warily and rarely with a direct entreaty from the advertiser. Instead, she relies on peers and trusted sources for her introductions. At the same time, she actively engages with the brands she likes and actively discourages her network from doing business with brands she dislikes. She wants companies to challenge her, understand her, and inspire her through the content they create. She wants stories that move her, excite her, and delight her. (2012)*

Given this scenario, all brands should be asking themselves, "How can we engage Alex and others like her today?" **When consumers have endless choices of content and screens, plus endless access to information and insights, why should they stop to listen to your message?** For every technology designed to interrupt a media experience or a search for information, people will find a way to block, ignore, or skip it. And if the interruption is egregious, be prepared to hear about it from empowered consumers. As John Miller, president and founder of Scribewise, puts it:

> *We have entered the era of preference marketing, and the audience will not buy from you unless you've created a relationship with them and demonstrated why they should choose you. The audience has access to so much information, much of it conflicting, that it rarely accepts anything at face value. You may claim that your service is the best, but the prospect can*

easily access your competitors, your customer reviews, and other third-party information sources. (2013)

What is the solution? Beyond advertising *could* and *should* be something people want and seek out because it provides value. J. R. Smith, executive chairman at NURO and partner at Evolution Equity, writes:

The trouble is that nobody opens their digital door to receive an ad. They will, however, invite information across their threshold, provided that it promises to be of value to them. In 2020, the successful advertisers will be those who years ago—like, right now—stopped treating consumers as so many targets and marks. In an online universe populated by consumers armed with the desire, the regulatory support, and the technology to be aggressively selective in the choices they make, advertisers will be obliged to treat consumers as decision makers. (2012)

Some brands are already bringing the R.A.V.E.S. model to life in their content, design, and interaction. One example is an initiative undertaken by a McDonald's in Madrid in early 2013. Upon realizing that patrons of neighboring restaurants and shops were taking advantage of McDonald's' free wi-fi, McDonald's incorporated witty messages and discounts into the names of their networks to entice the wi-fi users to come to McDonald's. The wi-fi networks names appeared in order as such:

"If all you want is free wi-fi,"

"Just stay where you are."

"But if you also want a good meal,"

"come to McDonald's."

They extended the experience to bus stops throughout the city, using such network names as, "This bus stop has free wi-fi" . . . "So does McDonald's" . . . "And it's more comfortable there."

The wi-fi network names became marketing messages. They reached people in an unexpected, funny, and unobtrusive way and through a novel touch-point while offering value and boosting the brand's playful image.

How is it **R.A.V.E.S.**?

The initiative is **relevant** to users who are in the act of an exchange with McDonald's—using their wi-fi in physical proximity.

It is **respectful** of people in the tone and unobtrusiveness of the message.

It offers several possible **actions**—keep using free wi-fi, or come to McDonald's for a discount. Even if a person chooses to keep using free wi-fi, they have been made aware of McDonald's' generosity, which might inspire them to patronize the restaurant in the future.

It offers **value** in all three of its dimensions: monetary (a discount); cognitive (an unexpected offer and awareness of McDonald's offering free wi-fi), and emotional (surprising and funny).

It is an **exceptional experience**—simple and useful. Someone might expect that being "caught" using free wi-fi would lead to being charged or cut-off. McDonald's chose to extend humor and generosity instead.

It provides a **shareworthy story**—unexpected and funny, exactly the kind of story that people like to share with their friends and that builds good will.

And finally, McDonald's is taking advantage of every possible point of interaction with people. Of course they have print ads, television ads, billboards, and online ads, and have the most recognizable symbol in the entire world, but they don't overlook the many other avenues where they reach and impact their audience and potential patrons.

All communications that brands have with people can achieve this level of effective content, design, and interaction. **It is the way to engage consumers like Alex, who are suspicious of inauthentic messages yet open to being surprised and delighted.**

Many successful R.A.V.E.S. examples take place in the real world instead of on screen. Brands have always taken advantage of spaces where people are captive audiences, such as in airports and bus stops. These days, as people are immersed in their mobile devices and disconnected from their surroundings, brands have to work a bit harder to get noticed. But mobile devices and innovations in out-of-home advertising technology (such as QR codes and geofencing) provide unique opportunities for engagement.

In early 2013, Qualcomm Mobile did a "We Make Life Better with Mobile" stunt where they put up a poster at a bus stop in Los Angeles with questions such as "Bored?" "Seen It All?" and "In a Hurry?" followed by instructions to visit a web address. When the person visited the site on their mobile phone, within a few minutes different surprising forms of transportation and entertainment appeared at the bus stop—a Ferrari, a dog sled, a bus full of circus performers—to take the passengers to their destination and provide some unexpected fun.

Qualcomm took into consideration the state of mind of people waiting in public at a bus stop and provided an "opt-in" experience that made their campaign relevant and respectful; they offered an action to take (engage with the ad or not) and provided value—entertainment and transportation. **It was an exceptional experience for the participants and witnesses and had a surprising story about the potential of mobile technology.** Videos of these events went viral just a few days before Qualcomm announced the launch of a new product (Hepburn, 2013).

When advertising and all other touchpoints are R.A.V.E.S., people are more likely to enjoy it, appreciate it, share it, and act on it. Let's take a closer look at the five components of the R.A.V.E.S. model, which are brought to life in the graphic created by Alex Hall, president of the Americas at Tigerspike *(see Figure 5.2)*.

Figure 5.2 Alex Hall, Adspotting

Adspotting

Wharton
The future of advertising program

Choose life in 2020.

Choose any screen size you want for whatever, whenever & wherever.

Choose shows, movies and games you want when you want.

Choose who joins you on each screen to share the experience.

Choose touch screens with gesture, voice and mood controls thrown in.

Choose to switch from one screen to all screens to no screens at the touch of a button or through a single spoken word.

Choose to watch the same thing on every screen in every room of your house.

Choose to have something different on each screen – switching between each to embrace the ADD generation.

Choose from endless content, data and options; making choice a challenge.

Choose a whole new set of Digital Withdrawal Disorders (DWD). Choose weekend retreats offering no wifi or technology.

Choose multi tasking over ADD, because a positive spin is better than acknowledging you have no discipline.

Choose services that get you what you need faster, and filter relevant content before you get distracted.

Choose shorter sports matches, shorter movies, shorter e-books and shorter meals.

Choose whether you want advertising to accompany the experience.

Choose to pay for the right not to receive advertising.

Choose the right to dismiss advertising that bores you and isn't relevant.

Choose to pause a show with a word and to buy something from the freeze frame with another.

Choose not to choose and have content presented to you because the web can tell what mood you're in.

Choose your own Personal Technology adventure.

Consumerism will continue to grow and digital advertising will increasingly be requested and controlled by the consumer. The consumer will choose exactly what experience works for them with the limited time they have available. To be effective, advertising must complement that experience- through product placement, sponsorship or something yet unknown. Own the content, the utility or the experience on digital platforms and it may be possible to win over the consumer. Just choose the associations carefully, because we have a lot of options and dismiss irrelevancy in a flash.

Relevant and Respectful: We're Not "Targets," We're People!

> *Advertising will be a unique relevant communication experience the consumer "seeks" out because it will mean something to them . . . advertising will become Experiential Communication.*
>
> — Denise Larson, *President, Leap Media Investments (2012)*

In the digital age, relevance and respect are each essential elements for effective touchpoints including advertising. The speed and breadth of digitization, mobilization, and big data analytics enables communications and connections between brands and their audiences to be tailored in myriad personalized fine-tunes, making messages more relevant to us as unique individuals. At the same time, as empowered consumers we demand not only that the information or entertainment is relevant to us but that we see, hear, or experience it only when we choose to.

As George Musi, managing partner, analytics, insights, and attribution at Mindshare, explains:

> *As the consumer becomes more complex and sophisticated, they will deride intrusions, and demand highly personalized communication, offers, and experiences (that they actually value)—based on who they are, where they, what they've purchased before, etc. Consumers will become increasingly intolerant of ads that lack direct and immediate relevancy to them as individuals. Delivering relevance will no longer be an option—it will be a necessity! (2013)*

How to Be Relevant

All advertisers hope to reach the right person at the right time with the right message, and increasingly sophisticated technology combined with data analysis will make this more possible than ever in the years to come. Mark Holden, worldwide strategy and planning director for PhD UK, delves into this future scenario:

> *Forrester has termed the next few years as "The Great Race for Relevancy." This new social data combined with clearer content marking will be interrogated with powerful new algorithms. There will be a movement from link-based to answers that are algorithmically based, where search engines will actually compute the right answer. By 2020, we will be approaching a point where Google can give direct and accurate answers to questions like: What time is Guess Guess Guess on? Who plays in goal for LA Galaxy? Who is the favorite to win the Superbowl? What black suits are on sale at Zara?*
>
> *From here something magical starts to happen. . . .*
>
> *The Internet Wakes Up*
>
> *Beyond 2020, Google's algorithm will improve to the point where it can answer questions that are more nuanced and geo- and time-based: Is the*

stimulus package working? Which is Yui's best song at the moment? Did the council approve the town hall closure? When should I leave to get to Beijing by 8 P.M.?

At this point the Internet becomes an intelligence that will make its current guise seem incredibly dumb and disorganized. We won't know how we lived without it. (2012)

We are not quite there yet, but there are several levels of relevance that brands need to consider today.

The goal of relevance is to reach specific individuals. General demographics and television time-slots no longer cut it when trying to communicate with people who juggle multiple screens and identities (family, work, social roles) throughout the day. Advertisers must get to the basics: Who are you? What are you doing? Where are you? What time is it? Why are you doing it? And how?

A recent Pantene initiative—dubbed the Weather Program—encapsulates the value of such fine-tuned relevance. The company recognized that women often blamed their hair products for being ineffective when the weather was bad. In partnership with Walgreens and the Weather Channel, Pantene produced a "haircast'—geo-specific advertisements for a weather-specific hair product that appeared when an individual used the Weather Channel app. The ad then linked to a discount for product purchase at Walgreens. Rather than overwhelming consumers with products they didn't need, or already owned, Pantene found a way to preempt, and genuinely meet, consumer needs (2014).

As we know, we are receptive to different messages when we are in work mode during the day, parenting mode in the evening, or when we're walking past a Starbucks at 2 P.M. **Messages relevant to time, location, and personal preferences can be very effective, but they are not sufficient for optimal effectiveness: mood and state of mind must also be taken into consideration, just like human interaction: "Is this a good time to talk to you about . . . ?"**

As Jacques Bughin, director of McKinsey & Company, Brussels, and David Edelman, global co-leader of digital and marketing and sales of McKinsey & Company, Boston, write:

Digital media drove a shift in marketers' budgets to "always-on" digital media, such as search, display, and social. The marketing on-demand world of 2020 will evolve to be "always relevant." For brands and their agencies, that will require a much more sophisticated and targeted approach to address the ubiquity of touchpoints so that they can be there at a consumer's moment of need—no matter where or when it is. And, they will invest in massive analytical capabilities to support the brand's stewardship of their customers' information. As a renowned internet services leader recently said at McKinsey's 2011 Chief Marketing and Sales Officer Forum: "Ads need to answer questions". (2012)

Big Data analytics have the potential to develop an understanding of who we are; mobile technology has the potential to serve people with ads relevant to the time and their location; and our personal mobile devices can determine what we are doing and how to reach us. This leads us to the most relevant advertising message possible—the one we choose.

Make it Personal

> *[P]repared advertising campaigns as a one-way form of communications should be banished. Advertisers should create connections that count based on real-time, "tradigital," relevant, data-driven, human-centric, agile communications. There must be a purpose behind the brand that shares values with the consumer.*
>
> — Lisa Colantuono, *Co-President at AAR Partners (2013)*

In the Convergence Marketing study of consumer preferences from 2000, years before social media existed in current forms, it was determined that people wanted the five following things from advertisers: customization, community, convenience and channel options, competitive value, and tools for choice. Fourteen years later, these five categories define effectiveness in the digital age. If they haven't already, advertisers must ask themselves whether they are providing people with any of these five options (Wind and Mahajan 2002).

There are two main ways to personalize consumer experience. First, provide a platform for people to customize a product or service themselves. One of the earliest examples of a mass customizable platform is NIKEiD, which was launched in 1999. Originally an online service that allowed people to customize sneakers based on a few limited choices of colors and styles, the platform expanded to a large range of personalization options in stores and online. NIKEiD brought in huge revenues for Nike and showed the enormous potential for co-creation (Wong, 2010).

The second way to personalize an experience is to use sophisticated data analysis to make assumptions and predictions about what someone would want. Amazon's recommend feature, which suggests products you might like based on your previous purchases, and the My Yahoo homepage, which uses social media data to personalize the categories of news and information that appears on your home page, are current examples. The predictive analytics required to automate this personalization still have room for improvement.

Of course, automated personalization online walks a fine line between relevance and invasiveness. Facebook uses algorithms to determine what advertisements might be relevant to users depending on their stated preferences and behaviors, but these ads can be perceived as insulting when they miss the target since social media platforms like Facebook are intensely personal.

Similarly, the problem of "retargeting" plagues the online experience. When we make purchases online, we are often "followed" across websites with banner ads for the very products we have either already purchased or decided explicitly not to purchase. Tom Goodwin, SVP of strategy and innovation at Havas Media, said on our radio show, **"Retargeting is like a clock running slowly."** This lack of relevance within the context of online personalization can be incredibly frustrating. Personalization in the future will require advertisers to switch from using past data to predictive analytics, in theory to great effect. To quote Goodwin again, "By making fairly sensible guesses about what people are likely to do, we can give the right message to the right person at the right time. Offering someone an Uber when it's about to start raining will be really powerful" (Marketing Matters April 2014).

Terry Young, founder and CEO of Sparks & Honey, discusses how predictive analytics will create a "quantified everywhere" advertising renaissance in 2020:

> *The combination of quantified, sensor-based data, social data and transactional data will create a real-time marketing nirvana for the advertising industry. It will also open up new media spaces by turning currently unavailable physical environments into new storytelling experiences. Screens will be everywhere via new materials and projection technologies, sensors will be embedded in ALL physical objects and link ALL objects together into a unified network, and the average consumer will have enhanced sensory capabilities via the ever increasing computation power of 2020 Smart devices. (2013)*

R-E-S-P-E-C-T

> *The new marketing—in which the basic unit is now a story supported by sharing—can finally satisfy deep desires we all recognize: to be among friends in communities governed by mutual respect and shared ideals.*
>
> — Jon King, *Owner and Principal Consultant, Content Corporation (2012)*

Consideration of people's needs and state of mind is at the core of the respect that could/should characterize advertising in 2020. While messages can be tailored in the relevant ways, advertising always risks coming across as "creepy," the technical term for crossing the line without full disclosure. Avoiding this line is a conscious choice: The Qualcomm Mobile experience, for example, gave people an "opt-in" opportunity with their enticing messages rather than just dropping a surprise on them that might not have been welcome.

> *All brands can make moves towards inspiring a greater respect. Being true to the viewers, creating or being associated to content they like and with which they share common values, conveying messages only to viewers willing to receive them are some of the ways to gain respect. . . . New opportunities everyday can be seized by brands to get closer to the viewers, without being intrusive. Tomorrow's winning brands will probably be the most tactical*

ones, succeeding in establishing a close relationship not only with viewers, but with each viewer.

— Timothy Duquesne, *Screenwriter/Consultant, We Support Creators (2013)*

Being respectful means giving people the option to choose to hear the message or participate in the experience, being aware that people are heterogeneous and experience ads from many different points of view, expressing gratitude when people choose to receive and/or interact with your message.

Ad blocking represents the individual's vote against the advertiser's traditional bargain: "I make the content available to you, so you have to put up with whatever I choose to make you endure." Perhaps by simply creating content that follows the R.A.V.E.S. guidelines, business and revenue models of publishers, platforms, advertisers and other intermediaries could find alignment.

Imagine all of the advertising now that doesn't feel respectful. Think of the "ins": intrusive, inconvenient, insulting, invasive, inappropriate, inconsiderate, incomplete, indiscriminate, insensitive. How do the "ins" make people feel? Brendan Foley, divisional vice president, online business unit, Sears Holding Corporation, writes:

Women today drive 85 percent of all brand purchases made by households, represent the majority of the online market, and account for a greater percentage of social networking activity than men. According to recent surveys, however, many women feel misunderstood by marketers, receiving messages that don't resonate with their interests or how they want to consume information. (2012)

Crossing the Line

By 2020 the data flow will render both life and media flows more visible to advertisers, agencies, media owners, and increasingly citizens, too. As such, privacy issues will come even more to the fore, and establishing the appropriate protocols and protections will be essential in order to maintain trust.

— Hamish Pringle, *Non-Executive Director, 23 Red (2012)*

The era of big data creates many opportunities for a new level of intrusiveness. A colleague who had recently moved her family to a new city was sent a promotional email from The Gap with the subject line "Putting off packing? This should help." While we know that our online activities inform marketers of our preferences and general whereabouts, the promotion was perceived as intrusive and overly personal, not to mention several weeks too late. There is a balance, of course, that has to be achieved between people and the brands they communicate with. Miles Nadal, chairman and CEO of Peerage Capital, explains:

As consumers, we are now beginning to understand exactly what we are gaining, and sometimes giving up, in exchange for this balance. As advertisers,

> *we're always hungry to know more, and always in danger of upsetting that balance. We're navigating a meritocracy. Consumers will ultimately control the exchange, if not at the outset, then in the long run. (2012)*

Tom Morton, director of strategy at co:collective, warns about what might occur if there is not a balance—a future "Dumb Over-Targeting Scenario" where *"brand and media owners will pursue consumers through emerging media channels with barrages of offers based on half-correct algorithms. To paraphrase Russell Davies, it will be a Blade Runner future, brought to you by Groupon"* (2012).

Crossing the line of relevance is one way to annoy people. Cindy Gallop, founder and CEO of MakeLoveNotPorn, IfWeRanTheWorld, and Behance, describes another way:

> *From "you can download this for free, if you just watch these ads," to "you can make your calls for free if you just agree to receive ads to your phone," and the pre-roll ad countdown: "Just 10 more seconds to go, nine more seconds to go, bear with us, eight more seconds to go," all these messages are driven by, and what they communicate, that advertising is a very bad thing. And that therefore people have to be tricked, cajoled, persuaded, begged, bribed or blackmailed into watching it. (2012)*

And today, empowered consumers will happily let brands know when they've crossed a line of respect. In Singapore, when an insurance company created a Facebook page about an unusual couple in love they garnered over 3,000 followers. When it was revealed that the couple were actors in an insurance commercial, the negative backlash was so bad that the actors in the campaign were personally threatened and the insurance company never revealed itself. When today's empowered consumers feel duped or manipulated, they speak back (Chansanchai 2011).

We don't stand for intrusion and manipulation in interpersonal relations, so why should we in communications with brands and the companies behind them? Instead of all the "ins," imagine if all the potential was going in the opposite direction? To make advertising respectful, be on-demand; considerate of people's time, energy, emotions, and intelligence; and sensitive to differences.

> *The brands of 2020 are essentially all in the same business regardless what they produce or sell—customer advocacy, service, and satisfaction. There is less room or tolerance for disconnect between a brand and its audience.*
>
> — Sam Hanna, *International Director, Athenaeum Worldwide (2013)*

Actionable: Sounds Good, Now What?

> *Messages in the future will need to be smart. If they do not integrate fulfillment and payment mechanisms so that people can take decisions immediately,*

> *a lot of sales will be lost. Brands and agencies must look at each message as a potential point of purchase.*
>
> — Ravi Kiran, *Cofounder and CEO, DazzleToday, VentureNursery, and Friends of Ambition (2012)*

Touchpoints, including advertising, in 2020 should take advantage of the many ways audiences can immediately and easily take action. Social media offers reverberating options to tweet, like, post, comment, share, pan, react, and more. Viral ads can reach millions of people across the globe at incredible speeds. Innovative payment options collapse the purchase journey to one click. Learn more, opt-in, opt-out, try on, borrow, watch, explore, request, save, later, tag, rate, respond, recommend, remind, schedule, co-create. . . .

Brendan Foley envisions actionable "permission-based marketing" in 2020:

> *As Jane goes about her day, her ad service engages her across all the devices she uses—the dashboard on her electric car, her cell phone, tablet, personal computer, and digital television. It's easy and intuitive for Jane to take action on her terms—whether she's video chatting with friends and buying through one click a product she sees on a primetime drama they're watching online or saving an alert delivered on her cell phone for an upcoming movie playing at the local theater in the mall where she's shopping. It's hard for Jane to imagine a world without her personalized ad service, which explains why she takes action on the ads she sees more than 20 percent of the time. (2012)*

Innovations in out-of-home advertising provide many interesting actionable opportunities. For example, Samsung placed posters at various out-of-home environments (shopping malls, airports, movie theaters, etc.) with Near Field Communication (NFC) to promote their new Galaxy S3 phone. Users could download free content (songs, stories, videos) by tapping their phone on the NFC-enabled posters. Only Samsung users could access the content. NFC, Geo Fencing, and QR codes provide all sorts of intriguing ways for brands to offer on-demand content and experiences to people with mobile devices (Funaro 2012).

Another example of an actionable touchpoint is Nike's Summer 2014 Fuelbox event, a fun game-like experience and opportunity for users of Nike's Fuelband personal-fitness trackers. Nike placed temporary vending machines in locations around Manhattan where users could exchange points accumulated on their Fuelbands for rewards such as hats, shirts, and watches. The points had to be earned that day, encouraging users to get some exercise to get free gear (Kumparak 2014).

Nike hinted at the locations of the Fuelboxes via the @nikenyc twitter account, using social media to broadcast and amplify two messages simultaneously: a reward for existing customers and a statement of ongoing support for the

Fuelband platform in general. It was a clever way to reiterate Nike's commitment to a branded lifestyle; an invitation to exercise and reap the rewards.

Valuable: Give People What They Need, Want . . . or Something Even Better

> *As large parts of society continue to lose trust in once reputable institutions as well as corporations, brands will have to extremely carefully manage their relationship and image with their core customer base both in a broader social responsibility context as well as in one on one interaction.*
>
> — Thomas Burkhardt, *Global Brand Builder, Thomas Burkhardt Branding & Strategy (2013)*

Touchpoints in 2020 are seen as creating value in the eyes of its audience while driving long- and short-term value for the advertiser. Transforming advertising and all touchpoints into something that provides value in and of itself creates a positive impact on culture and society.

> *Adapting to a world where scale depends not just on media budgets but on ideas that have velocity requires a philosophical adjustment. Instead of asking "what do we want to say with this content?" brands should begin by asking "why would someone choose to consume this content?" "Content" is a key word, because choice-based impressions rely on a breadth of solutions, many of which don't resemble what we've come to think of as ads.*
>
> *To do: Determine the types of content your audience desires, and build the capability to create it (or find partners who can).*
>
> — Adam Cahill, *Founder, Anagram LLC;* *Baba Shetty, Chief Strategy and Media Officer, Digitas (2013)*

As we saw previously, valuable has two dimensions: cognitive and emotional. Touchpoints can engage us on both levels. They can provide monetary value (coupons, discounts), education, information, entertainment, or all of the above. Moreover, these dimensions can apply to either the individual (save money, be "in the know," get the latest gadget, wow your loved one) or society at large (environmental, social, or political impact).

Touchpoints providing several dimensions of value was an important change that many of our contributors emphasized. Maria Sipka, CEO and founder of Linqia, explains:

> *Advertisers must transform their messaging from selling to informing, entertaining, inspiring and/or educating. This approach earns the advertiser attention, loyalty, and permission to build new and ongoing valuable relationships. It's no longer about investing the lion's share of the billions of dollars into clever, beautiful and expensive commercials and advertisements.*

> *The guardians of these budgets need to delve into the hearts of their brand, business, or organization and repackage the wealth of value that has been built over the life of that entity into relevant content and experiences that can be shared and repurposed to an engaged audience of people. (2012)*

Cognitive value appeals to our brains: this solves my problems, is good for me financially, makes sense to my life and what I am trying to accomplish. Yet, more and more is known about the heart as ruler: we make emotional choices and then follow them up with cognitive rationales: I respond to advertising that makes my life better, gives me a sense of identity and self-worth, and has a positive psychological impact on my sense of well-being.

Seth Godin explains how creating something that people value is a key to success in the digital age:

> *The only asset that actually gets built online is permission. Permission to talk to people who want to be talked to, delivering and anticipating personal and relevant messages to people who want to get them, and connecting them to one another. That's all we can build and what we should measure. Not how many people thumbed up some video we made, but instead how many people want to hear from us. (2012)*

And, in the digital age, it is not only important that people would want the content, but also vitally important that they would want to share it with others. As Peter Field, president at Field Consulting puts it, *"social media are personal, their appeal driven by the ability to connect people with others. Brands that want to thrive in this space have to earn their welcome through the continually refreshed offer of social currency: ideas that people want to share with others"* (2012).

Ads that are funny, moving, or inspiring are the ones that people like to share and are the most likely to go viral. In his recent book *Contagious: Why Things Catch On*, Wharton professor Jonah Berger suggests six principles for developing contagious, or shareable, ideas based on his research findings, using the acronym STEPPS:

Social Currency: make it cool to talk about

Triggers: make it top of mind

Emotion: make them feel something

Public: make it visible

Practical Value: make it useful

Stories: make it tell-able. (Berger 2013)

An idea or story is only "contagious" if it can be easily shared and retold, and people love to share things that make them feel something. Kmart capitalized on this with their "Ship My Pants" campaign. To highlight the value of their free online delivery service—and address their reputation of frequently being out of stock of items in store—the company produced short YouTube clips where people were incredulous about being able to "ship their pants/bed/drawers," right there. The funny, low-budget campaign went viral, gaining 15 million views in just eight days (Warc 2014).

These different components of value suggest that the worlds of logic and emotions must be married with all the senses and muses from music to scents, visuals to touch, virtual to reality. As discussed earlier, these have been demonstrated to build long-term effectiveness for brands. **Monetary value motivates consumers to make purchases, but it won't necessarily be enough to motivate them to repeat that purchase, or to recommend an object or service to peers.** Pearse McCabe, CEO of Dragon Rouge NY explains,

> *Marketers need to look at the spaces where their target audiences live, how they operate, what problems plague them, what they value and why. A successful brand story must tap into these spaces, bring ease to these operations, solve these problems and support these values. A rich, genuine story will not only explain a brand's identity, it will relate to consumers' own stories and undercover opportunities where the two connect—in other words, show what you can do for them on both and emotional and rational level. (2013)*

Finally, value can be co-created, rather than zero-sum. In his book *Doing Both*, Inder Sidhu, senior VP, strategy & planning for worldwide operations at Cisco, provides years of evidence to demonstrate that when managers make decisions that achieve more than one positive objective, outcomes are significantly better than those that assume that trade-offs and win-lose options are required (Sidhu 2010).

Patagonia provides a great example of how brands with purpose create win-win scenarios for society and for their bottom line. The company launched its "Don't Buy This Jacket" campaign in 2011, encouraging customers to reuse and recycle their Patagonia gear instead of buying new Patagonia products. Patagonia's legendary founder and owner, Yvon Chouinard, embodies his company's message with his lone-wolf adventurer lifestyle, lending credence to what might otherwise come across as a gimmick. Plus, Patagonia makes their fleece jackets out of recycled bottles, powers their headquarters with solar electricity, and donates a percentage of their revenue to environmental causes. The results of the campaign: "In 2012, after 9 months of their 'buy less' marketing, Patagonia sales increased almost one third, to $543 million, as the company opened 14 more stores" (Stock 2013).

The Patagonia example probably resonates with Dr. Carl Marci, chief neuroscientist at Nielsen Consumer Neuroscience:

> *Modern neuroscience clearly demonstrates the tremendous importance of nonconscious processing in the brain. The emotional centers receive and*

process information from the senses prior to the cognitive and more rational centers, exerting considerable influence on advertiser relevant brain activity. These include the powerful role of emotional responses generated in the brain and experienced in our bodies to direct attention, enhance learning and memory, and ultimately drive behavior. Because the emotional centers occupy distinct areas of the brain and lack direct connectivity to the language centers, stated or self-reported responses from consumers are incomplete and often biased by both social context and complex cognitions. This interference clouds recall and confuses projections of behavioral intent. Research needs to do a better job of guiding advertisers to stories full of emotional triggers and relatable characters while integrating benefits and subtly addressing features. Advertisers need to embrace a new understanding of the neurosciences that complement and extend traditional measures. (2012)

Exceptional Experience: Make It Memorable

> *In the future advertising will equal experience. It might be an experience that is shared, as in "I was there, you should be there!" Or it might be an experience that is created by the individual, "I'm creative, innovative, visionary," and in effect, advertising becomes 'my personal channel' to market these capabilities.*
>
> — Kenneth Nisch, *Chairman, JGA (2012)*

In 2020, people will not make distinctions between the touchpoints they have with a brand. All will be expected to be excellent. And an exceptional experience with one brand becomes the de-facto standard for all experiences.

> *We now know for a fact that the most important triggers that motivate a positive preference for a brand lie below the surface of the targeted audience's consciousness. These hidden triggers—we call them "cues and codes"—can range from an individual's positive response to certain colors, logos, music, or—and this is the most effective means of motivation—to an arresting, creative, presentation of a brand experience. Consistently presenting the audience with brand experiential "ideas they can see and feel" will be a prerogative for commercial persuasion success in 2020. Apple doesn't serve coffee—but they always serve the best experience in town.*
>
> — Mac Cato, *Chairman, Cato Consulting Group (2012)*

Many brands today are striving to create these best experiences. Virgin Atlantic provided an exemplary exceptional experience in New York City in July 2013. The airline set up a red park bench in Times Square, and whenever someone sat on it they were greeted by flight attendants and given all manner of first-class services (a gourmet meal, champagne, digital and live entertainment). While this experience was unlikely to convert regular people into first-class international fliers, it provided the masses with an unexpected and well-executed glimpse into the kind of preferential treatment offered by the airline, and certainly distinguished Virgin Atlantic from other airlines (Gianatasio 2013).

Another example is Adobe, who set up a live photo-shop stunt in Finland to promote their Creative Day events. In many ways Photoshop is synonymous with inauthenticity: "photoshopping" implies airbrushing away flaws in celebrity photographs and manipulating the real into the ideal. **Adobe took these criticisms head-on and created a funny and unexpected experience for real people in the street, reminding us in a light-hearted way about the creative potential of these photo manipulation tools** (Gianatasio 2013).

Zappos, whose "Deliver Happiness" slogan has driven several out-of-the-box experiences, also produced an exceptional live experience. On the day before Thanksgiving in 2013, the company turned a baggage claim in the Houston airport into a Wheel of Fortune style game. If a passenger's luggage landed on a panel representing a prize—various types of Zappos merchandise—they won it. Zappos chose Houston because it is one of the company's biggest markets of loyal customers, and held the crowd-pleasing event on one of the busiest and most stressful travel days of the year. It was a no-strings-attached surprise that bolstered Zappos's image as an innovative company that cares about people (Diaz 2013).

These three brands took a risk of confronting unsuspecting people in public places. Their events had to be well-planned and executed in order to make the right kind of impact and create an exceptional experience for those involved, as well as for live witnesses and all of those who might have watched the events unfold on social media. **However, an exceptional experience can be something as small as a positive experience with a sales representative online or in person.** As Ralph Oliva, executive director of ISBM and marketing professor at Penn State Smeal College of Business reminds us, this front line of customer experience is crucial: *"Smart firms will be able to differentiate themselves as we move toward 2020 by actually allowing something that's rare today: genuine human contact between their employees and their customers in meaningful conversations"* (2012).

Most compelling about the exceptional experience is the win-win. The Forrester Customer Experience study, conducted since 2007, measures the effect of three criteria that on the bottom line of the company/organization:

- How **effective** were they at meeting your needs?
- How **easy** were they to do business with?
- How **enjoyable** were they to do business with?

A portfolio of the top 10 performing companies had 8 percent higher word-of-mouth recommendations, 38 percent lower churn, and 54 percent higher additional purchases for a total annual impact of $4.7 billion than a portfolio of the bottom 10 performing firms. **For the six-year period from 2007 to 2012, the Customer Experience Leaders in the companion Watermark study outperformed the broader market, generating a total return that was three times**

higher on average than the S&P 500 Index ("Customer Experience Affects Your Bottom Line" 2013).

> *As more businesses aspire to become Experience Brands, CEOs will champion enterprise-wide brand experience visions. Experience Branding exemplars will be the most powerful brands in the world—less because of the advertising spend—than because their customers have taken them to new heights. Customers love Experience Brands because they enable them to live better lives. These brands will measure their success based on quality of life metrics and the degree to which they have become trusted advisors. Customer co-creation, sharing "their brands," and providing real time feedback about their experience will enable employee focus and compensation/rewards. Chief Experience Officers will be appointed to steward their organizations in bringing their brands to life in important ways. Several CEOs have already established these roles reporting directly to them. And, this is just the beginning.*
>
> — Michelle Bottomley, *Chief Marketing and Sales Officer, Mercer (2012)*

With all of this evidence pointing to its effectiveness, we should all ask ourselves whether we are providing exceptional experiences, in both expected and unexpected places, for the people we seek to serve.

Shareworthy Story: Tell Me Something Worth My Time and Energy

> *The narrative architecture of advertising needs to evolve away from propositions wrapped in anecdotes to three-act stories through which a protagonist brand evolves.*
>
> — Tim Flattery, *Executive Creative Director, MEC (2012)*

Many of our Advertising 2020 contributors emphasized the power of storytelling for brands. As Pearse McCabe puts it:

> *Storytelling is the most direct and lasting method to connect with consumers—after all, it is the most fundamental way that we communicate as a species. Stories are the way we process and share information; they create meaning, establish relevance and evoke emotional response. Stories are the way we make sense of the world around us, the way we understand how and why things work. Sharing stories is how we connect, discover commonalities and differences, and figure out ways to work together. (2013)*

With an overload of communications vying for our attention in 2020, the element of delight, essential to the human spirit, is most likely to break through an overload of messages. Yet delight falls flat if not connected to a story that can withstand the scrutiny of the empowered individual. Is the story manufactured or is it based on something that employees would tell and tell with pride? Does the story connect with what is important to an audience, as well as with each member of the board of directors?

Storytelling has always been central to brand communications as the primary, and primal, means of connecting with people. As Mark Morris, international partner of The FiftySeven, writes,

> *Storytelling moves communication from interruption to participation, from repetitive manipulation to value creation. People still want solid facts but today they choose to engage with a brand on their own terms. Therefore, if informational benefits are important to brand engagement, they must be exposed in the right context.* ***Cognitive psychologist Jerome Bruner said, "A fact wrapped in a story is 22 times more memorable."*** *So, if a brand's story contains facts that differentiate, it becomes essential for those facts to be delivered in ways that people are open to listening to. (2012)*

Michael Kassan, chairman and CEO of MediaLink, agrees:

> *Constant change is business as usual in a digital ecosystem, where new challenges and opportunities are constantly emerging, everything is in perpetual motion and moving at blinding speed, and not even definitions stay the same. But the need for good storytelling in any form (or any length—even 140 characters) remains. (2012)*

Crafting a story about a brand or product, is, however, not easy. Without an engaging character or narrative, a story will not resonate. Kirk Cheyfitz, co-CEO and chief storyteller at Story Worldwide, explains:

> *Instead of ads as we know them, advertising [in 2020] will be brand stories—fairy stories, news stories, epic stories, histories, romances, and so on. These stories must be so entertaining, informative, engaging, and valuable to the audience that people actually seek them out, choosing to see and hear them. Importantly, these stories must also do three critical things at once:*
>
> - *Narrate a brand's core proposition;*
> - *Tap into the deep core interests of the brand's audiences* and *thus, the reasons the brand should be important to people; and*
> - *Work to accomplish the brand's business goals. (2012)*

Stories don't have to be verbal, of course; they can be told visually, via rich experiences, and by integrating all relevant touchpoints to add up to a holistic, consistent, and lasting narrative. Jonathan Mildenhall, CMO at Airbnb puts it like this:

> We need to focus on the evolution of storytelling. We need to move from one-way storytelling to dynamic storytelling. What is the definition of dynamic storytelling? Well, it's the development of incremental elements of a brand idea that get dispersed systematically across multiple channels of conversation for the purposes of creating a unified and coordinated brand experience. (TheCognitiveMedia 2011)

Taken with all the other R.A.V.E.S. elements, compelling storytelling can overcome the indifference that most people have toward the messages of brands. A recent venture in the UK by Laphroaig Single Malt Whiskey demonstrates the effectiveness of a shareworthy story when coupled with the other R.A.V.E.S. elements. In May 2014 Laphroaig launched "Opinions Welcome," where they filmed real people tasting their whiskey and used their reactions, many of them very negative and funny, in their ads. The dramatic reviews featured prominently in the ads include:

> "A symphony of smoke. Tastes like a burning hospital."
>
> "It's like being kicked in the face by a horse that's been galloping in a peaty bog."
>
> "I think they let the cows in that one."

The comments are unexpected for their blunt honesty and humor. The brand took a risk, but by respecting their audience—not everyone agrees on what tastes good—they generated good will as well as a laugh (Griner 2014).

Storytelling, Storydoing and Storyscaping

As the Laphroaig campaign shows, an effective way of creating an engaging story is by doing something interesting and then telling the story about it. This strategy, referred to as "story doing," carries within it the means to create interest and enthusiasm among a wide audience. Ian Wishingrad, founder and creative director at BigEyedWish, writes:

> *A story is the foundation for every great brand, and so few have them today. Unfortunately, we live in an era where no one has the time, patience, or talent to develop a great story, so we rely on being buzz worthy. Clients think, "at least they're talking and tweeting about us." To some degree, that's true, but having a few good PR hits over a month is*

> *not a long-term solution. The solution is telling your story consistently across all media. (2012)*

Laphroaig's "foundation," for example, is that it's an acquired but celebrated taste, and their print ads and videos support that story.

Taking it even further, Gaston Legorburu and Darren McColl, among our collaborators, have created the notion of "Storyscaping" whereby brands create immersive worlds for their audiences and generate emotional connections based on live and on-line interactions (Legorburu and McColl, 2014). They discovered how something special happens when people become involved with the story and contribute to its creation. Their methodical, thoughtful approach to multisensory participatory events is an inspiring example of bringing these theories to life.

By requiring future advertising to achieve all the elements that have come before *and* deliver an element of surprise as part of an authentic story communicated through every touchpoint, then brands will embrace the lesson that journalists and storytellers have understood for the last 30,000 years.

> *By 2020 consumers will fully own advertising. They will shape its creative, its messaging, and decipher what its utility should be. Brand managers and advertisers will no longer have the pleasure of deploying any portion of a push strategy.... Brands will thrive or barely survive based on the experiences they are able to bring to consumers and the emotions they will evoke through these. Needless to say that as consumers are transformed and empowered to own the brands we as advertisers and marketers so carefully try to protect, the "truth in advertising" will obtain a new meaning.*
>
> — Michelle Taite, *Senior Global Brand Manager, Unilever (2012)*

Brands no longer need to think about being manipulative or aggressive to get attention; authentic and creative stories open up channels of communication with people. Imagining "advertising" in 2020 affords us the opportunity to set a standard for today in hopes of achieving all that it could and should be by 2020 . . . if not before. What would the world look like if this were achieved? How would people feel about brands and advertising? What financial and social benefits would be afforded employees and shareholders? How could "advertising" be redefined? What if advertisers were named person of the year by *Time* Magazine for these transformations? Creating R.A.V.E.S. advertising through every touchpoint has the potential for achieving this transformation.

> *Most positively we are headed inexorably towards a new era of truth. Truth in what products do, truth in how and by who they are made, truth in the opportunity cost of their manufacturer, truth in performance and, yes, truth in advertising.*
>
> — Rob Norman, *Chief Digital Officer Global, GroupM (2012)*

Figure 5.3 Beyond Advertising in Action: The R.A.V.E.S. Content Principles

Beyond Advertising in Action
THE R.A.V.E.S. CONTENT PRINCIPLES

IBM WATSON FOOD TRUCK
Agency: Ogilvy & Mather
Effie Award: Gold—B2B 2015

OBJECTIVE/PROBLEM TO BE SOLVED
IBM wanted to demonstrate the creative B2B potential of Watson to skeptical developers and start-ups.

APPROACH
IBM installed Watson in a food truck called Cognitive Cooking and parked it at Austin's SXSWi in 2014. Menu suggestions were solicited via twitter, then Watson's algorithms and understanding of the foods' chemical flavor compounds produced unexpected and unheard of food combinations and recipes.

THE RESULTS
IBM successfully demonstrated a real-world application for cognitive computing systems and how they can come up with creative ideas and solutions. Thousands of developers contacted IBM to see what they could build with Watson's help.

LESSONS AND OBSERVATIONS
IBM created a R.A.V.E.S. experience to demonstrate the capabilities of their product in an unexpected, creative, surprising, and impactful way.

CITATION: Effie Award Winners, 2015

Key Takeaways

- **Relevance, Respect, Action, Value, Experience, Story—brought together, these concepts form the foundation of advertising for, not advertising at, individuals.**

- **The personal—a sense that an ad is talking to you, in a language you relate to, about something that matters to you—underpins each of these terms. And importantly, to personalize is not to target: it results in engagement by choice.**

- **As we all know, the personal is often private. There is an immense responsibility for all of us—whether in advertising or not—to respect individual boundaries. Thinking with R.A.V.E.S. helps us do that.**

- **Authenticity is as fundamental as the personal/private divide when aiming to build respect. The public, more than ever, is skeptical and informed: if we see something we don't like—be it invasive or disingenuous—we have myriad platforms to say something. So inevitably R.A.V.E.S. is not an option, it's a necessity *(see Figure 5.3).***

Chapter 6

The Expanded Power of Context: M.A.D.E.^{s}

A contextual ad is not only relevant in its content, it has temporal relevance, location relevance, and relevance in all other contextual dimensions. Therefore a contextual ad must reach the consumer at the right time, at the right place, through the right people (e.g., people he or she trusts). It will be much more effective. Advertisers won't need to be so intrusive, and ads don't have to be an annoyance. In fact, if an ad can be context sensitive, it may even become something desirable.

— Michael Wu, *Chief Scientist, Lithium Technologies (2012)*

In life, we know that timing is everything. Suggest something to someone or to a group of people at the wrong time or in the wrong place and the consequences are not only bad at the moment, but likely bad for the foreseeable future. We've wasted their time and we've wasted our own time, even if *what* we had to say might have been perfectly valid. We may never get a second chance if we are woefully off. Conversely, looking for, being ready for, and/or creating just the right setting and surroundings, when the person is in the right frame of mind and emotional state, increases the likelihood of positive outcomes for all. **Done consistently, thoughtfully, over time, in subsequent circumstances and situations, the positive connection, appreciation, and trust can be lasting.** Such is the power of context.

By 2020, brands will be held to the same standards as people, and they will have the wherewithal and self-interested, aligned motivation to deliver. Advances in science and technology give us an unprecedented ability to listen for and understand the psychological, social, and cultural nature of humans, and the ever-evolving technologies to predict, perceive, and deliver on these nuances. Retail shopping expert Herb Sorensen, scientific advisor for TNS Global, writes about how these advances enable digitally mediated sales, replacing the personal skills salespeople honed over the centuries:

> *The pre-self-service retailing involved mediated sales, where the proprietor or clerk mediated-assisted-expedited sales in the store. In contrast, self-service retail is largely unmediated. For online sales, the most effective selling is digitally mediated sales, where knowledge of the shopper, and of the merchandise, is used to algorithmically assist/expedite bringing the shopper to a decision. (2012)*

Publishers, producers, gamers, media properties, platform providers, retailers, technologists, architects, product, service, software and app developers, and their collaborators are continuously creating an exploding array of tools and techniques to leverage the richness of context across all touchpoints. As Lynda Resnick, vice chair and co-owner of The Wonderful Company and Ken Youngleib, associate creative director at Apple write:

> *[A]dvertisers will soon know so much about an individual's lifestyle and buying habits—and even their physical location—that they'll be able to deliver messages that are both customized and relevant in real time. The mom on her way to the supermarket will find on her smartphone a coupon for exactly what she's getting. (2012)*

Alain Heureux, former president and CEO of IAB Europe, puts it like this: *"In 2020 Advertising will still be based on emotions but [will be] much more efficient thanks to Technologies and Data: the holy grail of Reaching the Right People at the Right Place on the Right Moment with the most Relevant and Engaging message should become achievable . . . based on a Trustful Dialogue!"* (2012) Frederic Bonn, chief creative officer, North America at the Mirum Agency, emphasizes the significance of this capability, explaining that *"Brands that want to be successful will not only need to deliver value through entertainment, information, tools, services, and conversations, but will need to deliver that value consistently regardless of the location, moment, or point of interaction"* (2012).

So what do we mean by context? In order to change our mindsets for the future, we chose this term as the least anchored in the past to enable us to think as broadly, holistically, and dynamically as possible, to take full advantage of the many ways that we can enhance the value of what we have to say (content/substance) with *when*, *where*, and *how* we say or do it. **Context in the future will be as powerful as content. And rather than arguing about which one is king or queen, we believe that the savvy will take full advantage of what each can offer in value creation for the triple bottom line.**

Figure 6.1 The M.A.D.E.^{S} Guidelines for Context

	M.A.D.E.^{S} CONTEXT GUIDELINES
M	MULTISENSORY AESTHETIC AND DESIGN
A	AUDIENCE FRAME OF MIND
D	DELIVERY MECHANISM, INTERFACE, AND PLATFORM/ MEDIUM
E	ENVIRONMENT AND LOCATION
S	SYNERGY WITH OTHER TOUCHPOINTS

Being context savvy is equally important whether you are creating the context—for example, developing your website or customer service—or if you are engaging with a predeveloped context—for example, on a platform such as Facebook or Bloomberg Media, where you need to fit into the culture and the aesthetic.

On behalf of our Advertising 2020 collaborators, we've distilled six contextual design dimensions that expand the consideration of context for the future. Not all are relevant for every touchpoint. But given how powerful they can be, we advocate thinking creatively about each one and revisiting them frequently to see what else can be mined. We suggest that the context be "M.A.D.E. to the power of S", where synergy with other touchpoints can have exponential impact, or M.A.D.E.^{S}, for short *(see Figure 6.1)*:

- **Multisensory Aesthetic**: Beyond the ever-important look and feel, how can all five senses be considered and celebrated? How can they be used to enhance the contextual power and value?

- **Audience Frame of Mind**: What is the recent, current, and future emotional state, frame of mind, mood, role of the audience in the current context? Who are they with, what are they doing, and why?

- **Delivery Mechanism, Interface, and Platform/Medium**: What are the characteristics and properties of the particular interface, including physical place, human face, hardware, and software?

- **Environment and Location**: Where are they, what's taking place in the physical environment, and what's the tone and manner in the surrounding environment? What's the relevant vibe?

- **Synergy**: How can one context become exponentially more valuable for all by leveraging synergies with and among other touchpoints?

Multisensory Aesthetic

> *Brands will explore many senses in addition to audio and visual. Haptics, smell, and even taste will be used in advertising. With the proliferation of 3D printers, we will be able to print a model of a new car while haptic feedback will allow us to experience driving it on a mountain road. Cosmetic manufacturers will replace those scratch-and-smell inserts with smell-generating technologies.*
>
> — Scott Puopolo, *VP, Global Lead, Service Provider Transformation Group, Cisco Systems;* Leszek Izdebski, *Managing Director, Service Provider Transformation Group, Cisco Systems (2012)*

Once the domain of only physical spaces, the power of the five senses will be appreciated and optimized across all touchpoints. We can learn from the best of retailers who understand and fully leverage the power of look, smell, sound, touch, and taste to provide the right context-creating.

We all know the examples of context-wrecking. That insufferable music on hold. The annoying, blipping display ad. The musty smell in the store. The filthy tester. The stale sample. But done right, the music, the scent, the look and feel, the right flavor, and we are transformed into a new world. Imagine each touchpoint being designed with all senses in mind.

For this, there are many inspirational examples, such the Nike AirMax Day ad we came across in Ads of the World (MediaBistro, 2015).

> "Hong Kong is crazy about sneakers, it even has a street named after it. To celebrate Air Max Day, we created interactive installations that showed how this iconic sneaker has been a part of its popular culture since its debut in 1987. Five local-born artists illustrated how each Air Max model has a Hong Kong story for each year. To take people back in time, each installation had the five human senses of 'sight, sound, smell, taste and touch' hidden in the art. These multisensory installations virtually took people back in time to re-experience familiar local memories."

Another example of an innovative use of a sense came from Oscar Mayer's "Wake Up to the Smell of Bacon" campaign, developed by 360i. Over nine months, an iPhone plug-in device was developed that could literally wake users up with the scent of bacon: it released the smell when a special bacon-themed alarm clock app went off. Only 5,000 devices were produced, and users were encouraged to sign up on a microsite that featured a video spoof of a perfume commercial to create hype around the product. Smell, sound, sight; all employed to promote a brand's signature taste (Warc, 2015).

Likewise, a campaign in Argentina commissioned by the scientific research center the Fundación Favaloro expanded the senses involved in marketing by linking taste to visibility. "The Salt You Can See" aimed to raise awareness of the dangers of overconsumption of salt. Rather than simply producing PSAs filled with data, Agency Grey Argentina developed neon-colored salt that was distributed widely at supermarkets, restaurants, and public places, rendering the additive highly visible. The campaign was launched for World Salt Awareness Week, during which people could receive free health checks at Fundación Favaloro and were given saltshakers of the neon product. The campaign, which was supplemented with a social media presence driven by "#Salfie" (the Spanish word for salt, sal, blended with "selfie"), was widely successful, and neon salt will stay on the market—with all the sales proceeds going to the Fundación (Cannes Lions 2015).

We also gained a lot of understanding on the power of visual context from our research on native advertising. Our colleagues at Yahoo! Asia Pacific early on saw the potential of this emerging new alignment between publisher/platform, brand and audience. Native advertising is the notion that instead of something intrusive relative to the primary content on a site or media property, advertisements would look and feel more like the rest of what audiences were seeking and experiencing. A favorite analogy is *Vogue* magazine, where readers value the first third of the magazine's pages—where brands' advertise fashions, photography, and prose—at least equally to the editorial content.

What we found is the power of contextualization. **Content from brands that meet the same standards of the look and feel of the editorial content is more highly valued by audiences.** We appreciate advertising that is additive to our experience, rather than competing for our attention.

Audience and Individual's Frame of Mind

Research confirms the contextual importance of emotional, psychographic, and sociographic elements: how someone is feeling, what their frame of mind is and where they are in this moment relative to others. Several Advertising 2020 collaborators cited the work of Daniel Kahneman, who illuminates the power of the emotional part of the brain. Kahneman's book, *Thinking, Fast and Slow,* is structured around the metaphor of System One and System Two. Kahneman describes System One as follows: intuitive, automatic, effortless, and unconscious; it simplifies and shapes available information into narrative coherence; it is associative, impressionistic, emotional, nonstatistical, gullible, and heuristic. System Two, by contrast, is what we traditionally consider our "thinking" self: it is conscious, deliberate, effortful, slow, statistical, and suspicious. It takes System One's rough draft of reality and polishes it up with reasoned arguments and clear findings.

But System Two, in addition to being the more logical and rational of the pair, is also lazy. It costs a lot of resources (i.e. time and energy) to use. Because of this, instead of slowing things down and rationalizing them, System Two is often content to accept the convenient but inconsistent reality that System One provides it. Kahneman makes it clear that while System Two at times offers directional insight, System One—with all its heuristic shortcomings—is really the one at the helm (Kahneman 2013).

The ability to understand the nuanced aspects of these factors will have a huge impact on advertising. As Thomas Ramsoy, founder and CEO at Neurons Inc., and adjunct faculty at Singularity University puts it,

> *During the past couple of decades, cognitive neuroscience has provided dramatic changes in our understanding of human perception, attention, consciousness, memory, emotions, preference formation, decision-making, and social behavior. Becoming up to date on this knowledge will provide advertisers with new skills and tools for communicating with consumers in their struggle to obtain attention, preference, choice and satisfaction for their products and services. It will provide a crucial next step in the toolbox of advertising (2012).*

Erik du Plessis, non-executive chairman of Millward Brown South Africa, elaborates on this point. He argues that in 1995 we began to understand the importance of emotion; in 2012, we began to understand feelings—our perceptions of our emotions; and that by 2020 we will be able to discern *"background feelings like mood, personality, and probably culture"* (2012). Stephen Rappaport, senior consultant Stephen D. Rappaport Consulting, and Howard Moskowitz, founding partner and chief scientist, Mind Genomics Advisors, support these claims with the assertion that *"the analysis of personal mind genomes will lead to personalized advertising treatment based on mindsets."* They assert that *"the race is on to sequence the consumer mind's genome, to map and describe its mindsets in order to improve people's lives through scientifically based human-centered marketing and advertising"* (2013).

Technologies are emerging to discern someone's frame of mind by the cues and clues they give in real time, so that we can address them accordingly. Donna Hoffman and Thomas Novak, professors of marketing at the George Washington University School of Business, describe the following near-future scenario:

> *In stores and on city streets, we are seeing "smart signs," dynamic signage that tailors advertisements to consumers, using facial recognition algorithms. "Gladvertising" presents different ads to different consumers based on the customer's current mood as inferred by their facial expression. Cameras are being used to identify and target customers by age and gender with increasing accuracy. Kraft is testing a signage system in supermarkets where a camera recommends products based on consumer demographics and other factors such as time of day. As smart signs continue to converge with augmented reality that overlays digital information on physical objects, marketers will be able to identify particular consumers, suggest products just for them, and digitally augment them right there on the street! (2012)*

Other companies are experimenting with using voice recognition to evaluate our state of mind. Yoram Levanon, chairman and founder of Exaudios writes: *"Following years of research we . . . tested over 50,000 different talks (achieving more than 75 percent accuracy in western languages). Analyzing 10 seconds of a personal speech can tell us the person's emotional state without understanding the content"* (2012).

Social platforms (acknowledging that this term is likely to be obsolete by 2020) have a tremendous amount of information about your choices and are able to describe you in ways far more addressable than a generic message. As we write this book, we are just beginning to understand the potential of enlisting analytics to create relevant clusters for whom brands can personalize messages.

Kip Voytek, CEO of Rumble Fox, captures some of the value and nuance of big data by writing, *"Algorithms are the path to the marketing nirvana of right message + right place + right time (+ right price + right product + right geo + . . .) We can't see algorithms, most of us can't read the code that executes them—but we will be absolutely dependent on them for success"* (2012).

Audience Frame of Mind adds another, crucial dimension to Kip's list, as it takes into account not only the state of the individual, but how they might be influenced by who else is in their physical and virtual world at that moment. **I would talk to you differently if you were alone, in a study group, at a concert, sitting next to your child, at home engaged online, in a virtual game with your team from around the world, or viewing a demo of a product or service for work.** In each setting, you are a different mode: solo, student, concert-goer, parent, game competitor, business person. Wonderfully and understandably your frame of mind is altered by whom you are with.

> *Addressability' not only will become common, but will evolve from targeting an entire segment with one piece of advertising creative to further segmenting the audience and serving differentiated pieces of advertising creative based on the audience's characteristics. This personalization will manifest itself in different advertising spots appearing for different users, and in tailored product placement. Not only will one viewer see a different car, in a different color, driven by the show hero—he or she will also hear a different dialogue and possibly see a different scene. To avoid huge additional costs for advertising creative, production will use IOE to collect detailed metadata, including scene geometry, which will enable new rendering approaches for partial automated dynamic modifications of video based on the viewer's segment.*
>
> — Scott Puopolo, *Vice President and Global Practices Lead;* Leszek Izdebski, *Director, Cisco Internet Business Solutions Group (IBSG) (2012)*

An example of advertising embracing and utilizing the knowledge of a specific audience can be seen in a recent US Navy recruitment campaign. Trying to fill spots in the cryptology division had been notoriously difficult: it required people with a high analytical foundation who weren't deterred by a difficult lifestyle. The Navy targeted a very specific audience, those individuals who "can't resist the scent of a nearly impossible puzzle." Using social media, they created a large-scale "war game" where players decoded various clues to find the coordinates of a fictitious hero. By actively enlisting—rather than simply listing—the skills they were looking for, the Navy's campaign reached 113,494 people, or 87 prospects for every spot they needed to fill (Olis, Martin & Goldstein, 2015). Casting a well-targeted and well-crafted net—as opposed to a wide and generic one—made for a far more successful campaign.

Audience frame of mind should also take into account where an individual is in relation to the brand. By 2020, none of us will be hounded by ads to buy something that we already bought, unless it is a refill. As Vince Schiavone, founder and CEO at AKUDA LLC, Listen Logic, puts it:

> *Today, individuals continually broadcast contextual signals telling the world exactly what they want, exactly when they want it. Technology now exists to understand these market triggers, as well as interest, emotions, and future intentions that advertisers need, through deep and continuous unstructured data analysis. In other words, the ability to deliver just right messaging, just in time. This level of deep, continuous, and immediate insight is the paradigm shift advertisers have been in search of for decades (2012).*

Likewise Scott Puopolo and Leszek Izdebski imagine a near-future scenario of personalization that offers people information or an experience they'll want and value:

> *Ad personalization will take many different forms, leading to greater user involvement. Brands will increasingly integrate with new types of apps associated with popular TV and movie characters. We will see new forms of marketing where apps currently positioned as extensions to the storyline will provide in-context advice by the show's characters. For example, through augmented-reality technology on a mobile phone, an app-based representation of a judge from "America's Next Top Model" will be able to assist in dress selection at a store. (2012)*

Delivery Mechanism, Interface, and Platform

Context also encompasses the means through which we connect. If we go back to our analogy at the beginning, we know there is a big difference if we connect in person versus if we call or text or e-mail or post or SnapChat. Or send a handwritten letter.

1. *The Device or Delivery Mechanism*
   Is it a mobile phone? A digital billboard? A newspaper? A container? A customer service agent? The product itself? An app? A social media site? The brand's website? An event or a happening?

2. *The Interface*
   Is it broadcast? Interactive? Touch screen? Motion-sensitive? Voice activated? Voice recognition? Ambient? A game console? Human? Augmented Reality?

3. *The Platform/App*
   Is it social? News? Entertainment? Productivity? Hobby? Neighborhood?

Each layer has increasingly robust capabilities as well as differing relationships with the audience. As we saw in chapter 2, mobile isn't necessarily on-the-go, as 68 percent of all smartphone minutes take place in the home (AOL, BBDO, & InsightsNow 2012). Additional research emerges daily about the differences in how we relate to our variety of mobile devices, and this will continue to evolve. The key is to have an open mind to the art of the possible. Here are some of the scenarios our contributors envision:

> *The combination of quantified, sensor-based data, social data and transactional data will create a real-time marketing nirvana for the advertising industry. It will also open up new media spaces by turning currently unavailable physical environments into new storytelling experiences. Screens will be everywhere via new materials and projection technologies, sensors will be embedded in ALL physical objects and link ALL objects together into a unified network, and the average consumer will have enhanced sensory capabilities via the ever increasing computation power of 2020 smart devices.*
>
> — Terry Young, *CEO and Founder, Sparks & Honey (2013)*

> *Our lab-based research has identified a couple of key principles that are likely to play out over the next few years and still be important in 2020.*
>
> 1. *The first is the arrival of high quality video screens on multiple devices. This means that platform doesn't matter for television commercial advertising: TV is "everywhere," and every screen is potentially equally effective. When consumers watch video ads across multiple screens, frequency on any single screen is an illusory goal, and silo-based planning no longer works. Instead advertisers have to plan for reach, across multiple platforms, making the most of every exposure they achieve. Which brings us to our next principle.*
>
> 2. *Interactivity. The new screens are touchable, making more information and entertainment available, across more platforms, than ever before. Interactivity is the biggest change advertisers have to face, but the one for which they are the least prepared. Our current knowledge is based on the limited "request for information" interactivity that cable*

and satellite technology could deliver. Online television promises new experiential forms of interactive advertising that are more entertaining and game-like. Interactivity delivers metrics that supersede the exposure currencies of the past. Instead, advertisers need to choose their goals on a case-by-case basis. Interactivity can sift or persuade, or both. It can identify leads or loyals, or convert prospects into new leads. When different platforms offer different types of interactivity, sequence of usage is important, and advertisers need to research and plan for cross-platform synergies.

— Steven Bellman, *Researcher at MediaScience;* *Duane Varan*, *CEO MediaScience (2012)*

The future isn't social. Consumers are shifting from interacting with other people, through applications, to interacting directly with applications. This trend will accelerate as consumers become embedded in an "Internet of Things." In turn, these smart applications will not only interact with people, but also with other applications. Thus, social networks of tomorrow may be not be networks of people, but rather networks of applications that, guided by ambient intelligence, collectively respond to consumers in a social way. As products get smarter and as consumers shift from interacting with people to interacting with smarter applications, particularly in mobile and local contexts, consumers' interactions with each other—i.e., what it means to be "social"—may recede in importance compared to our interactions with smarter apps that "know" more and more about us. These shifts in the digital landscape will require advertisers of the future to think far beyond a model of advertising that, even now, still hews closer to broadcasting than to innovative, personalized, digital approaches for communicating with modern online consumers.

— Thomas P. Novak and Donna L. Hoffman, *Professors of Marketing, George Washington School of Business (2012)*

Environment and Location

Today, advertisers are increasingly using unexpected touchpoints within our environment to create powerful campaigns. There are a large number of examples, but here are two of our favorites.

The level of pollution in China is a major public health concern, and factories produce 65 percent of the airborne toxins. Xiao Zhu, an air purifier company, was seeking to enter the market. Working with Y&R Shanghai, the company developed the campaign "Breathe Again," where pictures of choking children were projected onto the smoke billowing from smoke stacks. While certainly aiming to gain traction in a saturated market, Xiao Zhu used the lived environment to reveal a normally innocuous presence, and increased public awareness about air pollution by 38 percent (Cannes Lions Archive 2015).

But environment doesn't have to be something quite so, well, environmental. Burger King's 2014 campaign, "Proud Whopper," is a good example of this.

To promote support for—and awareness of—LGBTQ rights during pride week, Burger King created a rainbow-colored wrapping for the Whopper, which revealed the text "We are all the same on the inside" once opened. People's reactions to the burger—which many thought must be somehow different to the "traditional" whopper—were filmed, and the video distributed online (Cannes Lions Archive 2015). By changing something seemingly irrelevant in our daily environment, Burger King made people register their position and try looking at things through a slightly different lens.

And this is just the level of environmental engagement companies are capable of today. By 2020, communications with audiences will have a far greater ability to be locally contextualized. This will be primarily driven by the extent to which sensors will pervade our world. Just think "smart and connected everything." Seriously. Everything.

> *Everything that is physical will have a real-time digital skin. The ubiquity of mobile devices combined with increased user interest in wellness applications will lead to value (both user and commercial) created around the quantified self, and the use of mobile wellness applications as digital skins around the person. While the intersection of personal health and advertising can be a touchy topic, smart advertisers will figure out ways to create authentic transactions that begin with the prudent use of personal information and provide the user with something of value to them.*
>
> *The enthusiasm around smart homes and smart appliances has never translated into a real market because it hasn't addressed the trillions of dollars of sunk cost in my old sump pump and your old washing machine. The ubiquity of cheap sensors and cheap networking is leading to software customized appliance skins from companies such as Twine. The ability to have a real-time pulse on the local appliance universe has advertising benefits that accrue not only the DIY brands and appliance manufacturers, but also an indirect but more significant impact on the level of analytics around the CPG industry. It has the potential of moving retail from destination to distribution. Instead of customers coming to a store to look at your wares, you can proactively sense their need (e.g., for a new dishwasher) and engage them in a personalized retail transaction.*
>
> — Venu Vasudevan, *Senior Director, Media Analytics and Systems, ARRIS (2012)*

Sensors will not only be on the equipment and appliances in our lives, but on our person and in what we wear, maybe even implanted as part of a personal operating system we control access to.

> *The successors of wearable technology like Google Glass will blend the digital and physical worlds. Ambient connectedness to information and one another will force us to redirect advertising dollars from billboards and TV spots to the millions of people who are "wired." Opting in or out of brand communications will be more fluid based on a person's exact location and*

activity, shifting the current focus from hyper-local to in the moment. Apps like Ebay Now will become widespread, as will technology that anticipates what a person wants while in-store. In a future where all kinds of objects are internet-connected, instant gratification will take on new meaning—if it rains and you don't have an umbrella, the sensor in your wet shoes will send a signal to a retailer who will meet you with a rain jacket.

— Russell Dubner, *U.S. CEO, Edelman (2013)*

Driven by the increasing dominance of mobile devices, the next frontier in advertising will be using digital to give the real world web-style functionality with technologies such as near field communications (NFC), visual recognition (VR), and augmented reality (AR).

The ultimate outcome will be the ability to market the last three feet—to be there as the consumer's hand is reaching toward the shelf—and to recognize her or his choices and needs in order to deliver critical information from the brand story precisely at the point of decision.

— Kirk Cheyfitz, *Co-CEO and Chief Storyteller, Story Worldwide (2012)*

But of course we don't have to wait for the full deployment of these connected technologies. **And we may very well see a trend toward sensor-blocking if these potentially beneficial connections are abused.** The fact that a significant percentage of the world's population are rarely without geo-locational devices—smartphones—gives the carrier and app world tremendous contextual data on our environment. And this is just the beginning of locational ways of understanding and relating to a person's context.

Today's mobile technology serves multiple functions, including check-in, location sharing, hyperlocal news/information, and near limitless access to the Internet and applications.

Even so, the industry continues to mature to deliver new ways for consumers to interact with mobile devices, as they cross between the physical and digital world. As these interactions expand, so does our ability to paint a more accurate picture about the consumer journey. The result is insights that can help brands inform decisions across the entire marketing spectrum.

Location signals will be everywhere and will increase the value of users and apps. It will be on all the time, unless otherwise specified through user control within the device. Given this fact, safety and regulation must and will inspire use, protection and ultimately acceptance.

— Duncan McCall, *CEO and Cofounder, PlaceIQ (2012)*

Synergy

As we think about the design principles for each touchpoint, perhaps the most important is to build into the design of each the capacity and functionality to work seamlessly in concert with the others. **Not only is the whole greater than the sum**

of its parts, the interaction among the parts makes the whole exponentially greater than single executions. As Carl Marci, chief neuroscientist at Nielsen Consumer Neuroscience writes:

> *Advertising will take advantage of synergy across media platforms and communication vehicles to support products, brands, and services all the way to the point of purchase and beyond. Experts use the "emotional pull through" that cross-platform communications offer. They reach consumers where and when they are involved with media. This means bridging them emotionally through an advertising experience that feels natural and genuine, while leveraging the technology powering everything just below the surface. (2012)*

The synergies of contextual design elements creating an emotional pull through is a compelling goal. Daniel Parmar, director of digital strategy at Merkle, expresses a similar concept using a real-life example:

> *The focus is going to be on ongoing conversations, building on previous interactions and not differentiating based on the medium. Else, this would be like a person introducing himself to an old friend by starting the conversation with "Hello, my name is so-and-so." Even first interactions can be orchestrated with some knowledge of the customer, in a noninvasive way. The ability to tailor and sequence conversations will become more accurate and encompass virtual and physical interactions. The most excellent customer journeys are those that do not differentiate between digital and physical. (2015)*

To close this section, we leave you with this not-so-distant future vision from Terry Young:

> *Imagine passing someone on the street who is wearing an amazing pair of sun glasses. A digital ad for that item could appear as you pass by and simply by indicating you want it, the glasses could be digitally delivered to your 4D printer where it would be manufactured and assembled. The speed at which we go from the digital world to the physical world and back again will be nearly instantaneous. (2013)*

Continuing with our analogy from the outset of the chapter, the better we know someone, the better we can use all the means at our disposal to create the best environment to get our message across. And yet, we also know that we are most vulnerable to those who know us best. Those who know our foibles, our weaknesses, our predilections, our most ardent hopes and dreams.

Hence the flip side of being able to know so much that we can contextualize our message and connections and actions as brands: it can enable what we do not want: intrusive, manipulative, underhanded, duplicitous, deceptive, insidious, heinous, illegal, destructive advertising.

The Future of Advertising community has grave concerns about the potential misuse of technology relative to the rights and privacy of individuals. Aligning objectives and outcomes with individuals and society, as described in Chapter 3, becomes essential. Keeping people safe and harm-free must be at the top of the contextualizing consideration set. Ethical standards, and the governance to ensure them, are paramount.

As wonderful as this highly connected and therefore highly contextualized world can be, let us not forget the other meaning of environment—our natural environment of air and water and wind and earth and the great outdoors. Unplugging. Getting caught in a rainstorm without an umbrella and splashing in the puddles. All on our own without any help from brands. **Let there be a future where we can be free of brand connections as well. Let us have the wisdom to know when not to be present. In the future, this restraint may well be the most important value creation gift of all.**

Figure 6.2 Beyond Advertising in Action: M.A.D.E.^{S} Context Principles

Beyond Advertising in Action
THE M.A.D.E.^{S} CONTEXT PRINCIPLES

DON'T RAISE MONEY, MAKE MONEY—DEPAUL UK
Agency: Publicis London
Warc 100: #14, 2014

OBJECTIVE/PROBLEM TO BE SOLVED

Depaul UK, a homeless charity for youth, struggled with a crowded UK charity scene dominated by a small number of large organizations—point six percent of the charities got 60 percent of donations in 2013. Homelessness, although it afflicted 80 thousand young people a year, was an unpopular issue.

APPROACH

Market research showed that people most sympathized with the homeless when they were moving, and it was found nearly 3.8 million households had moved in the past two years. Depaul created a box company and printed the stories of homeless people who had been assisted by the charity on the box, as well as websites where people could find more information about the charity itself.

THE RESULTS

The company cost £7,417 to set up in March 2013, and has generated nearly £20,000 of revenue to date—enough to provide beds for over 300 homeless people.

LESSONS AND OBSERVATIONS

This initiative exemplifies M.A.D.E.^{S} Reaching people in the right context—time, place, frame of mind—is an essential component of a successful strategy. Synergies between the components boost overall effectiveness.

CITATION: Warc 100, 2014

Key Takeaways

- **Where we "are" goes far beyond time and place—what we can smell or hear, whether we're stressed or relaxed, if we're feeling happy or sad—all these facets, changing moment to moment, influence how we see the world. Context is a microcosm.**

- **Technologies and methodologies are developing that allow us to respond to these micro-contexts: embracing the diversity they enable is crucial. A TV ad transposed onto a mobile device ignores the shift in scale, scope, and individual experience the different platforms offer.**

- **Our surroundings are an important aspect of context, and our ability to sense and respond to an individual's environment is rapidly changing. The Internet of Things, wearable tech, and sensory technology opens vast opportunities for enhancing the way we experience the world.**

- **Technology and scientific research have made us better equipped to contextualize marketing, and will continue to do so. But this ability demands extreme caution: the line between engaging and invasive should always be treated with respect, and everyone deserves the right to unplug *(see Figure 6.2)*.**

Part III

What to Do Now to Get Ready for—and Co-create—the Future

Young doctors in training are often instructed as follows: 'Listen to your patient. He's telling you the diagnosis.' The same advice is now and must continue to be followed by marketers. Listen to your customer. He or she is telling you how to innovate. How to retain loyalty. How to drive sales. The customer is doing that through social media, in person, on your website, and over various channels. By listening to what made the customer dissatisfied or happy, or learning what would make the customer even happier, marketers are learning about where they need to innovate.

—Zain Raj, *Chairman and CEO, Shapiro + Raj (2012)*

In addition to the question, *What could/should advertising look like in the future?* we asked a second question of our Advertising 2020 contributors: *What do we need to do now to get ready for that desired future?* In Part III, we distill Jerry's decades of work at the Wharton School and augment it with insights from our 2020 collaborators to provide key elements for transformation. The concepts are intended to be valuable and actionable regardless of your title, your role in or out of the current advertising and marketing ecosystem, or where you are in the world.

In parallel with current approaches, the best place to start is by experimenting with three new approaches *(see Figure III.1)*:

1. Embrace a culture of adaptive experimentation

2. Leverage all aspects of organizational architecture for change

3. Transcend silos and barriers with aligned objectives, open innovation, network activation and orchestration

Chapter 7 makes the case that the most important, fundamental mindsets and capabilities for the future come from embracing and instilling a culture of adaptive experimentation. **Adaptive experimentation is critical to learning, measurement, innovation, and improved decisions.** This implies a creative culture that gives permission to fail and take risks for the sake of continuously learning what works, what doesn't, and what could work even better. As Jerry emphasizes throughout his teaching, it is the only way to learn the causal impact of approaches and spending. This applies not only to approaches with audiences, but to new organizational approaches as well.

Steve Bellman and Duane Varan from MediaScience explain:

> *When the future is not like the past, historical methods are of little use. Instead, what is needed is lab-based research to test new ideas, and the variables that make them work.... The brands that do best will be the ones that invest the most in R&D, and more importantly have the agility to implement its findings. A good analogy is Olympic cycling: once one team adopted carbon-fiber frames and disc wheels, every team had to follow, or get left behind. (2012)*

Figure III.1 Update and Expand Mindsets and Capabilities

IV.
UPDATE AND EXPAND MINDSETS AND CAPABILITIES

Embrace a Culture of Adaptive Experimentation	Leverage All Aspects of Organizational Architecture to Effect Change or Start Fresh	Transcend Silos and Barriers with Aligned Objectives, Open Innovation, and Network Activation and Orchestration

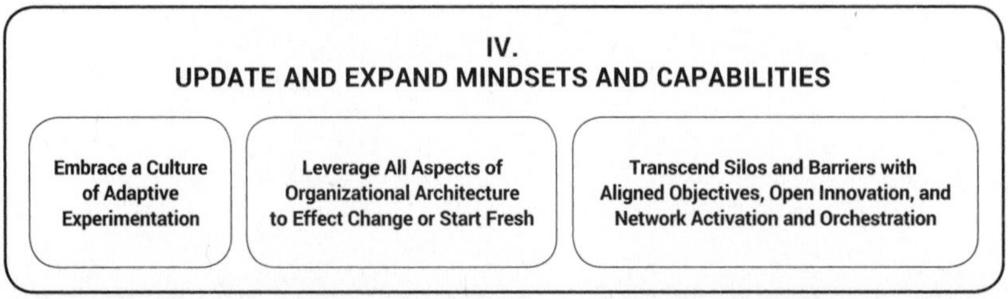

Chapter 8 lays out the framework for creating parallel paths to move forward with existing structures and processes while experimenting with changes to the organizational architecture that encompasses:

- Culture and values
- Governance and business models
- Structure and processes
- Value creation processes
- People, mindsets, and competencies
- Physical and virtual facilities
- Resources
- Technology infrastructure
- Metrics/Dashboard, performance measures, and incentives

Chapter 9 creates a framework for identifying the silos that will likely thwart new approaches and suggests approaches for bridging them. Open innovation, as both a mindset and an operational model, is one of the critical game changers of our time. It brings the advantages of diverse disciplines and innovative solutions at a fraction of traditional costs and time. Network activation and orchestration capabilities offer a means to bridge traditional silos inside and outside an organization and weave together collaborators and touchpoints for new means of value creation.

In Chapter 10, we conclude with an invitation to join the *Beyond Advertising* movement by adopting, experimenting with, and sharing the lessons learned from the approaches and philosophies of the book.

Exciting change is happening—we can all feel it. This book, thanks to all its contributors, has prepared us to embrace it. The first step is self-evaluation: once we see our perspective for what it is—a mental model for looking at the world—we can move beyond it.

Fluidity and connectivity are at the center of our world today, and they are central to working towards the future as it could/should be. By finding ways to connect, honestly and respectfully, within our organizations and with the people we want to reach, we can move towards that future.

We've created a visionary starting point and laid out a roadmap to help create this future *(see Figure III.2)*. Now its time to build up evidence. Identify, experiment, and share your results: the future is, above all, the best of individual initiative and collaborative power.

Figure III.2 The Beyond Advertising Roadmap: Creating Value through All Touchpoints Model

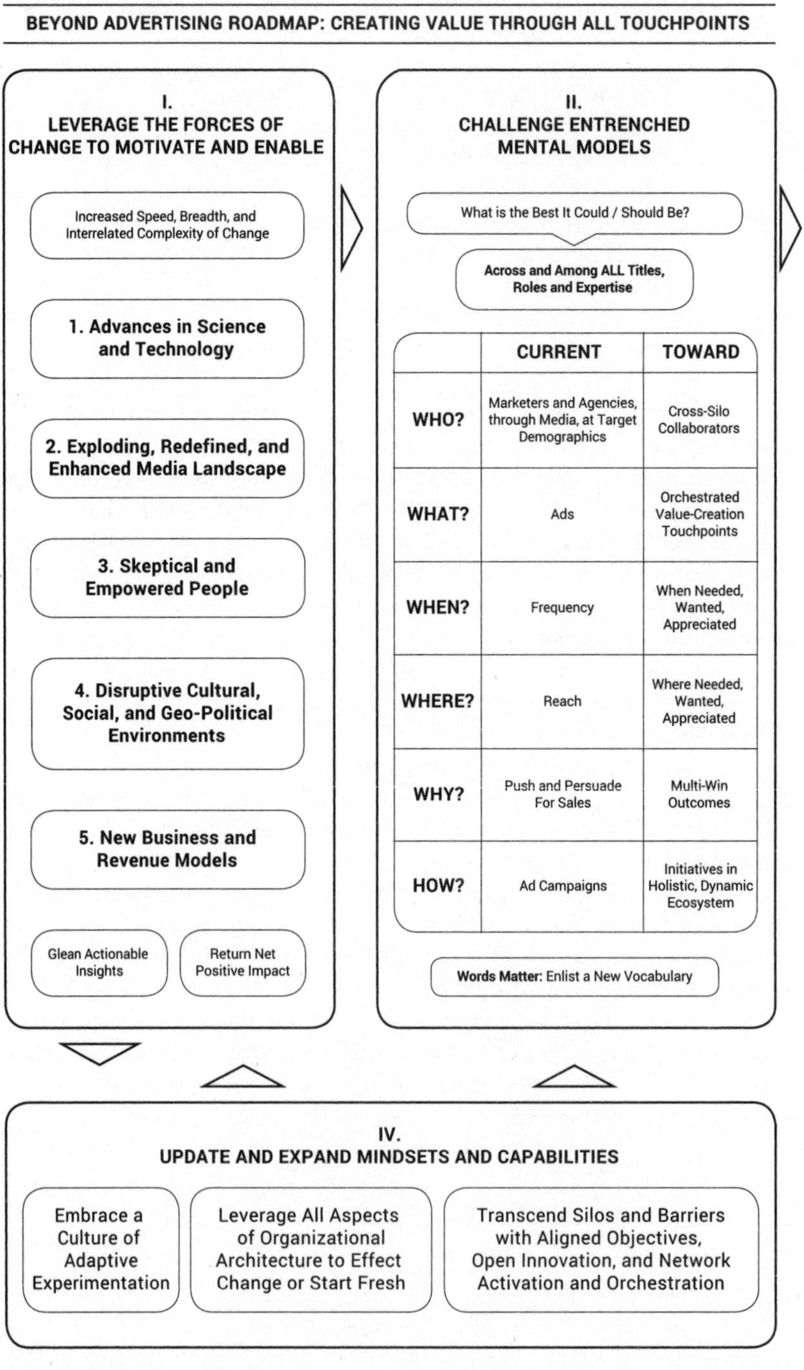

	CURRENT	TOWARD
WHO?	Marketers and Agencies, through Media, at Target Demographics	Cross-Silo Collaborators
WHAT?	Ads	Orchestrated Value-Creation Touchpoints
WHEN?	Frequency	When Needed, Wanted, Appreciated
WHERE?	Reach	Where Needed, Wanted, Appreciated
WHY?	Push and Persuade For Sales	Multi-Win Outcomes
HOW?	Ad Campaigns	Initiatives in Holistic, Dynamic Ecosystem

Figure III.2 (*continued*)

III.
ALL TOUCHPOINT VALUE CREATION MODEL

An ongoing, synergistic orchestration and optimization of all touchpoint value creation among an enterprise, the people in its network, the people it seeks to reach and serve, and the societies and cultures in which it exists and has responsibility.

1. Aligned Objectives for Multi-Win Outcomes with Short Term and Long Term Impact

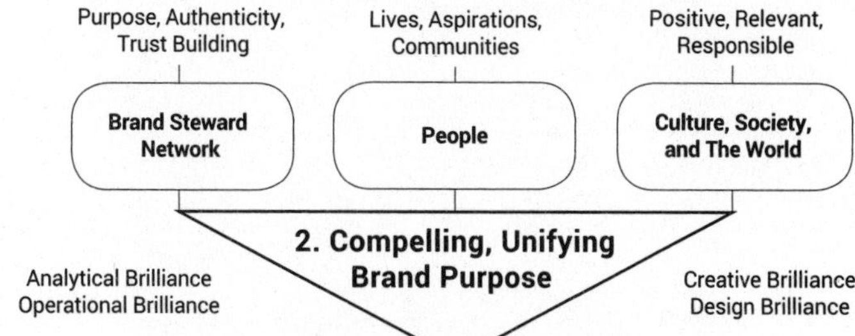

3. Orchestrated Across ALL Touchpoints

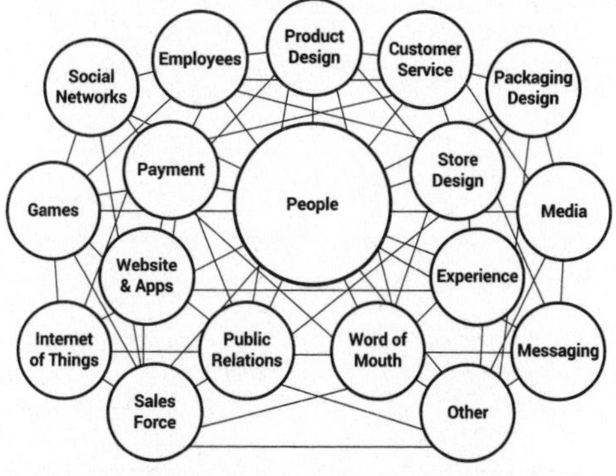

4. Touchpoint Value Creation

Maximized Context +	Maximized Substance
M.A.D.E.[S]	**R.A.V.E.S.**
✓ **M** ultisensory	✓ **R** elevant & Respectful
✓ **A** udience	✓ **A** ctionable
✓ **D** elivery Mechanism	✓ **V** aluable & Value-Generating
✓ **E** nvironment	✓ **E** xceptional Experience
✓ **S** ynergy	✓ **S** hareworthy Stories

Chapter 7 Embrace Adaptive Experimentation

While John Wanamaker's notion of overspending on advertising was over 100 years ago, it is still the case that most companies do not have a good idea about their optimal advertising resource allocation.

— Russell Winer, *Professor of Marketing, Stern School of Business, NYU (2012)*

If there is one notion that those of us in the advertising and marketing world can agree on for the future, it would be that we could and should be—once and for all—unshackled from this oft-cited quote by Wannamaker. We believe that day has already dawned. The availability of relevant data and information, the technology to capture and process it, the focus and guidance from human insights and caring, and the creative sparks to bring it to life through all touchpoints of the product or service set the stage. The only missing ingredient: creating a pervasive culture and capability for adaptive experimentation. Here's why.

Imagine investing €10 million in an advertising campaign and at the end of the year, the return was a 30 percent increase in sales and a 10 percent increase in market share. How much should be spent on the next campaign? Increase expenditure, reduce it, or keep it the same? And how to justify this choice to the CFO?

For a long time, the only answer has been "I don't know." Without additional data points, we can't identify what worked or why, so we can't make informed decisions for the future. This is not an enviable position, but unfortunately it remains a common one.

However, there is hope. Professor Winer explains:

> *This is changing . . . with more and more attention being paid to the development of sophisticated market response models and the pressure that CEOs and CFOs are putting on senior marketing personnel to demonstrate the ROI of marketing expenditures. . . . The beauty of digital advertising is that it is both measurable and has significant potential for controlled field experimentation. The combination of these two characteristics of advertising in 2020 will result in much more efficient allocation of marketing resources in general and of advertising spending in particular. (2012)*

Jerry is passionate about this topic, too, and in this chapter, he guides us in understanding and adopting this disciplined approach of experimentation to continuously increase our understanding about what works and what doesn't in an ever-evolving touchpoint landscape.

Don't wait until 2020 to realize the vision that Winer describes. **Adopt the philosophy of adaptive experimentation now and transform long-held ideas about risk and failure into practices that embrace creativity and innovation.** By adopting a culture of adaptive experimentation, organizations and the people who run them can leverage the benefits of unpredictability to consistently adapt to new challenges and opportunities, and what is otherwise known as waste—spending without learning or improving.

Adaptive experimentation is the design and implementation of continuous and ongoing real-world experiments to *learn* and improve business decisions and strategies over time. **Importantly, adaptive experimentation is not a one-time strategy or investment but rather a continuous improvement philosophy.** Common terms used to describe similar ideas are test and learn, rapid eval, or sense and respond. The strategy is closely related to the current trend towards "design-led thinking," where long-standing design practices—launch and iterate, collaborative play, data visualization, and prototyping—are used to tackle social, environmental, economic, and urban planning problems.

How Experimentation Leads to Answers and Innovations

Adaptive experimentation can be applied to any important decision area. What is the optimal budget allocation across markets and platforms? Which message results in the highest rate of conversion? Which product design contains the features most important to the customer? How do these variables interact and change across consumer contexts? Adaptive Experimentation can test each element of the All Touchpoint Value Creation Model.

In addition, by conducting experiments systematically over time, one can develop empirical generalizations—findings that hold under a wide range of circumstances and across a range of variants. Oft-cited examples of companies that successfully use adaptive experimentation include Google, Facebook, and industry disrupters like Uber. The audacious experiments and achievements of Google's famous X Labs read more like science fiction than the research and development agenda of an Internet company: self-driving cars, balloons that broadcast wi-fi around the world, and contact lenses that can measure glucose levels. In a profile of the X labs for *Fast Company*, Jon Gertner observed a culture that used "rapid eval" to test multiple ideas—rejecting most of them—and noted that **"Failure is not precisely the goal at Google X. But in many respects it is the means"** (2014). And Google's X Labs do not exist in a silo. The entire company, from Google's genesis as a project to organize the world's information to its investments in universal Internet access, is a model of experimentation: it's hardwired into their culture.

Another company that functions in a continual state of experimentation is Facebook. In 2014, Facebook launched the Airlock platform for testing and refining new features on its ubiquitous mobile interface. Two developers from the company, Ari Grant and Kang Zhang, describe the philosophy on constant experimentation:

> After we ship a new update, it's important for us to understand how new features perform, the fixes improved performance and reliability, and improvements to the user interface change how people use the app and where they spend their time. In order to analyze these objectives, we needed a mobile A/B testing infrastructure that would let us expose our users to multiple versions of our apps (version A and version B), which are the same in all aspects except for some specific tests. [Airlock] lets us compare metric data from each version of the app and the various tests, and then decide which version to ship or how to iterate further. (2014)

Uber also makes important decisions based on the results of experiments. During the summer of 2014, the company was in competition with Lyft for the New York market. According to the *New York Times*, Uber put a strategy in place to run pricing experiments to understand how price-sensitive the demand for rides was. The price was cut up to 25 percent for a short amount of time and the company measured the increase in ride volume. The motivation behind the experiment was greater than knowing price sensitivity: Uber hoped to gain insight into trigger points for consumer behavior and product demand. The experiment enabled Uber to understand when and how to adjust prices to ensure the optimal outcomes for customers and drivers. This valuable learning could take place in real time thanks to Uber's sophisticated analytics and data mining. According to founder Travis Kalanick, the company runs these kinds of experiments on an ongoing basis to perfect its pricing model (Irwin 2014). Perhaps not all their experiments are role model, but their learning through experiments is worth attention.

Mike Ewing, executive dean of the Deakin Business School at Deakin University reminds us that iteration isn't unique to the twenty-first century—far before app-based cab services, experimentation was taking place in the media industry:

> *In 1902, circulation figures for the French daily newspaper L'Auto were low relative to those of its chief rival, Le Vélo. The editorial team of L'Auto held a crisis meeting to identify a strategy to increase circulation. It was suggested that the newspaper organize a multistage bicycle race around France. The editor of L'Auto was originally unconvinced by the idea. Nevertheless, the paper's financial backers supported the strategy, and in July 1903, the paper organized (and reported on) the inaugural "Tour de France." Coverage of the race had an immediate impact on circulation figures; sales of L'Auto increased from 25,000 before the race to 65,000 immediately after. L'Auto would go on to out-sell Le Vélo, and the "Tour de France" would become the world's premier cycling race—with phenomenal global media coverage, advertising, and sponsorship. (2012)*

Back in the twenty-first century, Procter & Gamble is one of the most accomplished practitioners of adaptive experimentation and innovation in the CPG realm. Many of their products, including Pampers, Swiffer, and Crest White Strips, were category-defining disruptive innovations. Each year, P&G conducts "some 20,000 studies involving more than 5 million consumers in nearly 100 countries" (Brown and Anthony 2011).

These experiments, many of which start at a small scale in a specific region, enable the company to continually generate breakthrough innovations and stay ahead of their competitors. Bob McDonald, chairman, president, and CEO, observes, "We know from our history that while promotions may win quarters, innovation wins decades" (Brown and Anthony 2011).

So how does adaptive experimentation work? **Simply put, in contrast to a single action (and whatever result that action may generate), experimenting with variations can tell what effect each action is having, and what to do next.** Refer back to the example concerning the optimal budget size for a campaign that started this chapter. The business-as-usual model of investing €10 million in a budget provides little guidance on whether, and how, to increase or decrease the spend for the next year. Instead, an advertiser could design a simple experiment where certain channels or markets receive a €5 million budget and others a €10 million or even €15 million budget. Measuring the marginal effectiveness of each change in expenditure can give management insight into the marketing strategy and yield higher return on investment in the future.

In Figure 7.1 we demonstrate the utility of a single dimension approach to advertising in contrast to the insights to be gained from generating multiple data points.

The graph on the left shows the results of a single action: that such an approach yields little information about how to improve your actions for better results is apparent. In contrast, the graph on the right shows three different

Figure 7.1 Contrast in Insights

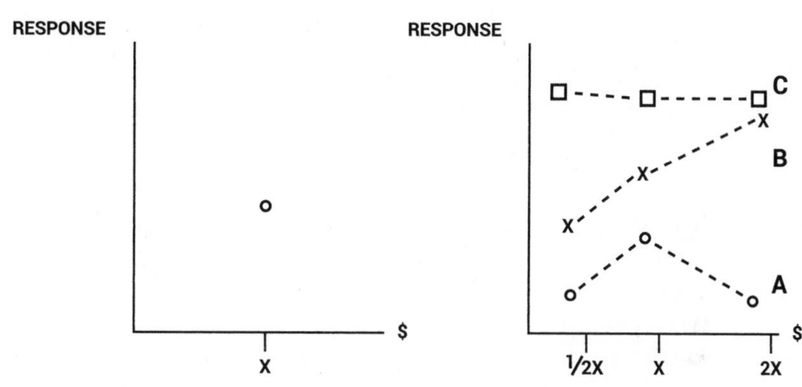

actions—one with X amount of money spent, one with half that amount, and one with double that amount. The results of these three actions give clear insights into the impacts of different amounts, reveals what works best, and, therefore, the best course of action for the future. But the key to adaptive experimentation is to continue experimenting, to continue pushing possibilities, even when results seem conclusive. If results map onto line A of the graph, continue advertising at level X and add other variables. If the results match line B on the graph, push the test out to 3X or even 4X. And if the results map onto line C, experiment with both 1/4X and 3X.

One of Jerry's classic and compelling examples of experimentation is brewing company Anheuser Busch. In the 1960s, the firm decided to experiment with budget levels—ranging from zero spend to triple spend—in different markets, with adjustments in media mix, frequency, and supplemental advertising. The continuous experiments found that decreased spend in the short term did *not* have a negative impact on sales, and that a complete stoppage of television advertising for a short time actually *increased* sales in some cases. **The strategy of alternating normal spend levels with periods of zero advertising spend is called flighting and may not have emerged without the experimental spirit displayed by Anheuser Busch during that decade.**

In Figure 7.2 we illustrate a more complex experiment design called the Latin Square Design. The diagram shows three dimensions (A, B, and C), which could, for example, represent message, dominant touchpoint, and distribution—each at three levels.

Of course experiments can include any number of factors at different number of levels, and are not limited only to only three variables. We've included Jerry's more detailed explanation of experimentation, as well as references to free, open, online courses to learn more, in Appendix 4.

Figure 7.2 Latin Square Design with Three Dimensions at Three Levels

		B		
		1	2	3
A	1	C_1	C_2	C_3
	2	C_2	C_3	C_1
	3	C_3	C_1	C_2

Seven Benefits of Adaptive Experimentation

Adaptive Experimentation results in (at least) seven significant benefits, which together yield the best insurance against the risks inherent to a complex and changing environment *(see Figure 7.3)*.

First, experimentation with appropriate controls is the best way to **establish causal relations between actions and results**, allowing organizations to garner concrete information and deep insights about their strategies. In contrast, market response models can demonstrate that there is a correlation between certain actions and results, but cannot prove that the actions were the cause of the

Figure 7.3 Seven Benefits of Adaptive Experimentation

	SEVEN BENEFITS OF ADAPTIVE EXPERIMENTATION
1	Identify the causal relationships between actions and results
2	Learn to make better, more effective, and more efficient decisions
3	Initiate bold and innovative actions
4	Co-create and collaborate with customers and partners
5	Force measurement and accountability
6	Create a creative and innovative organization
7	Achieve a competitive advantage

results. As Randall Rothenberg, president and CEO at the Interactive Advertising Bureau, puts it,

> *[W]e must become much more adept at picking out the signal from the noise. We have to understand that technology alone will not get us there. Human interactions and skills are required to identify and understand significant marketplace trends, and then to test them scientifically. We need more than a processer and an algorithm to make sense of the massive daily volume of census-based information, and to pick out, for example, exactly which sentiments are transitory and which will still be relevant by the time the company produces, distributes, and advertises the new product. (2012)*

Second, once we learn to understand the impacts of our actions we can make **better, more effective, and more efficient decisions, thereby reducing risk.** Horst Stipp, executive vice president global business strategy at the ARF, regards this as an urgent need:

> *As discussed at Wharton Future of Advertising meetings and at many ARF conferences, the most urgent problem today is the lack of good measurement for many of the new distribution channels, and a lack of valid data that limit marketers' ability to make well-informed decisions on advertising strategies. As the future is getting more complex, a major effort in this area is becoming even more urgent. (2012)*

In the current environment, decisions need to be made quickly, and understanding causality means those decisions can be made upon proven causal relationships as opposed to intuition or retrofitted market response models. As Anant Rangaswami, editor at Storyboard notes, *"We will have vast mountains of data on what content is being consumed, on who is consuming the content and where and when the content is being consumed—and, frighteningly, on whether the content is liked or disliked"* (2012). Finding ways to quickly understand how our actions influence this content is essential. And, thanks to the continuous nature of adaptive experimentation, we can continually build on our knowledge of causal relationships thereby making better decisions, reducing risks, and capturing unique opportunities.

Third, adaptive experimentation encourages **true innovation and bold actions.** When conducting experiments people are freed to conceive of wholly new concepts and test them—we salute the many skilled researchers who dedicate their time and expertise to this process. Khayyam Wakil, chief belief officer at Thynk Tank observes: *"In this fabric of technology, tides shift, power sways, and companies rise and fall in popularity in what seems like the blink of an eye. The companies that are taking matters into their own hands and risking big are now producing the content themselves and winning big"* (2013). Already the companies that we consider icons of contemporary innovation are deeply engaged in innovation. To quote Gareth Kay, cofounder at Chapter SF,

> *[Greatness] comes from experimentation and learning from placing little bets rather than ponderously trying to birth perfection. Google's a great example of this (originally a project to index Stanford's library) as are Starbucks and the way comedians and musicians try out new material. It's what gets Pixar from "suck to nonsuck" through huge amounts of early iteration and feedback sessions every day around rushes. (2013)*

Fourth, **experiments encourage codesigning and collaboration with customers, partners, and other parts of the organization.** Sharing control can, of course, feel risky. Thankfully experimentation offers a controlled learning opportunity that allows people to step outside their comfort zone. Engaging customers as co-creators is critical but often viewed as risky by the leadership team; when presented as an experiment it may be more likely to be accepted. Organizations can also be strengthened by bringing together people from different sides of the spectrum. Writes Carl Marci, chief neuroscientist of Nielsen Consumer Neuroscience, *"Researchers should work closer with creative directors to accelerate the learning exchange, support ideation, and enhance the efficiency of creativity"* (2012).

Fifth, experiments require measurement, which encourages the development and application of analytics, **driving a shift toward data-informed decision making and a culture of accountability.** The path toward understanding how efforts impact the bottom line is through rigorously measured experiments; without measurement one cannot conduct experiments. Implementing process measures for fact-based decision-making inspires organizations to look beyond traditional industry metrics and gain a deeper understanding of firm performance, employee performance, and customer behavior and satisfaction. For Hayes Roth, former chief marketing officer at Landor and now principal at HA Roth Consulting LLC, *"We already have more data at our disposal than we can usefully assimilate as marketers—and this will only grow by quantum leaps in the decade to come. The challenge is how to discern that information which has the most relevant value and what to do with it"* (2013).

Sixth, adaptive experimentation sends the signal that it is okay to fail as long as learning is gained, fostering the creation and development of a **creative and innovative organization.** After all, no one should expect every experiment to succeed. Whether an organization has innovation and a startup mentality in its DNA, or is trying to recapture the fail-fast-and-cheap mindset, adaptive experimentation provides a rational framework for testing and evaluating ideas before expending significant investments.

In an episode of our radio show, *Marketing Matters*, R/GA's SVP of technology Will Turnage discussed the benefits of this approach, saying, "When the goal is rapid-fire iteration, you might come up with no ideas, or you might come up with some really great ideas, but you will definitely start thinking about the technology [or anything else] in an entirely different way." The process, he points out, could be as simple as the exercise of pairing a technology with unexpected adjectives: "Thinking about a 'sad tweet' or a 'sarcastic car alarm' can suddenly create a whole other understanding, one that is hugely generative" (Marketing Matters February 2015).

By encouraging a culture of innovation, organizations avoid risk-averse behavior that leaves them vulnerable to new entrants. Richard Wise, brand anthropologist at Geometry Global, and Watts Wacker, founder and director at Firstmatter, write, *"At work, run lots of experiments—don't think you have to do everything perfectly. Don't freak out if you have a bad experience. Don't let it turn into a trauma that blocks creativity"* (2012). "Failure" then isn't a bad word—we prefer to think of it as part of the iterative process. If the goal is *learning*, lessons can be taught through success and failure both.

Finally, conducting experiments **provides a competitive advantage** in the marketplace because the one conducting the experiment is the only one who knows what's going on. Competitors will witness actions and results, but without knowing the experimental design they won't be able to link the two. This is particularly true for complex experiments with many variables.

Of these seven benefits, which seems to be the most relevant for your organization or venture? Which would have the most impact? What additional benefit can you envision that would warrant this approach?

Using adaptive experimentation as an ongoing strategy leads to continuous learning and better decisions over time. The field of direct mail, now enjoying a renaissance of "owned media" and a direct connect, has embraced and continues to benefit from constant experimentation. By tweaking and testing variations in the greeting, message, image, style, or tone of the postcard or letter, online and offline, companies garner—and gauge—different engagement rates so that communications are continuously refined and improved, for both sender and recipient.

As Karsten Koed, CEO of Gorm Larsen & Zornig, and Morten Gad, creative director and partner of Gorm Larsen & Zornig, observe, *"Today, everything digital is in a constant state of beta. We develop, we test, we launch and we repeat and iterate in order to constantly improve our communication. In the future, this process will speed up and eventually it will happen in real time. Those who iterate will survive!"* (2012). **While a single experiment could lead to some of these benefits, the real benefits—a more creative and innovative culture, a discipline of measurement, improved insights about the causal impact of our activities, making better decisions—can be more pervasive if adaptive experimentation is adopted as a management philosophy.** As the results of an experiment come in, management will evaluate and decide what to do—continue, expand, modify, or kill—without deeming *any* experiment a failure. This approach will inherently require organizational experimentation. As Thomas Burkhardt, global brand builder, suggests, *"Besides investments into technology and big data, the* *biggest—and potentially most difficult—challenge for companies and agencies will be the changes required to skill sets of individuals and experimentations with new and potentially radically different organizational structures"* (2013). But more on that in Chapter 8.

How to Implement Adaptive Experimentation

Adaptive experimentation holds the promise of significantly improving brand and organizational management. One key role of adaptive experimentation is to establish a culture of learning and exploration throughout the organization. However, before experiments can be designed, implemented, and adapted, there may be significant institutional and individual resistance to change.

Today, research shows that about 70 percent of change initiatives fail to meet their goals. The topic of change management has been the subject of many books and conferences over the last few decades, but Jerry's extensive work on transformational leadership with executives and organizations around the world suggest that many still face significant obstacles in implementing well thought-out solutions to challenging business problems.

How can established, slow-to-change organizations adopt the mindset of experimentation, learning, and iteration necessary to allocate significant resources toward uncertainty? He offers four steps:

1. *Challenge mental models*
   The riskiest business decision in today's environment is to continue with the status quo. Seek alignment around the upside of challenging and improving upon the current approaches for everyone involved.

2. *Gain buy-in*
   Start with low-risk, easy-to-understand experiments that demonstrate the value of an "always testing" mindset. Consider selecting experimental questions that align with existing marketing efforts instead of creating entirely new projects. And when the experiments demonstrate results, make consequential strategy changes. Highlighting the cost-effectiveness, relevance, and accountability of your experimental marketing initiatives will help generate organizational buy-in and may lead to larger budgets for more ambitious testing.

3. *Provide incentives and rewards*
   One of the most common obstacles to change is, well, the fear of change itself: job loss, wage insecurity, an unfamiliar role, intimidating new responsibilities, a bigger team, a different schedule, a different office.... Find concrete ways to remove these legitimate barriers to new approaches. To mitigate these concerns during the experimentation, ensure that people in experimental units are compensated at the same rate as those in the most successful. Incentives, rewards, and recognition

cement alignment and motivate collaborators to become champions instead of resistors.

4. *Institutionalize experimentation to balance short- and long-term learning* Include numerous key experiments as part of any strategic plan and budget. Adaptive experimentation will yield short-term results and feedback and must also be designed to understand and refine the broader importance on growth and profitability of brand effect over time. An adaptive experimentation vision and plan should be connected to the normal conduct of business: it must be linked to the budget and strategic plans.

Once the initial resistance to experimentation has been overcome, the most difficult obstacle for new ideas can sometimes be a lack of will to change the current resource allocation. The Three Innovation Horizons approach *(Figure 7.4)*

Figure 7.4 The Three Innovation Horizons

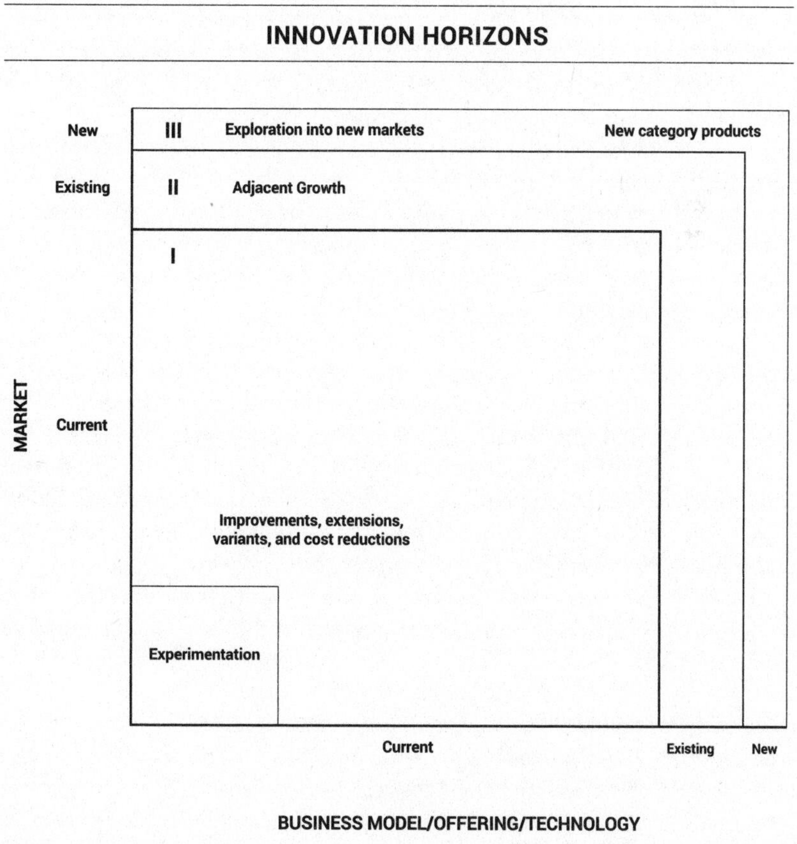

is a useful model for thinking about determining allocation of resources and managing uncertainty, regardless of the size of the organization.

Thinking through innovation horizons pushes us to be forward-looking. In the featured example, Knowledge of Technology expands from horizon one, technology a company already uses; to horizon two, existing technology a company doesn't use but can start to consider; and out to horizon three, technologies that are completely outside the scope of a company's current focus. These developments connect with the expanding market on the vertical axis, which grows from existing market, to existing but untapped market, to a new market. The arch where these points meet form innovation horizons, and show that by remaining focused solely on horizon one—the current situation—companies are limiting their potential for growth in the near and distant future. We recommend that 80 to 90 percent of resources should be invested in the current horizon, but at least 10 to 20 percent be dedicated to exploring new opportunities in horizon two and three. Moreover, part of each experiment should take place in each of the three areas.

Coca-Cola offers an example of management in relation to the three horizons. They have a 70-20-10 rule of experimental budget allocation. Seventy percent of the spend is focused on the "now" or established strategies, 20 percent is focused on the "new," and 10 percent is focused on the "next." This commitment to adaptive experimentation is key for remaining competitive.

Take a moment to consider your own organization. **How much are you currently investing, in terms of time and money, in the different horizons? How do you develop, prioritize, plan, and execute new ideas when the effectiveness is unknown?** Does your firm have experimental processes in place? If so, are they followed with careful tracking and accountability? How do you scale successful experiments across the organization?

If you are unsure about some of these questions, you're not alone. Forrester Research has found that just 3 percent of marketing budgets are devoted to experimentation and 25 percent of marketers dedicate nothing to such a process (Ramos 2014). With business-to-business marketing budgets predicted to rise by 6 percent in 2014, there is certainly room for some growth without compromising on existing priorities. Claudia Lagunas, senior director of Global Digital Marketing for Visa writes, *"Bold moves need to be made in terms of allocating proper resources to tools that can help improve the ability to adapt or redesign a campaign or a business to keep relevancy.... Allocate budgets for experimentation and innovation, as this can be the key to keep your brand relevant and fresh on a permanent basis"* (2012).

Developing and Implementing the Experimental Design

When using the adaptive experimentation approach, confidence in having a correct understanding of the causal relationships between variables is critical. Strategic and carefully thought-out design is therefore essential. Here, Jerry outlines the basic principles of experimental design to ensure reliable results. Appendix 4 provides a bit more detail on the 10 steps of experimentation and provides references for free online Coursera courses, such as Design Thinking for Business Innovation (offered through the University of Virginia), or Interaction Design (offered through the University of California) to better understand this process. In the meantime, here are the 10 necessary steps for successful experimentation:

1. Decide on the objective of the experiment
2. Select the innovative experimental variable (ATP, R.A.V.E.S., M.A.D.E.^{S}, etc.)
3. Select a control group
4. Define the unit of analysis (country, state, city, store, individual)
5. Structure the performance measures and length of experiment
6. Decide on the experimental design including the execution of the test and control stimuli
7. Design the implementation
8. Analyze the results (ANCOVA)
9. Present the results as a story and as an integral part of the dashboard
10. Decide on the required actions (scale up, kill, something else); develop the next round of experiments

Done right, insights and knowledge gained from experiments far outweigh the cost and effort invested. **The most important takeaway is that experiments should build on each other for ongoing development and decision improvement.** And one can always extend experiments to get more specificity from your results.

To approach the future from a position of strength, invest in experimentation and adaptive capabilities and translate the results into practical and widely implemented initiatives to truly improve business performance.

Adaptive Experimentation in All Touchpoint Value Creation

Every element of the All Touchpoint Value Creation Model can be experimented with—any component or any combination of Aligned Objectives for a Compelling Purpose (Chapter 3), Portfolios of Touchpoints (Chapter 4), R.A.V.E.S. (Chapter 5), M.A.D.E.^{S} (Chapter 6). Be bold and creative, and choose aspects that really test your mental models. Uncovering the unexpected is the goal.

For example, WFoA is collaborating with Facebook, brands, and agencies on a series of tests to learn more about personalization at scale. The initiative aims to jointly research the brand impact of personalized marketing—going beyond traditional demographic models of age, sex, and gender to building segmentations based on interests, geographies, and so on, to reach a specific audience. Based on Facebook advertising best practices, the tests are exploring the effectiveness of targeted messages when compared against generalized ad creative. The answer may differ by company and even within an advertiser's portfolio. Through this analysis, companies can evaluate what is the best strategy for their brand(s). We may have the tools and technology to do so, but does it have an impact? Only an experiment such as this one can determine for certain.

Although adaptive experimentation is being used by some of the highest-performing firms to good effect, many firms have been slow to embrace it. There is perceived safety and comfort in conducting business as usual, in managing resources according to a preauthorized plan, and in minimizing variation and discouraging mistakes. **Change means risk—a scary word—but again, the status quo mentality is the highest risk strategy.** Experimentation is the most effective strategy for success.

The Ethics of Experimentation

While rigorous adaptive experimentation can deliver great benefits to organizations—and their audiences—no discussion of experimentation would be complete without addressing the responsibility that comes with managing and optimizing based on data about people's characteristics, behaviors, online and offline activity, and anything else trackable. These concerns represent the tug-of-war between offering heightened personalization and breaching consumers' privacy. In a briefing entitled "Why Marketing Should Be Personal," Econsultancy and Adobe remind us that "privacy isn't just a set of laws and guidelines; privacy is a feeling in the hearts and minds of our customers" (2014).

So, as we think about designing and implementing experiments, we must keep in mind that "a clear focus on customer value over immediate profits is the safest approach, and the most profitable in the long run" (Econsultancy 2014).

Careful ethical considerations, policies and awareness are essential. Recent examples of public responses to undisclosed experimentation is, unsurprisingly, strong. Facebook's 2012 study on its users' expressions of positive and negative emotions was met with public outcry: trust was breached. Subsequently, Facebook issued a statement and established a new framework for its research practices, including stricter guidelines for researchers, tighter review committees, a six-week training program for researchers, and a public centralized research website.

Similarly, concerns were raised over dating site OkCupid's experiments in testing response rates when certain factors, such as match percentage, were changed. As Dr. Pamela Rutledge, psychologist and director of the Media Psychology Research Center in Newport Beach, California, told thinkprogress.org, "I think there is a presumption—a naïve one perhaps—that the companies are acting to help the user achieve their goals rather than the awareness of that it is also the user serving the company goals.... Dating is so personal that it's hard to remember it's a business" (Quoted in Williams, 2014).

However, the question of ethical experimentation in business needs to be kept in perspective: Facebook's study, while highly statistically significant, was in reality very tiny. As Professor Tal Yarkoni, University of Texas at Austin, writes:

> The largest effect size reported had a Cohen's d of 0.02–meaning that eliminating a substantial proportion of emotional content from a user's feed had the monumental **effect of shifting that user's own emotional word use by two hundredths of a standard deviation.** In other words, the manipulation had a negligible real-world impact on users' behavior. (2014)

And the experiment itself only measured *expression* of emotions: no link between expression and actual emotional state/behavior was definitively established. This point emphasizes the importance of respect and relevance we have been discussing throughout the book: people may see "manipulation" as acceptable or as a violation of their privacy based entirely on how respected they feel and the level of trust that has been earned and must continue to be earned.

Figure 7.5 Beyond Advertising in Action: The Experiment Imperative

Beyond Advertising in Action
THE EXPERIMENT IMPERATIVE

INGLORIOUS FRUITS AND VEGETABLES—INTERMARCHE
Agency: Marcel
Effie Award: Gold—Positive Change Europe Single Market 2014

OBJECTIVE/PROBLEM TO BE SOLVED

In 2014, the European Union made it a priority to combat food waste. In France alone, $545 worth of food per person was being thrown away, 40% of which was fruits and vegetables.

APPROACH

Intermarche, one of the largest supermarkets in France, decided to tackle this problem by showing that 'ugly' vegetables and fruits could be just as tasty. Intermarche bought produce that would have normally been thrown away by growers and called them "Inglorious Fruits and Vegetables." These were given their own aisle and a 30% price reduction to make them more appealing to customers.

THE RESULTS

During a local test, point of sale traffic increased 24%. Due to positive feedback, the initiative was rolled out in the group's 1,800 national stores. During the nationwide October launch, 1.5 tons of 'ugly' fruits and vegetables were sold within the first month. Following the launch of the campaign, three other large French retailers created similar initiatives.

LESSONS AND OBSERVATIONS

Taking risks and experimenting can yield unexpectedly high results. Start small, get feedback, and iterate.

CITATION: Effie Award Winners, 2014

Key Takeaways

- **Adaptive experimentation paves the road to innovation. Remember that experiments don't have to be large scale from the get-go: start small, adapt, and evolve, and the potential for innovation will become evident.**

- **Experimentation allows us to understand—and take some control of—variation. By consciously adapting certain factors and carefully measuring the results, we can understand the present, and better predict the future.**

- **Experimentation can take many forms, and testing any combination of the insights from previous chapters can help us understand how to best adapt and evolve. Set a clear set of parameters, have a control group, and then use your imagination.**

- **The bottom line benefits aside, experimentation can have dramatic and positive impact on the ethos of a company. When experimentation is celebrated and "failure" is replaced with "learning", workspaces become more productive, cohesive, and creative.**

- **Human testing, no matter how benign, should be approached with ethical awareness. People's data may not be physically part of them but it still warrants careful treatment and respect *(see Figure 7.5).***

Chapter 8

Leverage Organizational Architecture

Through the understanding and activating of data and their supporting technological architectures, we as advertisers will create rich, intimate, highly personalized, and culturally resonant experiences for the people and communities that care about our brands. These experiences will help transport people and communities from their current state to a desired state (within reason), and these folks will in turn thank us by becoming brand loyalists.

— Loren Grossman, *Chief Experience Officer and President of the CXM, Annalect (2012)*

Implementing a comprehensive All Touchpoint Value Creation Model as described in Part II, which fully leverages the five forces of change put forth in Part I, has profound implications across the entire organization—large or small, agency or advertiser, media provider or research firm. As our 2020 collaborators identify these implications and necessary actions, they collectively touch on all aspects of an organization, its people and its processes. We urge you to peruse their recommended action plans to get the full richness of their insights and perspectives at wfoa.wharton.upenn.edu/ad2020/. Indeed, many, if not most, of these 2020 visionaries are walking their talk, and are already putting their forward-looking concepts into practice and pioneering new approaches with the clear objective of helping to create a more desirable future.

In this chapter we provide a high-level framework for implementation, based on Jerry's years of transformational leadership research and work with senior executives, to capture all aspects of an organization that can be leveraged for change. We then provide examples from our collaborator community to provide a sampling of their recommendations.

Challenges to Change

Before we get to these recommendations for action, we acknowledge that change is rarely logical, methodical, sequential, or easy. Often, even with the best of plans, it can be messy, surprising, and infinitely frustrating. Even with the promise and control of an adaptive experimentation approach that we discussed in Chapter 7, existing strictures and structures can stymie new approaches.

As we go to press, Joe Plummer, senior advisor to the Wharton Future of Advertising Program, alerted us to another study that describes just how great the challenge remains. The subtitle of the *eMarketer* article reads, "Resources, measurement and coordination limit multichannel marketing."

> In a June 2015 study by Lewis PR, 84 percent of senior marketers worldwide said multichannel marketing was a key focus of their current marketing strategy, and the same percentage intended to increase marketing spending on such campaigns in the coming year. However, marketers may not be getting the support they need to actually implement such efforts, despite recognition from upper levels—86 percent of respondents said senior leaders at their organizations endorsed multichannel marketing, and 25 percent were using it because of pressure from the board.
>
> When asked about the biggest challenges to multichannel marketing, nearly a quarter of respondents said they lacked the time and resources to develop and execute multichannel campaigns, and the same percentage struggled to get buy-in at the board level. Similarly, other issues related to a lack of investment in tools needed to manage multichannel campaigns as well as a limited understanding about the process as a whole. ("Why Marketers Haven't Mastered Multichannel" 2015).

And this is just the "multichannel" aspect, and doesn't even address the other touchpoints of product design, package design, customer service, and more that the ATVC model encompasses. As Shelly Palmer puts it, *"The pace of change will never be as slow as it is today, so buckle-up and get ready for a wild ride!"* (2013)

Where to Start?

The most pragmatic way to implement the ATVC model is by focusing on those elements of the organizational architecture that are most critical to its implementation, then removing barriers or creating a separate organizational unit to implement the model or its parts. And some may be ready for a more radical approach or are in a position to start fresh.

Given that each of us is at a different stage in the journey, here are two perspectives. The first acknowledges that it may be more practical to start new initiatives for change in parallel with existing approaches. The second recommends a more radical approach.

Ipsos OTX CEO Shelley Zalis suggested at a recent WFoA executive roundtable in L.A. that some may be more successful by continuing on with day-to-day operations, while creating a *parallel effort* to carve out time, energy, and resources to begin to explore new approaches. Ideally, this would be experimentation with a capital "E" that we describe in Appendix 4, but experimenting with a small "e" may be the necessary first step. We learned firsthand about the "launch and iterate" approach from Cindy Goodrich and Sofia Buschmann, our Google collaborators on our Fast. *Forward* YouTube channel launched in 2009. We first talked about the idea in July and had the site up and running by the end of August. It continued to evolve to be one of the first channels to feature thought leaders from around the world sharing insights in two- to three-minute conversations ("Will the Future of Advertising Be a Blend of Old and New Media?" 2009).

On the other hand, Cindy Gallop tells adland: "Blow Yourselves Up and Start Again."

> *"You need to blow yourselves up and start again. You need to think about it like that. You can't stick on solutions, you can't just add bits on, which is what everyone's doing.*
>
> *"You need to restructure from the core. This is actually what you are already doing anyway as a process of attrition, when you lay people off, when you shut down divisions. Turn that into an opportunity.*
>
> *"At the moment you are breaking things down, actually use that to completely redesign from the ground-up to start again." (2012)*

There are also times when we can clearly see major opportunities, inefficiencies, unmet needs or deficiencies that offer a window for change. This means taking advantage of more nimble approaches such as launch-and-iterate, rapid prototyping, start-up mentality, skunkworks, innovation labs, hack-a-thons, paid time for innovation, and a plethora of ways that innovation and creativity and new team mash-ups are happening. Sometimes before the formal experimenting can happen, which should be the goal, innovation and initiatives to learn must get started.

Artem Zhiganov, product marketing manager at ZVooq in Russia, explains this relative to the agency world, but the suggestions transcend:

> *Startup ethos can change ideology, business process and sales policy of such an agency:*
>
> - *Lean methodology helps to break creative strategies into hypotheses for testing them with MVPs and iterate in real time according to the data collected*

- *Dynamic briefs are updated during campaigns, keeping the team in the know about the hypotheses and upcoming creative pivots*
- *"Always in beta" paradigm helps to reinvent relationships between the agency and the client (e.g., validated learnings as the main KPI)*
- *Collaboration principle disrupts the traditional process with physical colocation of project teams, mixing developers with creatives, and so forth*
- *Cloud-based solutions enable us to do everything from anywhere and make the office asset-light (2013)*

Nine Levers for Organizational Change

Regardless of where you begin, implementation of the ATVC will likely require reconsideration of all nine components of the organizational architecture, represented in Figure 8.1.

Any architectural change should consider the principles of speed, agility, continuous innovation, and transparency, reflecting the needs of all stakeholders and strive for a win-win-win outcomes. And crucially, given that the

Figure 8.1 Levers of Organizational Change

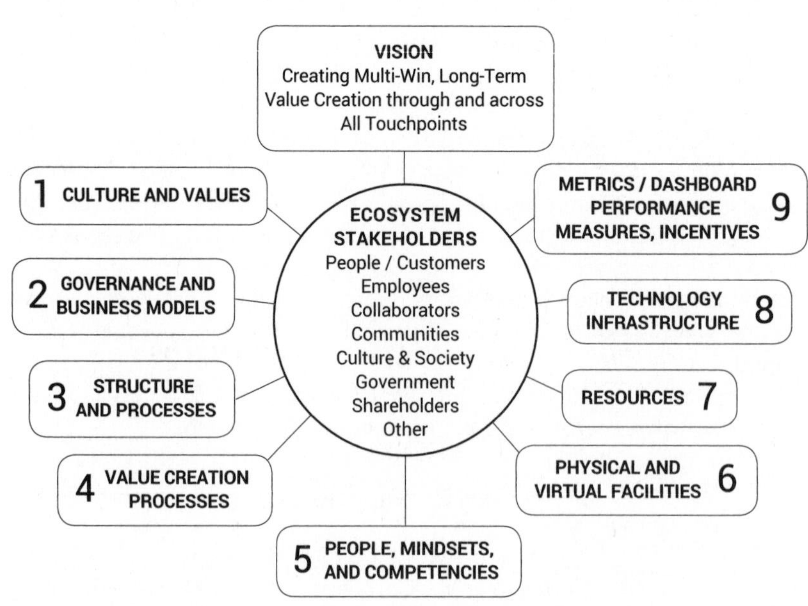

entire system is interconnected: it cannot fully achieve its potential if only one part of the organization embraces change. **Just as a doctor who focuses on only one body part might make a faulty diagnosis and provide insufficient treatment, an organization that focuses only on one unit, risks becoming disconnected and ineffectual.**

Lever 1: Culture and Values

> *The future of advertising will happen inside out. The companies that will flourish will care intensely about their cultures, knowing that purpose makes profit, and it all starts with their people.*
>
> — Mark Pollard, *EVP, Director of NY Planning, Edelman (2012)*

Embracing the Beyond Advertising Roadmap and the All Touchpoint Value Creation Model means getting at the very heart of an organization, its people and its collaborators to refine or redefine its culture and values. They will need to reflect the new mental models and key principles we have advocated throughout this book and permeate the entire organization.

Increasingly, the culture within an organization will no longer stand in isolation of the broader evolution of culture. Steve Stoute, founder and CEO, Translation, foresees, *"The pace at which our culture is changing will have such broad and sweeping implications to marketing that it will be truly an opportunity for innovative thinkers and new ideas to flourish"* (2012). Given the ATVC model and the perspectives of our contributor community, the following principles should be at the top of the list of culture and values needed to flourish *(see Figure 8.2)*.

Here are some of our 2020 contributors developing these key concepts:

> *. . . One of the most difficult things for both agencies and marketers is to understand that in the social space, it is not they who own the Brand, it is the consumers who do so and if you have to win in this space, you have to let go of control. You can provoke and fuel conversations and debates, but*

Figure 8.2 Beyond Advertising Culture and Values

BEYOND ADVERTISING **CULTURE AND VALUES**
Transparency and trust
Creativity and collaboration
Win-win-win orientation
Human-centricity
Speed and agility

at the same time be honest and transparent in all your interventions. You have to recognize that consumers will help you build your Brand, but if you try misguiding them, they can also kill your Brand.

— Sanjay Thapar, *CEO, Bates India (2012)*

The Relationship Era, and its extraordinary results, is built on trust. Companies still stuck in the mire of the Consumer Era often make the critical mistake of thinking of trust as just another mechanism for influencing transactions. They view it as a means to an end, and many squander it as quickly as it accumulates.

— Doug Levy, *CEO, MEplusYOU (2013)*

Privacy concerns will likely contribute to this change. A 2013 consumer survey by LoyaltyOne shows that more than half of consumers do not trust their data in the hands of companies and 46 percent find it unacceptable that a company tracks their habits. Add to that mounting pressure to give consumers the chance to opt-in to digital advertising and data sharing (rather than opt out) and marketers will likely find themselves designing creative not just for a brand, but for the "opt-in" button.

In other words, advertisers won't simply be tasked with creating demand for a product—they will be tasked with creating demand for the ad.

— Bryan Pearson, *CEO, LoyaltyOne (2013)*

The Future of Advertising is Collaborative… it's unlikely that creativity will be limited to the creative director and copywriter—the number of influencers on any given ad will continue to increase.

— Chris Yeh, *VP, Marketing, PBworks (2012)*

. . . All advertising/marketing campaigns would be 'performance with purpose'—meaning that they would make a difference to the environment, community.

— Richard Lee, *CMO, PepsiCo China (2012)*

Advertisers should create connections that count based on real-time, "tradigital," relevant, data-driven, human-centric, agile communications. There must be a purpose behind the brand that shares values with the consumer.

— Lisa Colantuono, *Co-President, AAR Partners (2012)*

But what do we need to do differently as we approach 2020? First is to accept that it's not business as usual. The speed of change means we need a completely different mindset. The digitally-connected world is a dynamic and social space where media are constantly ebbing and flowing, seething or simmering—and where consumers regularly acquire new beliefs and behaviors which don't come to them though advertising or other traditional information sources. Whatever else Modern Marketing is, it has to be actively sought out by consumers – and then shared by them with others because the brand adds real value to their lives.

— Sally Williams, *Global President, Business Development & Client Relations, Omnicom (2012)*

As trends change and new competitors emerge, companies have had to adapt and pivot... Consumers have proven that they can shift their behavior rapidly as new services enter the market and new products find ways to captivate them, and advertisers and their agencies need to become just as agile in how they react to, predict or provoke these changes if they hope to remain relevant, and provide their clients with quantifiable results.

— Brent Chudoba, *Vice President and General Manager, SurveyMonkey (2012)*

What are the cultural principles and values that would define your ideal organization?

Lever 2: Governance and Business Models

The standard today is not an elaborate media plan filled with an alphabet soup of CPMs and GRPs. Nor is it a clever advertising execution. It is how to make the most of all the moving parts and pull them together into a customer-relevant, all-embracing, up-to-the-minute, real-time experience.

— David Jowett, *President, DAC Group Europe (2013)*

Corporate activities are being evaluated in a far more public and comprehensive way, and the leadership practices of every organization must reinforce a forward-thinking collaborative culture and value system. This requires a change of the mind set of "control" – instead of traditional control, empower employees and customers and collaborators, co-create with them, and share with them the benefits with a win-win-win orientation.

All facets of leadership and governance can be guided by the All Touchpoint Value Creation Model. Ideally, the CMO, CTO, CEO, HR, operations, board of directors—everyone should be working in tandem and with shared objectives. The voice of the customer and other stakeholders should also be heard in the governance structure of the organization. And as more and more companies consider business models that extend beyond stock price to include social impact, such as B Corporations discussed earlier, the triple-win alignment of the All Touchpoint Value Creation Model becomes possible.

We are particularly inspired by Rory Sutherland, executive creative director and vice-chairman, OgilvyOne London, who imagines an all-star leadership team to create the culture of a reimagined agency of the future: *"Let's say Buckminster Fuller, Howard Luck Gossage and Thorstein Veblen, perhaps...*

This entity would be able to recruit most of the Gen-Y talent from advertising colleges because it would be principally motivated not by self-enrichment but by a sense of higher social purpose. It would devote most of its energies to using advertising techniques, behavioural science and Darwinian theory to solve social problems – housing, welfare, economic and environmental challenges.

And he goes on to reimagine the agency business model:

It would be written into the agency's founding charter that it could never grow beyond the Dunbar number. All profits would be spent on R&D or distributed to the staff in the proper anarcho-syndicalist manner.

This seems like a recipe for business disaster. I completely disagree. It is an old-world idea that you get profitable first and then make yourself famous. Today it works the other way round. Hence the high-profile, socially valuable work of the agency would be a loss-leader for highly paid public speaking and consulting roles.

The agency's offices would be in Singapore, London, Santa Barbara and Vail. People would only work two weeks out of three, according to the new Dymaxion method. (2012)

Several contributors envision a future of more women in positions of leadership/governance in the industry. As Michele Cerwin, principal of mCerwin Consulting, writes:

The demographic research, purchasing power, behavioral indicators, online and offline engagement in the topic, and the type of talent required in the new agency model, all point to the need for increased female leadership in the future of advertising. The commonly touted facts that females represent over half the population, control 85 percent plus of purchasing power in the U.S., and engage in social media at a higher penetration than males, combined with the fact that, according to Catalyst, companies with the highest representation of women on their top management teams experienced better financial performance than companies with the lowest representation, make the following predictions almost unexcitingly too obvious. (2012)

And as we will discuss in greater depth in Chapter 9, business models will need to evolve to fully leverage, orchestrate and co-create value with the various networks of employees, customers, partners, media, and investors. What are the governance and business models that would inspire you to strive for win-win-win outcomes for the success of the organization, for people, and for society?

Lever 3: Structure and Processes

The structure (traditionally more fixed) and processes (traditionally more fluid) of an organization work in tandem to align its resources, drive efficiencies and maximize achievement. As such, each player in the ATVC model, advertisers, agencies, individuals, non-profits, intermediaries, etc. should reexamine their structures and processes. In all likelihood, traditional hierarchical structures with only command and control processes are not likely to withstand the new Beyond Advertising principles summarized in Figure 8.2. New structures and processes will need to allow for agility and reaping the benefits both from decentralization and, when needed, the power that leveraging through centralization facilitates.

What makes an organization nimble enough to allow a great, R.A.V.E.S.-conscious idea implemented in a M.A.D.E.[5] context to align with the cultural zeitgeist when speed is of the essence? As David Jowett, president of DAC Group Europe, writes, *"In 2020, the ability to think quickly and act nimbly will be the greatest competitive advantage that a company can have . . . Agility will need to become a total cultural experience throughout the organization, from the types of people that get hired to the kinds of behavior that gets rewarded"* (2013). Arthur Fleischman, president and partner of st. john advertising, suggests: *"Act quickly. Great opportunities won't wait for long briefing, incubation, approval, and production cycles. There will have to be parallel work streams for spontaneous and opportunistic creative that addresses something going on in the brand and consumer's world"* (2013).

Beyond acting nimbly in response to cultural moments, the organizational structure ought to support the ability to create real-time, personalized experiences. The Econsultancy/Adobe study discussed earlier supports this assertion: "The advantages of real-time personalization are also clear from this research. Those who can personalize in real time report an uplift in sales which is 33 percent greater than those businesses who say the type of personalization they carry out isn't instantaneous." Given these incentives, agility—the ability to provide real-time personalization—ought to be a "total cultural experience" in every organization ("Why Marketers Haven't Mastered Multichannel" 2015).

Several agency executives shared their visions for how agencies should be restructured to adapt to the demands of the future. Alessandro Panella, chief strategy officer at Grey Germany, together with Uli Veigel, Founder of Uli Veigel Brand Consultancywrites:

> *The agency of the future will be a lot more involved with a client's business. It will move upstream in the value creation chain. It will partner with clients to define the business problem at hand. Based on that it can develop creative solutions (that go beyond communication) with a greater business and cultural impact. To make this work, agency staff will spend more time sitting right next to their client counterparts (marketing, consumer research, or product development). The agency/client relationship would greatly benefit from this for at least three reasons.*
>
> 1. *Greater process efficiency: Going upstream will create better briefing in less time and the increased transparency will ensure that both sides have a better understanding of the task at hand.*

2. *Increased sense of ownership: The sooner agencies get involved the greater will be the sense of ownership of the briefing.*

3. *Better/quicker knowledge sharing: Agencies often have specialist knowledge (design packaging, consumer knowledge, etc.) and the client's organization can profit a lot more from that knowledge by letting them join the process a lot earlier. (2013)*

Consider how structure can bring efficiency, a sense of ownership, and better/quicker knowledge sharing among co-workers. Scott Goodson, CEO and founder of StrawberryFrog, writes:

> *I believe that the new agency model demands a new talent culture, with idea generators valued at all levels across all disciplines, but ultimately working together in a way that means that the agency of the future will be structured differently and staffed differently, and agency organ-o-grams will look very different to the traditional hierarchies still operating today. (2012)*

Pierre Soued, CEO, regional managing director of Havas Worldwide Middle East, explains it this way:

> *By 2020 digital agencies will not exist; we will all be digital, we will all be marketing, we will all be social—we are Communication Agents. Work will be based on a client-centric model and system and achievements will be focused on performance more than ever before. There must be technology at the heart of this to develop new and innovative communication offerings and mindsets. Deep-dive research capabilities with predictive analysis resources across multi-platforms, screens, and contexts will be a part of the everyday working reality. Instilling creativity and innovation at the inception of an idea to integrate media at the birth of the process rather than at the end will be the norm, to both aggregate disruptors and meet clients' ever-changing demands. In this super-speed world, 2020 will be upon us like it was yesterday and only the smartest and most agile agencies will adapt fast enough to face these big and numerous upcoming challenges and realities. (2014)*

How should the structure and the processes of your organization be reimagined to unleash the full power of the five forces of change described in Part I and the new value creation model outlined in Part II?

Lever 4: Value Creation Processes

> *The world of advertising is changing fundamentally and irreversibly. The advertising concepts, rules, methods, and processes optimized for the physical world are inadequate for the digital world, and vice versa.*
>
> — Arvind Rangaswamy, *Professor of Marketing, Penn State (2012)*

As each touchpoint is reconsidered as an opportunity, if not a mandate for value creation, there are repercussions throughout the ecosystem of players involved in the value creation. No single model emerged, but several contributors see a fundamental shift Beyond Advertising.

Saurabh Sharma, planning partner at Ogilvy & Mather, Beijing notes, *"As advertising evolves, it would look and feel a lot less like advertising and that is what will help it grow and add more value to businesses, brands and the society.... Advertising companies will make money not only on communication and engagement ideas but more. Constant need to improve the product and service for the end user will need more hands that the product development teams. This will lead to advertising companies having their own product intellectual property disciplines."*(2012)

Barry Wacksman, EVP, chief growth officer at R/GA, suggests that agencies will need to help clients become "Functionally Integrated," whereby products and services "blur together" in ways that deliver greater value:

> *If we only make ads, we won't be able to help clients grow. Rather than just making ads, we see our key role evolving to help clients create the entire ecosystem of value, to help them become Functionally Integrated. Doing this will require agencies to develop the ability to conceive of new functionally integrated products and services, delineate the business strategy, develop the underlying technology and user interfaces, create the brands, bring them to market through advertising and communications and integrate them back into the broader digital ecosystem of mobile, social media, retail stores, and live events. These are all the required pieces for the creation of functionally integrated ecosystems as well as the future of the agency business (2012).*

And from our cultural anthropologist contributor, Bill Mauer, dean, School of Social Sciences, director, Institute for Money, Technology and Financial Inclusion, UC Irvine, a thought-provoking aspect of the value creation process: cashless payments and the trail of data they generate:

> *The point of sale is already no longer a just till but a portal into a vast, quickly privatizing commons of transactional records. Money itself, in all its forms, is a gigantic database of transactions, a living and moving history of people's and things' and algorithms' interrelationships and meshed, interwoven subjectivities. And barter is back: a new marketing channel, and for business to business transactions. (2012)*

The processes involved in value creation must be rethought and redesigned. Following are some of the key questions to consider when designing a value creation process for the future *(see Figure 8.3)*.

Value creation is the core precept of the relationship of the future between brands, people and society. How does, and could/should, that infuse the interactions and processes of all involved?

Figure 8.3 Value Creation Process

VALUE CREATION DESIGN CONSIDERATIONS
• How are you getting **insights about the changing environment**?
• Who is leading the **decision-making** processes? The **creative** processes?
• **Which departments** are playing which role in these processes?
• Can your current processes create **multi-win outcomes** that benefit all of your stakeholders?
• Do your processes allow the incorporation of **open innovation** and reduce reliance on employees alone?
• Do your processes allow for taking advantage of **globalization,** for example establishing teams in locations around the globe in order to maintain a 24/7 project focus across time zones?
• Are you outsourcing at the cost of **missing opportunities** to interact with customers in need?

Lever 5: People, Mindsets, and Competencies

> *Technology will advance, but the ad business will always require the strategic and creative skills of actual humans. People who are smart, agile, flexible, and adaptable; those who have the ability and energy to constantly learn and relearn.*
>
> — Steven Landsberg, *Founding Partner and Chief Creative Officer, Grok (2012)*

Even though we encouraged our 2020 community to offer a future vision for what could/should be, this topic seemed to be of particular concern. Perhaps especially because we asked them to consider the best of what the future could hold, they recognized that to achieve it, they would need to do a better job of attracting and retaining people with the right mindsets, competencies and capabilities that perhaps we all need for the future. How can this newly imagined ecosystem define itself in a more future-thinking, exciting, and motivating way to attract the best people with these new mindsets and in particular those in the next generation?

A common refrain is how difficult it is to attract top-tier talent to the traditional advertising industry. As Richard Robinson, managing partner of Oystercatchers puts it, *"The challenge will be how to attract, develop, and retain the best and the brightest without the pay of Wall Street or the glitter of Silicon Valley. This has never been tougher and promises to get tougher still"* (2014). Tom Morton, director of strategy at co:collective, writes, *"Clients and agencies alike are short of enlightened data analysts and visionary product designers."* He offers this suggestion: *"Agencies will need to staff with designers, technologists, and user experience specialists, creating an appealing mix of smarts and humility that will attract new talent to advertising"* (2012).

At a CMO workshop we co-hosted with the ANA at Wharton in May 2015, the following key challenges were brought to the fore:

- Attracting and retaining modern digital talent
- Managing talent transformation while scaling business for growth
- Attracting leaders with "flexpertise"
- Sharing learning across the organization

These challenges are familiar to many of us. One success story comes from Nagisa Manabe, who as chief marketing and sales officer of USPS led the failing organization into its sixth consecutive quarter posting a profit. In terms of people and competencies, Manabe emphasized finding the right job for the right person; as a public company, the USPS has to work with a given pool of employees. With some honest assessments, Manabe and her team were able to fit people to the right roles. Everyone has talents: the key was ensuring that everyone's skillsets were well matched with their role.

Many of our contributors see multidisciplinary teams as essential to success in the future. Noam Lemelshtrich Latar, founding dean of IDC Herzilya, writes, *"In order to carry meaningful conversations advertisers should have a deep understanding of the social trends and to accomplish this they should employ a multidisciplinary team of experts from such fields as psychology, anthropology, linguistics and of various age groups." (2012)*

Rishad Tobaccowala, chief strategist for Publicis Groupe, is among our contributors who propose "upgrading the capabilities" of current team members:

> *Marketing will grow more important since it is about understanding and meeting customer requirements, and customers are becoming more empowered. The challenge will be whether marketers and agencies are capable of meeting the new challenge. Do we have the leadership, do we have the training and do we have the knowledge to deliver in the new world? Marketers working with each other, new partners, and academia must invest in upgrading the capabilities of their people in areas of next generation storytelling, comfort with data and technology, and the need for better collaborative skills. (2012)*

Carl Hartman, global client leader at WPP, supports this perspective:

> *Talent will need to change. We will need more "hybrids"—people who understand more than one vertical, who can begin to integrate specialties into a more accretive whole. Someone said there are only four people in the world who understand all the components of an iPhone. Those people are extremely valuable. The same will be true of agency "horizontal" experts who understand the whole. (2012)*

The Successful Network Orchestrator

Identifying the particular set of strengths and experiences that make an effective executive is a boon for putting together a successful team. We worked with Michael Distefano, CMO of Korn Ferry and president of the Korn Ferry Institute, to perform an analysis of Korn Ferry's extensive data in order to puzzle out the characteristics of successful network orchestrators. Network orchestrators are executives who are able to thrive in today's demanding and rapidly changing environment. (We examine network orchestration more closely in the following chapter.)

In Korn Ferry's assessments of more than 2.5 million professionals over a ten-year period, they identified a thorough and particular set of characteristics that stand out in successful high-level executives, which they organized into four dimensions of leadership and talent:

Competencies—skills and behaviors required for success that can be observed, such as decision quality, strategic mindset, global perspective, and business insights

Experiences—assignments or roles that prepare a person for future roles, such as functional experiences, international assignments, turnarounds, etc.

Traits—inclinations and natural tendencies a person leans toward, including personality traits such as assertiveness, risk taking, and confidence

Drivers—values and interests that influence a person's career path, motivation, and engagement such as power, status, autonomy, and challenge (Korn Ferry 2015)

For each of these four dimensions, Korn Ferry's analysis identified that most successful network orchestrators demonstrated particular strengths in each of these four dimensions that distinguished them from lower level managers.

Korn Ferry identified the following characteristics in the profile of a successful network orchestrator, which they call a "Best In Class" profile:

Competencies: Courage, Situational adaptability, Customer focus, Drives results, Global perspective

Experience: Crisis management, Strategy development, Business growth, Financial management

Traits: *Social leadership*: Empathy, Composure, Influence, Sociability, Affiliation; *Agility*: Adaptability, Tolerance for ambiguity, Risk Taking; *Energy*: Need for achievement, Persistence, Assertiveness

Drivers: Collaboration, Power, Challenge, Independence

One of the key takeaways from this analysis is the notable difference in traits that set apart the "Best in Class" Network Orchestrators. Figure 8.4 demonstrates the differences between the Level 1, 2 and 3 executives.

While the Director and Vice President profiles for Traits are practically identical, the CEOs demonstrate a much different set of these attributes. The largest difference, clearly, is in the "Social Leadership" category. This category includes traits such as empathy, composure, sociability, and influence. Successful network orchestrators also have higher levels of traits in the Energy category, including need for achievement, persistence, and assertiveness. The highest traits are persistence and need for achievement, and the lowest are in the Agility category including curiosity, focus, and adaptability.

Between the three levels, certain traits are essentially equal. In the Agility category, all executives have low levels of adaptability, curiosity, and focus, and higher levels of tolerance of ambiguity and risk taking. Assertiveness takes one of the biggest jumps in the move up to CEO, but not as big a jump as empathy, composure, influence, and sociability.

As might be expected, the traits demonstrated by the Best in Class Network Orchestrator CEOs are traits that emphasize the ability to connect with and lead through others and to generate a strong drive to take charge and excel.

A View to the Future

We believe that the holistic power of the All Touchpoint Value Creation Model, and the implementation of the Beyond Advertising Roadmap that supports it, will attract those who seek to make a difference in the world by bringing together a more productive and respectful future for the power of products & services and the brands that embody them.

As the silos between creatives, gamers, entertainers, activists, marketers, developers, technologists, sociologists and more blur, and the business models that reward their win-win-win mentalities proliferate, talented, inspired and resilient individuals will be drawn to the tremendous impact their efforts could yield.

How could these new concepts reinvigorate you, for starters, and those whom you would love to have on your team? What is the truly compelling "north star" vision that aligns, inspires, and motivates all those throughout the network?

Lever 6: Physical and Virtual Facilities

> *To meet the challenges of 2020, the advertising world will need to shift to agile creative development, with close working relationships between creative teams, partners, contractors, and clients.*
>
> — Chris Yeh, *VP, Marketing, PBWorks (2012)*

The collaborative essence of the ATVC model poses an interesting dichotomy about the facilities aspect of organizational architecture: the importance

Figure 8.4 Best In Class Network Orchestrators) Source: Korn Ferry, 2015

Best in Class: Network Orchestrator
Level: 1 Director level

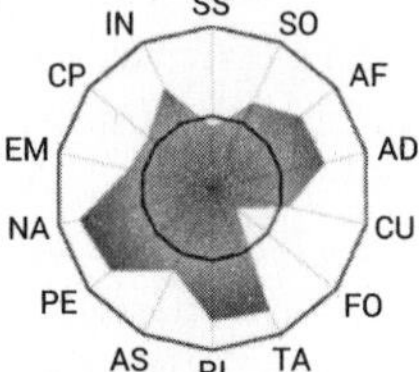

Social Leadership
EMPATHY (EM)
COMPOSURE (CP)
INFLUENCE (IN)
SELF-AWARENESS (SS)
SOCIABILITY (SO)
AFFILIATION (AF)

Energy
NEED FOR ACHIEVEMENT (NA)
PERSISTENCE (PE)
ASSERTIVENESS (AS)

Agility
ADAPTABILITY (AD)
CURIOSITY (CU)
FOCUS (FO)
TOLERANCE OF AMBIGUITY (TA)
RISK-TAKING (RI)

Best in Class: Network Orchestrator
Level: 2 Vice President level

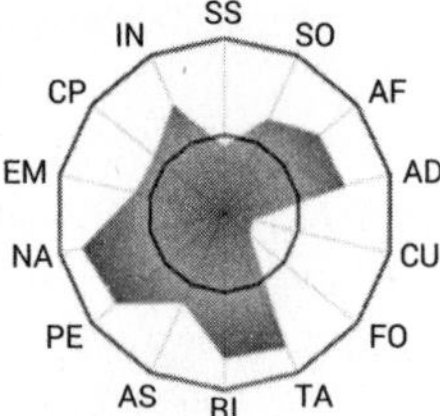

Social Leadership
EMPATHY (EM)
COMPOSURE (CP)
INFLUENCE (IN)
SELF-AWARENESS (SS)
SOCIABILITY (SO)
AFFILIATION (AF)

Energy
NEED FOR ACHIEVEMENT (NA)
PERSISTENCE (PE)
ASSERTIVENESS (AS)

Agility
ADAPTABILITY (AD)
CURIOSITY (CU)
FOCUS (FO)

Best in Class: Network Orchestrator
Level: 3 Executive level (CEO)

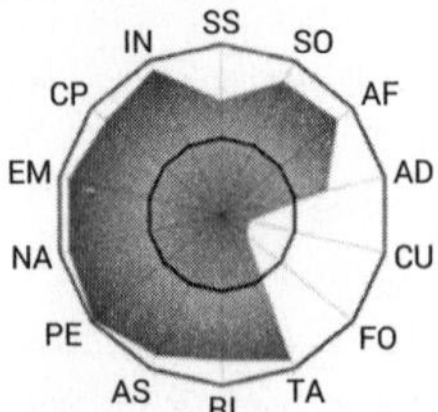

Social Leadership
EMPATHY (EM)
COMPOSURE (CP)
INFLUENCE (IN)
SELF-AWARENESS (SS)
SOCIABILITY (SO)
AFFILIATION (AF)

Energy
NEED FOR ACHIEVEMENT (NA)
PERSISTENCE (PE)
ASSERTIVENESS (AS)

Agility
ADAPTABILITY (AD)
CURIOSITY (CU)
FOCUS (FO)
TOLERANCE OF AMBIGUITY (TA)
RISK-TAKING (RI)

of both the physical space and the virtual space. In both manifestations, the facilities of an organization ought to reinforce the company's culture and values by encouraging creativity, empowerment, co-creation, and free-flowing communication. Many firms are specifically designing their workspaces in order to enable and encourage these values and the close working relationships that Chris Yeh promotes.

How to encourage more collaboration and communication? SEI Financial Services have been profiled for the open-space design in their headquarters. (Full disclosure, SEI is a major supporter of WFoA.) They eliminated private offices and cubicles, preventing artificial silos between people and departments and increasing spontaneous contact and collaboration ("Our Culture," 2015). **This open-space design dominates Silicon Valley companies such as Facebook and Google, and whether it leads to more efficiency or not has been debated. Nonetheless, it is a worthwhile experiment and a clear demonstration of the company's culture and values being integrated into the organizational structure at a physical, very visible, level**.

Yet increasingly, given the global and interdisciplinary teams, the character of virtual rooms become equally as important as our physical spaces. Our WFoA team, who has collaborated on writing this book from our various and evolving locations around the world, could not have survived and thrived without the online platforms that have been the lifeblood of our communications and conversations *(see more in the acknowledgements)*, in addition to our invaluable face-to-face time on campus together.

How much does the physical space and the enablers of virtual spaces fully reflect the unifying and compelling brand theme of your ATVC model? How much could changes in the physical and virtual worlds embody your value-creation community?

Lever 7: Resources and Resource Allocation

Understanding how best to allocate resources across traditional advertising channels to achieve optimal results has been a perennial challenge for marketers. This is now made far more complex by not only the exploding media landscape, but the key concept of the All Touchpoint Value Creation Model that emphasizes the orchestration of *all* touchpoints with current and potential customers, and hence the need for resource allocation to optimize their synergistic impact.

Indeed, this means thinking beyond the traditional budget silos of marketing to potentially reimagine a pool to encompass other critical touchpoints: product development and packaging, customer service, etc.

George Musi, managing partner, analytics, insights and attribution at Mindshare frames the challenge:

> *The core challenges of advertising remain, particularly in today's increasingly complex, fragmented, and multifaceted marketing landscape where the (always-on, always-present, always-connected) consumer weaves through*

a maze of digital, offline, online, paid, owned, earned media channels: How do we accurately measure advertising ROI and attribute advertising spend?

He goes on to describe what is needed to advance the field of impact analysis – broadly defined as attribution - a way of assigning partial credit (value) to all the different touchpoints along the consumer decision journey which have influenced a desired outcome, both in the short term and over time.

One thing is clear, given the number of options available to communicate and connect with consumers, there is a need for a transformation in the way marketing attribution, ROI analysis, optimization and forecasting is done. The ultimate goal is to have holistic marketing attribution – where every possible data point or variable in the world that may impact business or marketing performance has been observed and collected – that combines mix modeling (top-down; full market context) with digital attribution modeling (bottom-up; digital granularity) to help make sense of and navigate this complicated and ever-evolving marketing landscape:

- *Deliver "one source of truth" so that marketers aren't seeing two different pictures – one online and one offline – of the marketing world they work in;*
- *Provide a truly comprehensive evaluation of marketing performance (efficiency, effectiveness, optimization and ROI), rather than as a set of linear offline and digital channel results;*
- *Understand how all marketing works together in the ecosystem;*
- *Accurately and reliably value the true contribution and influence (equal or disproportionate amounts) of each channel, tactic and touch point toward a conversion;*
- *Understand the different roles that media plays*
    - *Introducers: Which media elements seed and capture interest of consumers?*
    - *Influencers or promoters: Which media channels provide frequency and reinforce the message?*
    - *Closers: Which media channels and networks contribute the most enrollments?*
- *Include both converting and non-converting paths to determine the value of a marketing touchpoint;*
- *Fine tune strategy and tactics to improve results (i.e., how to mix and match marketing activities across the customer journey; how to spend the next dollar betwen channels);*
- *Create an ongoing, iterative cycle, so marketers always have the most up-to-date insights and analysis to drive their planning and optimization decisions.*

Regardless of which attribution approach one embraces, it is critically important that:

- *All available data is captured across channels, devices and touchpoints;*
- *It includes other factors and dimensions (such as an advertiser's non-trackable marketing activity and the factor of uncertainty);*
- *It considers a company's business model, current marketing campaigns, marketing objectives, sales cycle, customers' activities, time of year/seasonality, product category, customer loyalty, initial and final touchpoint channels, length of conversion path, etc.;*
- *It continually gets tested, re-calibrated and validated for extended periods of time (2015).*

In addition to the need for attribution to consider all touchpoints beyond the traditional paid, earned, owned, the imperative remains for adaptive experimentation to ensure continued learning about how touchpoints *interact* for maximum impact over time, with the full set of relevant variables, resources, and resource allocation. While the typical demand is for more resources, our belief is that focusing on adaptive experimentation as a management philosophy will shift from demand for more resources to more efficient and effective allocation of resources both inside and outside the traditional boundaries of an organization *(see more on open innovation in Chapter 9)*. Advances in technology and especially increasingly intelligent and sensitive automation will allow us to do things better, faster, and more efficiently—without the traditional belief that there is a trade-off among these three.

What new models for resource allocation can be conceived to more fully leverage the suite of touchpoints and potential value creation across all impacted individuals in your organization's ecosystem?

Lever 8: Technology Infrastructure

> *Companies need new expertise, more agility, and new ways to work within an organization and partners. The Chief Technology Officer and the Chief Marketing Officer will need to be joined at the hip.*
>
> — Rishad Tobaccowala, *Chief Strategist, Publicis Groupe (2012)*

As we have emphasized earlier, the insights provided by technology fundamentally impact marketing capabilities and will continue to do so. As technology advances, our approaches to customer insights must change.

Organizations must create far more connected, smart and real-time decision support systems and dashboards with these approaches in mind. As Bob Kantor, chief marketing and business development officer for MDC Partners writes,

"If technology, and the depth of data it provides, is driving such significant change within the advertising industry, then we must learn how to integrate this competency into all departments, not make it a free-standing silo within the organization" (2012). In his *Fast Company* article "What Zara, P&G, and Berlitz Know about Agility," Faisal Hoque writes:

> To respond to changes in their environment, organizations must learn from various processes within different areas of the enterprise. Technology can enable these learning processes by supporting: (a) collection, distribution, analysis, and interpretation of data associated with business processes; and (b) generating response alternatives, decisions on appropriate courses of action, and implementing selected responses. (2012)

No longer an afterthought, technology infrastructure is among the most essential levers of organizational change and determinants of organizational success for the future, and must be developed as such. Richard Ting, EVP, global ECD, mobile social platforms for R/GA writes:

> *. . . brands must work quickly now to unify their customer data sets that currently exist in disparate environments like social CRM, consumers' social graph, and consumers' transaction history. Once this data is unified and the brand has a single view of the customer, only then can they provide more relevant and personalized brand experiences. (2012)*

In his 2020 scenario, Loren Grossman reiterates the importance of creating experiences for people that are M.A.D.E.[S] for R.A.V.E.[S], or in his words, *"rich, intimate, highly personalized, and culturally resonant experiences for people and communities"* (2012). Many of our contributors discussed the growing significance of personalization as a means to connect more profoundly and authentically with people. **They also highlighted, as Grossman does below, some of the barriers currently preventing personalization from becoming more widespread: not just how—but who—is able to turn the massive amounts of available data into useful information.**

Grossman describes this challenge as follows:

> *Big Data, as it has been recently dubbed, requires big and robust technology solutions and Big Data scientists that know how to read, synthesize, and use data to drive experiences, often in real time. Further, these data scientists will not succeed if they are only bolted onto the existing machine as a new component might be. Instead, they must be integrated completely and seamlessly into our advertising world so that the solutions they divine are not simply technologies for the sake of technologies but part of the DNA of the organic, brand-building, transformational experience. This will not be easy on the Big Data scientists; they prefer to work for IBM and HP. It will not be*

easy on the advertisers, who prefer entropy to rigor. And yet it is essential to our success. So if you do not have Big Data Scientists on staff, I suggest you go out and get some. Now. (2012)

A data infrastructure that captures incoming insights from all the primary and secondary information is essential but nowhere near enough. These must be guided by people both within and far outside of the fields of automation, programmatic, artificial intelligence, and cognitive computing who can ask the right questions, filter the responses, provide the right context, interpret the findings and continue to feed all this back in to creating ever more robust support systems.

The Architecture of Personalization

Many contributors discussed the importance of implementing just such an infrastructure. Amelia Torode, chief strategy officer at TBWA London, writes:

By 2020 we will have gone through a seismic shift moving from social technologies to truly smart technologies. This new smart Internet infrastructure will be the catalyst for a new era of smart advertising. We will witness the development of more personal "data/time/location" driven advertising. Better experiences, more relevant offers, and distinct consumer choice. In order to prepare for this, agencies should be looking now as to how they can build better data capture and planning into their businesses. The next wave of adland in-takes should be less cheerily client-friendly and more ferociously numbers-friendly. A greater respect should be given to number-gatherers, number-crunchers, and those who can create compelling stories out of numbers. (2012)

These "compelling stories out of numbers" are what make the personalized R.A.V.E.S. experiences that can be delivered in a M.A.D.E.[5] way, possible.

A recent global study by Econsultancy and Adobe on personalization, 'Why Marketing Should Be Personal,' brings us really close to what it is we are proposing. Mark Phibbs, vice president, EMEA marketing, Adobe, writes in the foreword:

> Companies need a personalization strategy in place and a clear plan of action if they want to improve the customer experience for everyone—from first-time visitors to loyal customers. A personalization framework should embrace all relevant customer touchpoints and devices, and not one or two channels in isolation. As the research below describes, the right blend between "man and machine" is crucial for achieving this. (2014)

The study found multiple statistics supporting the importance of personalization today, including a 14 percent uplift in sales by organizations who use personalization. Since our model is an idealized design, it doesn't completely exist yet, but solid research like this points the way forward. The organizational infrastructure that will improve customer experience across all touchpoints can be founded on a personalization platform.

The Econsultancy/Adobe study asked participants to identify the main barriers to personalization and found that:

> When asked to identify the main barriers to use (or better use) of personalization, half (52 percent) of those who don't target personalized content in real time said they are plagued by "technology which isn't integrated." Many companies invest in technology without even thinking about what customers expect and need, with no real personalization strategy in place. This often results in disjointed experiences, with technology becoming more of a problem than a solution. (2014)

What kind of listening, processing and proactive/reactive infrastructure informs and aligns those who make strategic and tactical decisions for your organization? How much priority are they given and how is that balanced with the strategic mission of the organization? How much does this prioritize the capability to protect and defend the wishes of each individual in the ecosystem?

Lever 9: Metrics/Dashboard Performance Measures, Incentives

> *From a measurement perspective, inputs are typically easier to measure than outputs, which are influenced by many factors. So, it is only human for most to succumb to creating a dashboard based on inputs. And while it is good to have that visibility and tracking ability, this should never replace the most essential dashboard: the one that regularly measures outcomes in terms of behavior or attitude. Marketers need to remain first and foremost outcome-centric, and link that to the WHY.*
>
> — Chris Burggraeve, *Founder, Vicomte LLC (2012)*

Metrics determine an organization's priorities. What is measured is what matters, so as we look to the future, we must consider carefully how success is defined and measured. In a world of the ATVC model, performance measures should be "outcome-centric" and look at the triple bottom line—impacts to the brand, individuals, and society.

New measurements and analytical capability need to be developed in order to fully align with the All Touchpoint Value Creation Model. How is the triple bottom line being measured and met? How will R.A.V.E.[S] content delivered through all touchpoints be kept as a standard? How can we continually improve the effectiveness of M.A.D.E.[S] context? As Pete Doe, media research and data expert at Nielsen warns, *"The vision of a closed loop system that guides people effortlessly toward purchase is for the most part likely to remain just a vision. The real world is a messier place"* (2012).

One rapidly emerging approach lies in the area of customer analytics. One of our sister organizations, the Wharton Customer Analytics Initiative (WCAI), led by Wharton professors Eric Bradlow and Pete Fader, focuses on the collection, management, analysis, and strategic leverage of a firm's granular data about the behaviors of its customers. They characterize customer analytics as behavioral, longitudinal, inherently granular, forward-looking and multiplatform, and they work with a variety of organizations to mine and monetize their customer data with predictive models. And just recently they launched, in conjunction with Wharton Online Learning, a new Business Analytics Specialization on the online education platform, Coursera. This specialization promises to be the first comprehensive set of courses designed to explore how data is used to drive better business decisions.

The incentives and rewards provided to an organization's many participants are another essential element of the All Touchpoint Value Creation model. And monetary rewards are not the only means of motivation. Recognition, for example, is extremely important. According to Edelman's global Trust Barometer survey, "a good relationship with employees is the third most important factor in sustaining confidence in a particular brand." It sat behind protection of consumer data and product quality control (Edelman.com 2014).

Consider the Publix supermarket chain based in Florida that has quietly become America's seventh-largest private company with $27.5 billion in sales in 2012 and industry-leading net margins of 5.7 percent in 2013–stunning results for a company that is 80 percent owned by its more than 160,000 employees. The company emphasizes the promotion-from-within philosophy that results in lower turnover and higher employee satisfaction—34,000 Publix employees have been with the company for more than 10 years, an unheard-of retention rate in the grocery business. These team members, who are compensated both through salary and stock options, are passionate brand ambassadors within the communities where Publix has a presence. Concerned about the success of Publix, WalMart has recently begun emphasizing its employee development opportunities ("Publix Announces Fourth Quarter and Annual Results for 2013," 2013).

In addition to the traditional metrics, how will organizations, including agencies, add new metrics to their dashboards to reflect the win-win-win objective and impact? David J. Moore, chairman of Xaxis and president of WPP Digital writes, *"Data is to media, what location is to Real Estate...As the number of attributes associated with a marketing campaign continues to rise, and the measures of success on various devices diverge, the most advanced algorithms and analysis will be required to define success"* (2012). Not to mention new social metrics that reflect changing priorities, as expressed by Amelia Torode, chief strategy officer for TBWA London: *"What is their environmental record, how do they treat employees overseas, what positive impacts are they committed to having on their community?"* (2012)

When it comes to metrics and measurements, Jerry recommends a simple dashboard, rather than one intended for a 747. Make it simple, include as many real time metrics as possible, and keep the North Star purpose and business success paramount so that short term, narrow, siloed objectives don't obscure the highly interrelated nature of the All Touchpoint landscape.

Figure 8.5 Beyond Advertising in Action: Leverage Organizational Architecture

Beyond Advertising in Action
LEVERAGE ORGANIZATION ARCHITECTURE

CITI BIKE—CITIBANK
Agency: Publicis Kaplan Thaler
Warc 100: #16, 2014

OBJECTIVE/PROBLEM TO BE SOLVED

After the world financial crisis in 2008, brand health for Citibank declined drastically through 2012, particularly in New York. At that time the city wanted to introduce a bike-share program as a supplement to existing public transportation options and to encourage citizens to be more active.

APPROACH

In 2012, New York approached Citibank for seed capital ($41 million over five years) for the bike-sharing program. To counter the high volume of resistance and negative feedback, Citibank promoted biking as "a new way to experience New York." Citi Bike was rolled out over the summer of 2013: registration was available online, and a mobile app provided users with available bike information, bike-friendly routes, and food recommendations through a *New York Times* partnership. The API for the app was open for New Yorkers to use, allowing for the development of different plugins for the apps.

THE RESULTS

Between May and July 2013, the campaign was incredibly successful. The bikes were used by celebrities and featured on *The New Yorker* cover. The bikes generated more than 125 thousand social media posts, with over 95 percent of social conversation trending neutral or positive. Projections for memberships were exceeded by 13 times, and the app was downloaded 150 thousand times. Citibank's brand health was driven to the highest levels since 2008, with 83 percent users associating the bike service with the company. As of 2014, New Yorkers have burned a collective 280 million calories pedaling.

LESSONS AND OBSERVATIONS

Taking on big challenges requires fortitude and persistence, full buy-in of the executive team, acting anticipatorily instead of reactively, and allowing adaptation as initiatives evolve. Being "controversy free" may no longer be an option with this model as advertising.

CITATION: Warc 100, 2014

Key Takeaways

- **Change is never easy: it makes the familiar strange, takes us out of our comfort zone, and requires skills we didn't know we had. But change is also hugely rewarding and empowering; the key is to make change a supported, well-led, inclusive process.**

- **Before initiating change, prepare for it: get buy-in through and across the organization, encourage dialog and discussion (not just among executives), and decide how best to proceed: is it best to evolve, or try to really disrupt?**

- **Value is not an output, something that can be produced and exported in a black box. Value creation must permeate the structure—physical and structural—of a business, must underpin the company culture, must guide hiring choices, and must inform team design. By seeing value as a multifaceted, interconnected project, big change makes sense.**

- **Change and value can and should be measured. Metrics and figures are an important part of this—how an experiment is playing out in terms of dollars is crucial—but an equally important resource is experience. Ask how people, both internal and external, are experiencing changes: human insights are invaluable when re-designing an organization *(see Figure 8.5).***

Chapter 9
Transcend Silos and Barriers

The more data we collect about consumers, the less we seem to understand what they really care about. This is partially due to the artificial silos we've created, dividing the client side from the agency side, dividing social from e-commerce from customer relations. Consumers don't think about those distinctions—they're artificial. Brands that want to be successful will not only need to deliver value through entertainment, information, tools, services, and conversations, but will need to deliver that value consistently regardless of the location, moment, or point of interaction.

— Frederic Bonn, *Chief Creative Officer, North America, Mirum Agency (2012)*

The unified and cohesive image that brands hope to leave in people's minds contrasts sharply with the corporate reality where traditional, owned, licensed, earned, shared, borrowed, and user-produced touchpoints are the domain of separate, siloed departments, often with competing interests. From the client/customer perspective, this results in strategies that are confusing, fragmented across touchpoints, and lacking in the synergies we recommend with the M.A.D.E.[5] principles. Unfortunately, while many see this and want to change it, they are encumbered not only by outdated mental models but by outdated organizational silos and artificial barriers to collaboration.

The 2015 "CMO Impact Study," undertaken by Kimberly A. Whitler, an assistant professor of marketing at the University of Virginia's Darden School of Business, in conjunction with CMO.com, highlights that the most successful companies integrate marketers and marketing insights into the broader company. By recognizing the valuable perspective marketing offers—and incorporating it broadly, rather than leaving it siloed—a whole company can be buoyed.

> The report surveyed 564 business executives, including 223 chief marketing officers or the equivalent, and mostly from U.S.-based firms. It found "a correlation between a correlation between companies in which CMOs have a higher profile and are more involved in overall strategy and firm success. On average, the companies with better marketing showed a two-thirds higher market share. (Cardona 2015)

The report also found that more than simply prioritizing a marketing strategy, better results were found in organizations where CMOs were included in strategy meetings. Eric Eden, senior vice president of marketing at technology firm Cvent argues that as all the members of the executive team have different perspectives, "success comes at the intersection of a healthy debate across these perspectives" (Eden, quoted in Cardona 2015).

At our WFoA October 2011 Roundtable on Orchestration, Ty Montague, CEO, co:collective, put it this way, "Technology is changing, but people are not changing. Our challenge is overcoming internal structural silos inside client organizations. Everything needs to start inside and flow outwards" (2011).

In this chapter we identify 12 persistent silos and offer four powerful approaches to overcoming the seemingly intractable challenge they present. Essentially, we have to broaden our understanding of an organization's goals and boundaries. First, boundaries and silos can evaporate if people can find common ground where all can benefit—the notion of **Aligning Objectives** that we discuss in Chapter 3. Second, the way to quickly access the incremental expertise and capabilities necessary to compete and innovate is through **Open Innovation**, a practice that in recent years has moved from an experimental approach to a widespread and requisite tool for all enterprises, regardless of size. Third, adding

Network Activation to business models opens the potential to more fully leverage the full-value exchange potential with networks of customers, employees, distributors, partners, investors, and more. And finally, **Network Orchestration** helps to ensure effective functioning of all the many moving parts and "connected partnerships": beyond a siloed world.

The Deadly Dozen Silos

As you've gathered by now, we and our Advertising 2020 collaborators are keen on eliminating the notion of "versus." In the future of advertising, beyond advertising, "and" will prevail—experience *and* fresh perspective, global efficiencies *and* local sensitivity, selling a product/service *and* not littering in the process. After they imagined this more desirable *"and"* future, our Advertising 2020 collaborators were pretty vocal, based on their personal experiences as pioneers, in identifying the seemingly intractable silos and barriers that make change and transformation so challenging. So let's just get these on the table and see the extent to which they resonate with your experience. We've named them the "deadly dozen silos" since they make implementing the All Touchpoint Value Creation Model so difficult, and therefore need to be addressed as an essential part of any action plan.

We frame them in Figure 9.1, followed by the way they are described by our 2020 contributors. Which ones are you facing and which should you prioritize? What is lurking as your twelfth hidden silo or boundary?

Deadly Silo 1
Objectives Silos: *Sales and Profit versus Positive Social and Cultural Impact*

> *I believe that the business model of the future is shared values, plus shared action, equals shared profit—social profit and financial profit.*
>
> — Cindy Gallop, *Founder and CEO, MakeLoveNotPorn, IfWeRantheWorld, Behance (2012)*

> *[A future agency] . . . would be principally motivated not by self-enrichment but by a sense of higher social purpose. It would devote most of its energies to using advertising techniques, behavioural science, and Darwinian theory to solve social problems—housing, welfare, economic and environmental challenges. This would create considerable fame for the agency, which they could then parlay into a source of revenue through public speaking and consultancy work for selected private-sector clients at a very high daily rate. . . .*
>
> *All of their work would eschew conventional notions of rational persuasion and focus on designing environments and choice architecture which lead to socially desirable outcomes through unconscious influence.*
>
> — Rory Sutherland, *Executive Creative Director, Vice Chairman, OgilvyOne, Ogilvy Group UK (2012)*

Figure 9.1 The Deadly Dozen Silos

THE DEADLY DOZEN SILOS	
1	**OBJECTIVE SILOS** Sales and Profit vs. Positive Social and Cultural impact
2	**SOLUTION SILOS** "We need a mobile app" vs. "What problem can we solve?"
3	**ORGANIZATIONAL SILOS** Us vs. Them
4	**GENERATIONAL SILOS** Extensive Experience vs. Fresh Perspectives
5	**OPERATIONAL SILOS** Product Management vs. Sales vs. Customer Services vs. PR vs. Marketing and Advertising
6	**EXPERTISE SILOS** The Creatives vs. the Analysts vs. the Strategists vs . . .
7	**RESPONSIBILITY AND ACCOUNTABILITY SILOS** Product/Service Sales Objectives vs. Responsibility and Accountability for Intended and Unintended Impact
8	**INTELLIGENCE SILOS** People vs. Computers
9	**NATIONAL SILOS** Global Efficiency vs. Local Sensitivity
10	**CULTURAL SILOS** What Makes Us Distinct vs. What Brings Us Together
11	**MEDIA/CHANNEL/TOUCHPOINT SILOS** Attribution Winners and Losers vs. Portfolio and Synergy Effect
12	**HIDDEN SILOS** The boundaries we don't yet see

Deadly Silo 2
Solution Silos: *"We Need a Mobile App" versus "What Problem Can We Solve?"*

> *We need to fully embrace the concept of making things people want rather than making people want things. It's not just about demographic shifts but new mindsets and behaviors.*
>
> —Michael Jacobs, *Managing Partner, Executive Creative Director, Our True North; Chief Creative Officer, iRGONOMIC (2012)*

The change (and opportunity) will come not from how advertising is done, but what advertising actually does. By 2020, the industry will not be helping clients sell physical stuff, but rather helping create and sell consumer solutions. In fact, it'll be more than that—it will be helping clients co-create those consumer solutions (with their own consumers).

— Guy Champniss, *VP, Marketing and Consumer Behavior, Enervee; Associate Professor, Henley Business School (2013)*

Deadly Silo 3
Organizational Silos: *Us versus Them*

An obvious solution [to the agency problem] is to separate each new discipline into distinct smaller creative units, pretty much like we have design agencies, brand agencies, and innovative digital shops today. While this allows for a status quo in how we organize our advertising agencies, and thus will be favored by the part of the business that is focused only on the next financial quarter, the drawback of this siloed attitude is that we lose the synergy effect of the individual teams enriching the thinking and development of one another.

The alternative approach is to revisit how we manage our agencies, knowing that the traditional team structure is optimized for marketing messages, but not, for example, for editorial- or design-led research and development.

Critical to success is how agency leaders choose to lead the new mix of creative competencies as they bleed into business transformation, brand creation, and client interaction.

— Frederik Andersen, *COO, Strategy and Operations, VICE Media Group + VIRTUE Worldwide (2012)*

Agencies and advertisers traditionally are organized by competencies and channels (i.e., work in silos across their respective channels). The last few years, during the sea of consumer change and media fragmentation, agencies have restructured their organization to be platform or channel experts—a display team, a broadcast team, RTB, online video, mobile, social—instead of becoming consumer experts. While there are of course broader campaign themes, the channels were largely independent from each other. But omnichannel demands a cross-functional team structure.

Agencies and advertisers will need to shift their paradigms, models, and traditions and break down and transcend the physical and metaphorical single-channel (internal and external) advertising silos dividing initiatives to embrace a 360-degree approach in order to connect with consumers—with holistic conversation, consistency of messaging, and (relevant, unified, customized and rewarding) experiences—wherever they are, whenever they want, and however they prefer.

— George Musi, *Managing Partner, Analytics, Insights, and Attribution, Mind-share (2013)*

Deadly Silo 4
Generational Silos: *Extensive Experience versus Fresh Perspective*

2020 has to be the decade that will finally recognize that the more mature minds are the masterminds of advertising. Like in Medicine, Law, Engineering, and Architecture, gray hair should mean authority. You might think—well, it hasn't always been like this. But yes, the market has become avid and hungry for younger talent. Yes, because Generation Y has amazing characteristics. But also, sorry for being so blunt, because this market is always looking to reduce manpower costs. Advertising is built with minds. And it is essential that the mature ones are part of this business that we are so passionate about. So let's quickly think every day about not only preparing the entry level professionals but also how to keep older guys updated and ally their experience, maturity, and wisdom with new trends and the everyday evolution.

— Vinicius Reis, *Partner, Chief Operating Officer, CP+B Brasil (2012)*

Not only is it personally satisfying to guide and nurture professionals of all ages, we gain immediate and long-term value to our industry. One of the most important aspects of retaining creative technologists especially is by providing an environment and culture in which they are constantly learning, improving their skills and being challenged to figure out how to bring a concept to life in ways that have never been done before.

— Nancy Hill, *President and CEO, American Association of Advertising Agencies (4As) (2012)*

Deadly Silo 5
Operational Silos: *Product Management versus Sales versus Customer Service versus PR versus Marketing and Advertising*

If technology, and the depth of data it provides, is driving such significant change within the advertising industry, then we must learn how to integrate this competency into all departments, not make it a free-standing silo within the organization.

— Bob Kantor, *Chief Marketing and Business Development Officer, MDC Partners (2012)*

The next few years should be spent recalibrating the relationship between marketing and I.T. More cross-disciplinary teams of marketing and I.T. experts and maybe new CMO (chief metrics officers) must develop.

— *Lisa Colantuono, Co-President, AAR Partners (2013)*

I almost see a new department called the Making Department that is a mix between media, creatives, planners, technologists and producers who spend most of their time tweaking campaigns in real time instead of revising campaigns long before launch.

— Calle Sjoenell, *CEO, Lowe Brindfors (2012)*

The artificial walls between planning and buying are collapsing, and the cycle that you are operating on is collapsing.

— Scott Hagedorn, *CEO, Annalect (2012)*

Deadly Silo 6

Expertise Silos: *The Creatives versus the Analytics versus the Strategists versus. . . .*

Professional silos abound, and productivity in marketing communications (MarCom) business intelligence, strategic planning, resourcing talent/suppliers, and archiving suffers greatly from a lack of an industry taxonomy and the common language and defined terms it can generate. Without considering the totality of Marketing Communications and the inter-relationships between disciplines and practices, the industry perpetuates these unproductive silos of expertise. By 2020, this problem will be rectified. Advertising will be redefined to encompass the total MarCom spectrum, and this redefinition will help tear down the existing silos that inhibit productivity and integrated advertising programs.

— Arthur Tauder, *Founding Partner, Thunderhouse (2012)*

Digital will not be a silo, or a medium. It will be a facilitator and an enhancer to our lifestyles. This will then drive a need for unparalleled integration within communication strategies. People and their embracement of technology is forcing the media, the idea, and the activation to collapse into one stream. Someone needs to lead this, but who? So we'll undoubtedly see media agencies adding creative to their strengths and vice versa. After years of agencies spinning off specialist brands, they will start to combine again in a "Big Crunch."

— Matthew Godfrey, *President, Y&R Asia (2012)*

Agencies are full of people who are in touch with their inner child. We don't need any more of them. But statisticians, business analysts, people who speak in math: those are the people who would genuinely expand the skills set of the average agency. We don't employ them not because they wouldn't make money, but because they wouldn't fit in. But perhaps it's us that need to fit in with them.

— Mike Follett, *Managing Director, Lumen Research (2012)*

Deadly Silo 7

Responsibility and Accountability Silos: *Product/Service Sales Objectives versus Responsibility and Accountability for Intended and Unintended Impact*

By 2020, organizations of all persuasions will have understood—some the hard way—that they can't hide. They live in the proverbial fish bowl and their actions often do speak louder than their words. The inexorable advance of technology will continue to offer up mountains of data to be analyzed that will then be used by friend and foe alike. Global researchers will have shown that brands that think about why they are in business instead of just thinking about what they are in business for will enjoy better financial growth and increased equity values. Jim Stengel, formerly P&G's top brand executive, wrote "Grow: How Ideals Power Growth and Profit at the World's Greatest Companies" on this thesis.

— Mac Cato, *Chairman, Cato Consulting Group (2012)*

Deadly Silo 8
Intelligence Silos: *People versus Computers*

The possibility of capturing consumer data digitally has allowed advertisers to leapfrog from mass media advertising to micro-targeting. Unfortunately, different data is stored with different digital media giants and is not being shared across domains. Advertisers advertising on a particular domain usually retrieve consumer data only from that domain, and as a result, they do ad targeting using information that does not completely describe the consumers. Advertisements then turn out to be less relevant and personalized.

So what do these mean? Indeed, there is an explosion of consumer data in the cloud that can be accessed from anywhere, anytime. However, such data is stored in silos, waiting to be organized into a complete and more compelling story. We may be good at collecting data today, but not as good at making sense of that data, yet.

But what if these data silos are broken down? What if information is allowed to interact across domains to form a dynamic, holistic, and complete understanding of every individual? What if information is aggregated and integrated to form our doppelgängers in the cloud? I think the potential for a new age of advertising is immense.

— Everlyn Lee, *Digital Planner, McCann Health Greater China (2012)*

Deadly Silo 9
National Silos: *Global Perspective versus Local Sensitivity*

Since 2015, it's like advertising has been on steroids. Even national borders have disappeared. Not everyone in India might be able to use the Internet, but it doesn't really matter now that every billboard is connected. Today, a brand's reach isn't about the big media outlets established in one country or another. Now it's all about giving the people what they want regardless of nationality, age, even sex!

The original advertising model was built on Western ideals and ambitions from decades ago. Last year, Africa became the fastest growing market for toothpaste, shampoo, and household cleaning products. It's no surprise: ["Western"] economies are growing at 0.00 something, and some African countries are showing 10 percent–plus growth rates. Brands had to adapt quickly to stay relevant, exciting, and alive. Brand leadership doesn't come from Europe or North America anymore. It comes from the people of planet Earth.

— Isabelle Quevilly, *Director, Brand Services, Brilliant Noise (2013)*

Deadly Silo 10
Cultural Silos: *What Separates Us versus What Brings Us Together*

By 2020, we should be seeing the death of the multicultural agency model. Even today, it is not necessary to have these silo businesses that collaborate to contribute to the client whole. I would argue that Wieden+Kennedy is perhaps one of the best African-American advertising agencies in the United States. Obviously, Wieden+Kennedy does not profess to be an African-American advertising agency, but the groundbreaking work that they have consistently produced for Nike and the Jordan brand has cemented iconic products into the culture of young urban teens—notably, the Air Jordan sneaker franchise. Yes, the Jordan brand features an array of African-American athletes, but that underscores the point that the best creative and most convincing product campaigns do not have to be born from an African-American specialty; agency, rather, an agency that integrates the perspectives of African-Americans into key roles drives greater business success. I predict that the specialty shops will become less of a necessity, and their argument for stand-alone existence will greatly diminish in light of omniculturalism.

To this end, all agencies should be thinking across cultural categories. They should have thought leadership in all aspects of American life with specific expertise toward the rare cases when ethnicity will be perhaps the most important strategic consideration (e.g. personal care products formulated for specific skin and hair) or when long-standing cultural biases will be necessary to unearth during the "insights" phase of the strategic planning process. However clients are inefficiently spending against these confederations of agencies to specialize in attuning simple human truths to gain market-share from specific ethnic groups when that investment could be more effectively targeted through other methodologies that are broader and inclusive.

— Steve Stoute, *Founder and CEO, Translation (2012)*

Women will be at least 50 percent of the communications community workforce . . . from executive suite to interns. Why? The "integrated" agency will be technology-enabled and remote-work friendly, which will allow "stay at home" women with children to be fully enabled contributors. Plus, the next five years will see more women in technology, and creative technology will subsume analog technology.

— Mike Donahue, *Founder, Connect the Dots (2013)*

Deadly Silo 11

Media/Channel/Touchpoint Silos: *Attribution Winners and Losers versus Portfolio and Synergy Effect*

> *Whilst the solution may seem simple, sadly, the barrier frequently comes from within: "silo" mentalities, and politics. The opportunity is to deliver seamless experiences across the silos, combined with creative curation to ensure high quality, and innovative, expression. The role of digital experiences within this holistic world cannot be underestimated and it seems clear that the potential of digital to augment, extend, and create whole new interactions will continue to shape companies.*
>
> — Jez Frampton, *Global CEO, Interbrand (2012)*

Deadly Silo 12

Hidden Silos: *The Boundaries We Don't Yet See*

Our contributors were able to identify these silos as they bumped up against them in their quest to innovate and excel, and many of them pointed out the inevitability of new silos developing as the world changes. This leads us to wonder: where else are there divisions that no longer serve us? What other silos are preventing us from accessing and taking advantage of unknown skills, insights, and breakthroughs? We encourage you to pause for a moment and take stock of what silos and boundaries might be holding you back from moving toward the ATVC model. Keep all these challenges in mind as you consider these approaches to transcend them.

Transcending Silos and Boundaries

The sub-optimization of silos and the limitations of boundaries must be overcome in order to progress. Here we offer approaches that will ameliorate disconnectedness by rethinking organizational boundaries: aligned objectives, open innovation, and network activation and orchestration.

Aligned Objectives

We believe the most powerful means of overcoming the challenge of silos is to find aligned objectives that transform boundaries and create win-win-win outcomes among all involved. Chapter 3 is devoted to this topic, so as a reminder, we offer these 2020 insights on the importance of alignment and common purpose:

> *This means we need to redefine the criteria from where and to where Advertising aims. While historically the commercial aspect has been central, we should refocus on the performative aspects of our practice. In the future, Advertising should expand its efficiency parameters, exiting the stronghold of the commercial, to be inserted into the core cultural spheres where people and contemporary world is created. These not only imply bringing people*

into the process, but also allow the process to enter the world of people. Advertising should become a social science that looks at reality from the context of consumption and its impact on people's lives.

— Vicente Valjalo de Ramón, *CEO, JWT Chile (2012)*

The day I saw Simon Sinek speak about the Golden Circle and reference the Law of Diffusion of Innovation, my world inverted. He goes through the WHAT it is that you do (as a company), HOW you do what you do, and finally WHY you do what you do. Sinek even draws parallels to the biology of our brains and the inner rings it mirrors to validate this theory. Simple idea, brilliant in fact, tap into belief.

— Khayyam Wakil, *Chief Belief Officer, Thynk Taynk (2013)*

Whenever I think about the future, I can't help but think about the world we're leaving for our children. Everyone on our planet could think a little more about leaving a world for our children that is not only hospitable, but sustainable and a better place. Right now, we're not doing that . . . the characteristic we could use a lot more of is purpose. If advertisers approached their business in this way, our advertising industry—and our world—would become a far better place.

— Max Kalehoff, *CMO, SocialCode (2012)*

To bring us to 2020, the new cross-silo and cross-boundary principles must reflect aligned objectives. If this were a test of future-looking readiness, how would you and your organization score and where do you see the greatest upside potential? **Instead of a silo mindset, imagine the transforming power of an alignment mindset, whereby "vs." in Figure 9.1 is replaced with "and", thus creating bridges between silos toward a common purpose.**

Open Innovation

Designing integrated physical-digital services, which deliver valuable and memorable brand experiences across a proliferation of connected interfaces, cannot be achieved within single units, no matter how compelling their specialist expertise. Neither can it be managed through the continuous acquisition of in-house capabilities. The idea of a genuine one-stop shop gets more expensive and less credible by the day, as the world gets more complex and interconnected.

All of which leads to the conclusion that—whatever else the future may hold—it has to include connected partnerships to supply the skills, innovations, insights, and necessary speed to market to compete. Connectivity has to be the watchword in more ways than one.

— Sally Williams, *Global President, Business Development and Client Relations, DAS, Omnicom Group (2012)*

"Connected partnerships" is another way of describing open innovation, a model that brings the benefits of outsourcing to all business domains, both large and small. As Williams mentions above, no company should operate as if it possessed all the resources necessary to navigate toward the future. Fortunately, there are more options than ever to tap into a vast global pool of problem-solvers and providers.

In 2001, a problem-solving company called InnoCentive discovered the pivotal power of open innovation when they found that the further the discipline of a problem solver from the discipline of a problem, the higher their likelihood of success. According to InnoCentive, "The global economy is forcing organizations to attack problems with all the brainpower they can muster both inside and outside the enterprise" (InnoCentive 2015). This may be the most powerful reason to experiment with and adopt open innovation. Since then, open innovation has turned mainstream, and numerous companies have sprung up that connect problems to problem solvers, such as IdeaConnection and NineSigma. In order to fulfill the need for diversity of expertise, every company should focus on establishing a portfolio of talent both internally (identifying, recruiting, developing, and retaining its own people) and through open innovation.

How to engage with open innovation? First, access open innovation by **using a firm that has activated its own network of open innovation talent** such as InnoCentive, co:collective, or Shout, a network of independent creatives. Connecting with these networks brings an instant breadth and depth of expertise and resources.

A second way to access open innovation is through **open competition**. Current successful examples of these include the X Prize Foundation, which rewards technological breakthroughs, and the numerous hackathons that draw together computer programmers and other developers to collaborate on projects.

Third, **internal corporate efforts** activate expertise of employees. In IBM's Jam sessions, the company's researchers, employees, and outside experts join together in virtual brainstorming sessions (IBM 2008).

A fourth way is to **enable a specialized community** such as the Apple developer community. How long would it take Apple, or any other company, to produce the thousands and thousands of apps on the iTunes platform? It would not have been possible for Apple to develop even a fraction of the apps that are currently available. Instead, they created a platform for developers to contribute to, thereby tapping into the broader world of creativity and innovation.

And fifth, connect through **customer-generated content**. As Chris Yeh writes:

> *Rather than building taglines from scratch, ad creators need to scratch the referential itch of the audience. One way of doing this is to involve the audience, as high-profile crowdsourcing campaigns like the Doritos Super Bowl promotion did. Even if the ads of 2020 don't always tap into direct audience input, it's unlikely that creativity will be limited to the creative director and copywriter—the number of influencers on any given ad will continue to increase. (2012)*

To resist open innovation today is to risk remaining at a resource and expertise disadvantage as the need for speed and agility will continue to accelerate. Need more convincing? There are dozens and dozens of inspiring success stories shared by companies around the world on IdeaConnection.com and current research on the topic abounds at openinnovation.eu and innocentive.com.

Network Activation

In 2014, Jerry and his collaborators Barry Libert and Megan Beck Fenley conducted research to assess the effectiveness of business models (based on the principal way an organization invests capital to generate and capture value). Of the four models they studied, detailed below, they found a networked organization to be far and away the most profitable and successful. They published their preliminary findings in an article in the Harvard Business Review in November 2014 entitled, "What Airbnb, Uber, and Alibaba Have in Common." The four business models are:

1. **Asset builders:** These companies build, develop, and lease physical assets to make, market, distribute, and sell physical things. Examples include Ford, Wal-Mart, and FedEx.

2. **Service providers:** These companies hire employees who provide services to customers or produce billable hours for which they charge. Examples include United Healthcare, Accenture, and JP Morgan.

3. **Technology creators:** These companies develop and sell intellectual property such as software, analytics, pharmaceuticals, and biotechnology. Examples include Microsoft, Oracle, and Amgen.

4. **Network orchestrators:** These companies create a network of peers in which the participants interact and share in the value creation. They may sell products or services, build relationships, share advice, give reviews, collaborate, co-create and more. Examples include eBay, Red Hat, and Visa, Uber, Tripadvisor, and Alibaba.

Their analysis found that Network Orchestrators outperform companies with other business models on several key dimensions. Advantages include higher valuations relative to their revenue, faster growth, and larger profit margins. They found that as of 2013, Network Orchestrators receive valuations on average two to four times higher than other companies. Furthermore, trend data over the past decade indicates that this valuation gap is widening. The degree to which a business model drives the gap between revenues and valuation is what they call "the multiplier effect" *(see Figure 9.2)*.

Companies with the highest multipliers were found to outperform less-valued companies on revenue growth, profitability, and return on assets for more than a decade (Libert, Wind, and Fenley 2014).

Figure 9.2 Network Orchestrators Lead the Pack on Price-to-Revenue

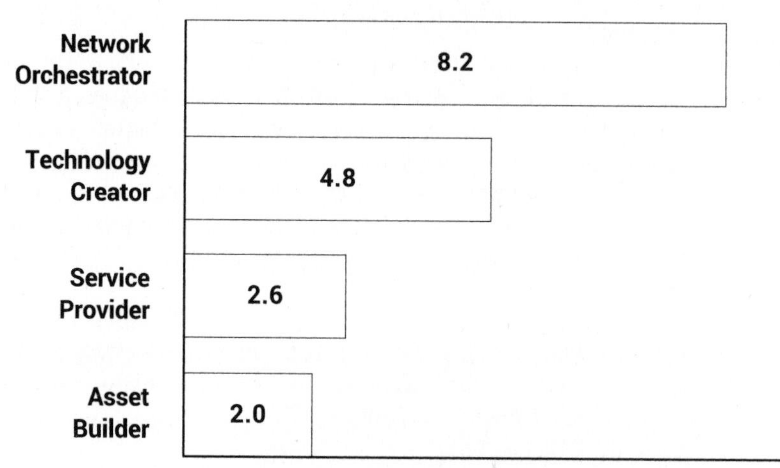

Source: Barry Libert, Jerry Wind, and Megan Beck Fenley (2014).

When looking beyond the impact of the business model on price-to-revenue ratio, they found that Network Orchestrators also outperform companies with other business models on both compound annual growth rate and profit margin. This seems to occur because the value creation performed by the network on behalf of the organization reduces the company's marginal cost, as described in Jeremy Rifkin's *The Zero Marginal Cost Society*. For example, TripAdvisor.com benefits from its customer's reviews and Airbnb leverages its network's housing assets (Rifkin Enterprises 2015).

Networks are sources of information, capabilities, and assets that lie in and around every organization. Most networks, however, lie dormant and untapped. To become a Network Orchestrator and create more value and better performance, leaders must connect to and activate their networks, tapping into new sources of value, both tangible (Airbnb's network of lodgings) and intangible (the expertise of Apple's Developer Network).

Approaches to Network Activation

How can those who are seeking to implement the All Touchpoint Value Creation Model leverage their various networks and augment their current business model to achieve the network multiplier effect? Here are four suggestions to get started:

1. **Assess the current business model.** Understand which business models currently exist within your organization and also the preferences and biases of the leadership team members who have created these models through capital allocation.

2. **Inventory network assets.** Take stock of your dormant network assets including customers, employees, partners, suppliers, distributors, and investors, and determine which have the greatest potential. Consider IBM—they have 400,000+ employees. Imagine leveraging each one as a touchpoint with an extensive network. Consider the expanded "who" of advertising we explored in chapter 2.

3. **Reallocate capital to networks.** Divert at least 5 to 10 percent of investment capital to activating networks. Take an experimental approach, as we explored in chapter 7, to early allocation and expect ongoing adaptation. This could be accomplished organically, through acquisition, or through partnership.

4. **Add network KPIs (key performance indicators).** Add to your standard financial and operational metrics new network-oriented indicators such as number of participants, their sentiment, and level of engagement. These KPIs will provide direction for your network growth and adaptation.

Network Orchestration

Expanding internally and externally beyond the marketing department to coordinate and optimize the interaction with people at and across all touchpoints, including open innovation and network activation, grows the challenge of how to orchestrate myriad components. Who will initiate and manage the connectivity required? How do we bridge silos that seem to be working at odds with one another? To quote Frederik Andersen, *"Management must cease to identify other disciplines as threats, but rather as stimulation for a constant flux of creative development that will not only sell products or change minds, but help define new audience experiences and relationships with brands"* (2012).

The concept of Network Orchestration aims to bring a unifying approach and mindset with six key elements, as illustrated in Figure 9.3.

Element 1: Select a Metaphor

An orchestra is, unsurprisingly, an apt metaphor. First, musicians must readily adapt to numerous conditions. Each musician must be a specialist in her own instrument and also be able to work closely with other instruments to produce the best results. At the same time, each section of an orchestra (the strings, the

Figure 9.3 Six Key Elements of Network Orchestration

	SIX KEY ELEMENTS FOR NETWORK ORCHESTRATION
1	Select a Metaphor
2	Include Current and Potential Customers in the Orchestra
3	Create Boundary-less Sections in the Orchestra
4	Include Emerging Markets and Trends in the Orchestra
5	Orchestrate on Solid Principles
6	Harness Technology to Enable and Empower the Orchestra and Orchestration

woodwinds) are a specialist group that need their own orchestration in order to work with other sections.

Think of the network required to orchestrate all touchpoint value creation as a collection of experts and specialist groups—what is the best way to bring them together? Do your vision, objectives, strategy, and unique context require a composer? An orchestra conductor? A jazz ensemble director? A leaderless team of equals as employed by the Orpheus or St. Paul Chamber Orchestras?

You might find other metaphors that work better for your context and conditions: curator, choreographer, coach, or even air traffic controller. Each metaphor has different implications for the role of the Network Orchestrator—the creator and leader in your organization.

Element 2: Include Current and Potential Customers in the Orchestra

"Customer-centric" organizations with a focus on CRM may actually have a higher risk of holding the unrealistic assumption that the firm is in control. In reality, as we have discussed, empowered and increasingly skeptical customers have great influence in the success or failure of a brand.

The engagement of consumers as co-designers, co-producers, co-marketers, content creators, and pricers is still in its infancy, but it is an area that is growing fast. Truly forward-looking organizations must engage customers through customer managed relationship (CMR) platforms—like the classic example of the Saber system that allowed travel agents to manage relationships with airlines—to provide *consumers* an effective, efficient way to manage their relationships with a company. No orchestration is complete without active, fully orchestrated engagement of customers and prospects. Once the network is developed, it's a multiway system.

Ayal Levin, strategy associate for Designit, and David Fogel, head of strategic research and business consulting department for Designit, discuss several ways consumers can be integrated as partners:

> ***Partnership in product development:*** *Share ideas with consumers, ask for their opinion, allow them to contribute in the development, testing, and production of new products. Volkswagen has proved, in their latest initiative "The People's Car," that collaborating with consumers in designing its newest model has enormous demand and potential.*
>
> ***Partnership in promotion:*** *Build consumer-centered communities through content and unique (branded) experiences and encourage consumer initiated brand advocacy. This may sound easy or mundane, but in reality this is the most difficult partnership to create as it requires a delicate balance between allowing them to "run" and "grow" the community, while maintaining certain branded elements. Nike+ is an example of one such community that enables the members (i.e., runners and athletes) to share their sporting experiences in a way that also promotes the Nike brand.*
>
> ***Partnerships in brand identity:*** *When Porsche decided to enter the SUV market, its consumers and fans protested, claiming their beloved brand changed its identity without consulting them. Marketing can no longer determine the brand identity on its own—consumers need to be part of the development of the brand's identity and values.*
>
> ***Partnership in decision making:*** *Following a decline in revenue and consumer protest to the changes led by former CEO Ron Johnson, JC Penney, in their recent TV campaign, apologized to consumers for changing their stores' pricing model and shopping experience. It is no secret that brands and companies rise and fall thanks to their consumers.*
>
> *Advertising will have the crucial role of creating and operating the platforms that will enable consumers to express themselves and be true partners to their beloved brands. (2013)*

John Winsor, head of the world's first advertising agency built on crowdsourcing, Victors & Spoils, was one of the first to put many of these ideas into action, helping brands activate their networks of fans and followers. In an interview with *Brand Equity Magazine* he described what he considers to be his greatest successes: "We created technology for Harley-Davidson, called Fan Machine, that allows fans on Facebook to participate in the creation of advertising ideas that we help produce. For Smartwool (an American clothing brand) we used social media to recruit their fans to become field-testers of the product. By doing so, Smartwool now has a community of 10,000 people that are field-testers, getting to try prototype products and giving feedback" (2012).

Element 3: Create Boundary-less Sections in the Orchestra

Each employee is a network unto his or herself. Hayes Roth, former chief marketing officer at Landor and now principal at HA Roth Consulting LLC, describes an example of an agency successfully orchestrating its employees:

> *Ford CMO Jim Farley has been an early and passionate advocate for just such a model with his marketing communications agencies, which in the U.S. is WPP's "Team Detroit." This is an agency without borders—walking its halls a casual visitor has no real idea where Wunderman (direct marketing) meets JWT (advertising) meets VML (digital) meets public relations, etc. This is completely by design. The agency and client practice "TRAIN:" Talent, Resource, and Insight Network, which means they find the best resources for any given project, whether within the Team Detroit/WPP construct or outside. Team Detroit then brings their curated selection of "best-of-class" talent in for whatever the project or challenge requires.*
>
> *This philosophy and structure provides Ford (and Team Detroit) access to top people and a highly collaborative creative environment while still contracting with a single agency. It ensures a ready supply of great creativity while maintaining single agency control and responsibility. As a result, the process breeds innovation and cooperation, focusing the team on the best solution possible, versus the best solution available within traditional agency confines. (2013)*

By treating their employees as an interconnected network of experts, rather than siloed and competitive departments, Ford elicits the best possible solutions.

Element 4: Include Emerging Markets and Trends in the Orchestra

As we cohosted roundtables around the world to understand and celebrate local innovation, we came to understand that the transformation of advertising and marketing has manifested in what should and could be seen as "international centers of excellence." Our session in New Delhi in 2011, organized by WFoA Global Advisory Board member Vaasu Gavarasana and attended by some of the most forward-thinking media, advertising, and brand executives in India, drove this point home. They discussed how the combination of cultural richness and challenges inherent in a market as large, complex, and diverse as theirs gave rise to some of the most powerful ideas to overcome these challenges and create a powerful source of empowerment and betterment through reimagined advertising—lessons that have universal inspiration and application.

Jerry's 2008 book, *Competing in a Flat World*, offers an in-depth example of a company successfully orchestrating for emerging markets and trends, the Li &

Fung trading company, which orchestrates over 15,000 global factories in over 40 countries without owning them, and yet consistently delivers products at the right price, place, and time. In the future, we have to see a world where companies are no longer competing firm to firm, but instead, network to network. Those with the strongest, most nimble networks, who also work toward the greatest positive impact on all its network collaborators as well as the culture and society and environment it inhabits, will yield the kinds of wins we all want to celebrate and reward (Fung, Fung, and Wind 2008).

Element 5: Orchestrate on Solid Principles

We invited Jay Reise, Professor of Music Composition at the University of Pennsylvania to our Wharton Future of Advertising Roundtable workshop on Orchestration to take us outside our field and bring an expert perspective on the topic. He defined six principles and best practices of orchestration:

- Virtuosity—cultivating individual expertise
- Context—knowing your role
- Adaptability—ability to accept change and improvise
- Awareness—of overall "composition" and other players' roles
- Communication—with all involved
- Solution-driven—concise, specific feedback on individual players' performance

Imagine that when each player in the network is following these best practices, the result is a masterpiece.

Element 6: Harness Technology to Enable and Empower the Orchestra and Orchestration

We would be remiss if we didn't reiterate here the importance and imperative of respectfully leveraging technology to realistically put into practice these principles of orchestration, given the inherent network complexity of the All Touchpoint Value Creation Model. As we discuss in the technology sections of Chapter 1 and Chapter 8, automation, programmatic, artificial intelligence, cognitive computing, and a growing body of tools and services offerings make it feasible to understand and make actionable people's preferences and cultural trends both in real time and over time (Wind 2012).

Key Takeaways

- **Silos in an organization are a persistent and pervasive obstacle to change and collaboration. The business world has long been one of stratification, hierarchy, and fiefdoms. Such rigidity no longer makes sense.**

Figure 9.4 Beyond Advertising in Action: Explore New Business Models

Beyond Advertising in Action
EXPLORE NEW BUSINESS MODELS

THE EVERYWHERE INITIATIVE—VISA 2015
Marketer: Visa
Open Innovation Contest

OBJECTIVE/PROBLEM TO BE SOLVED

Visa sought a way to adapt to changing technologies, promote innovation inside and outside the company, and develop new solutions to several of their marketing problems.

APPROACH

Visa launched the Everywhere Initiative to develop new relationships with startup companies and generate marketing ideas. In partnership with startup innovation platform Kite, three briefs were released to the startup community, focusing on digital commerce, millennials, and rewarding members. Finalists presented at the Visa headquarters competing for 50 thousand dollars to run a pilot with Visa.

THE RESULTS

The program allowed Visa to foster an environment of innovation and address specific marketing objectives. Nearly 400 applications were received, and 30 were ready to "be used right away," according to Claudia Lagunas, Senior Director of Global Marketing at Visa.

LESSONS AND OBSERVATIONS

Past success doesn't guarantee continued success. All companies must develop a culture of innovation and continuously adapt to the rapidly changing marketing landscape with new business models.

CITATION: Visa, 2015

- **To match the globalized, digitized world, organizations must embrace the very fluidity that defines it. Through a networked, orchestrated approach, this fluidity can be built into organizational structures, allowing people, teams, and ideas, to flow more freely.**
- **A less siloed space should not stop at an organization's door: the structure of the workforce is changing fundamentally, and talent can be accessed in new, exciting ways. The ability to bring in a fresh pair of eyes is easier—and more valuable—than ever.**
- **We've listed eleven silos we have identified in the contemporary workplace. The twelfth—the boundaries we don't yet see—may be the most insidious. A clear vision and courageous experimentation will help reveal, and break down, these barriers *(see Figure 9.4).***

Chapter 10

A Global Movement toward a More Desirable Future

Why do people start and join movements? . . . There's something happening around them that they're not quite content with, and they'd be interested in helping to change it (even if they're not entirely sure how).

— Scott Goodson, *Founder and CEO, StrawberryFrog (2012)*

We learned from Scott Goodson and the many wise people he features in his 2012 book *Uprising* that people don't join a movement because you tell them to. They feel a "restlessness" and they see a solution that motivates them to *take action* and join in. That's what we are hoping has happened for you when reading this book and the many inspiring insights from our Advertising 2020 collaborators.

The "we" that we have used throughout this book refers to all those who have a desire for a better future of advertising and are motivated to act upon it, collaboratively. **For starters, consider the power and potential of tapping into the advertising and marketing creativity, imagination, empathy, insights, strategy, planning, design, tech, and analytic talents and budgets, around the world, to collectively be a force of change to make a better future actually happen.** Given the nature of the five forces of change and the model that we collectively propose, there are a whole host of others, far beyond the traditional boundaries of advertising and marketing, who see the value of this approach and who, if we give them a compelling platform, *or* if we are open to joining forces with their equally compelling platforms, may well welcome our leadership and pioneering and co-creation. As many of you know, it is already happening, and you are already part of the change. We just want to give you good company and further encouragement.

As we go to press, we are sensing a global groundswell. Insights2020, a global marketing leadership initiative where Jerry serves as an advisory board member, focused on "uncovering the drivers of customer-centric growth," led by MillwardBrown Vermeer in partnership with ESOMAR, the ARF, Korn Ferry, Linkedin, and Kantar. They reached out to thousands of marketers around the world and came up with many findings consistent with, and inclusive of ours, including the importance of brand purpose, data-driven customization, and touchpoint consistency (Millward Brown Vermeer 2015).

At major industry conferences around the world, the themes are reaching beyond the topics of "mobile," "social," "local," "big data," and "IoT"—topics that have of course been necessary to get us to where we are today—to topics that open a greater discussion of what the relationship is and could be between brands; their collaborators; the people they seek to connect with and serve; and the culture, society, and world that presents untold opportunities for something more than a myopic focus on sales much less CPMs.

Our hope is that this book galvanizes the energies of those who have been involved and connected with the Wharton Future of Advertising Program to date, together with those who are inspired by this book and our collaborators, to take this effort to the next level—to make personal, professional, and organizational resource choices that could result in even more far-reaching impacts and implications.

Our hope is that this book can be the visionary starting point for thinking more comprehensively—beyond traditional silos of advertising and marketing—to a more holistic, enterprise- and network-wide view, seen from the vantage point of current and potential customers and associates and all those who are impacted by our choices, expenditures, and actions. Our research points the way to understanding how all people connections should be orchestrated in a way that is beneficial to all parties involved. By challenging our current mental models of "advertising", we can open our minds to what it *could* and *should* be.

With this newly co-created vision for the future, our hope is that we can leverage our respective time, talent, experience, wisdom, and resources to make it a reality. The model we have co-created to leverage the best of what has brought us to this point, while inspiring others to enthusiastically choose this pathway to realize their hopes and aspirations, will help us achieve that future. Let's take the advice of Rob Campbell, regional head of planning, Wieden + Kennedy Shanghai, and our very first contributor to the Advertising 2020 Project, to *"push, prod, provoke, create & prove ourselves. Over & over again" (2012).*

We are painfully aware that the moment this goes book goes to press it runs the risk of seeming dated in its examples, given how dynamic and rapidly changing our world is. Yet given our focus on an idealized future, we hope that its essential principles and concepts and inspirations will be worthwhile guideposts through 2020 and into the next decade. This book is therefore a testament to all those who took the time to co-create it, and represents a roadmap that we hope will be valuable even as the world continues to evolve. It is put forth at a pivotal moment in time. It celebrates and inspires those pioneers among you who will find the sting of the proverbial arrows in your back, but who will forge on, regardless of the naysayers.

The Wharton Future of Advertising Program's Advertising 2020 Project has been about standing on the shoulders of the past to look as far ahead as possible, and imagine what we as a community could and should create for a better future.

We very much hope you will join us and be part of a movement to make a better future happen. How to do so? Think and act differently. Stretch your mental models. Use a new vocabulary. Launch and iterate. Experiment. Then share what you have done, what you have learned, comment on others' learning, and stay up to date with new developments on our website: wfoa.wharton.upenn.edu.

Our hope is that there is a revolution in the making. And it promises to make all our lives better.

Appendix 1: The Backstory
The Wharton Future of Advertising Program and the Advertising 2020 Project

> *If we are not truly about reinvention, rather than tweaking, we should not even bother.*
>
> – Rishad Tobaccowala, *Chief Strategist, Publicis Groupe (2012)*

In 2011, the Wharton Future of Advertising (WFoA) Program was at a crossroads. We were four years into the Program's mission of reinventing the scope, practice, and value of advertising by bringing academic and practitioner visionaries from all corners of the world of advertising together. We had held two global research conferences to establish what had been recently proven about what works and what doesn't, and yet the research, by its very nature, was based on historical data in a world that was rapidly transforming. We wondered, would these findings still hold as things continued to evolve and change? We had held numerous roundtables and workshops around the world (New York, London, Paris, New Delhi, and Beijing) on topics such as the changing role of creatives in the digital age, emerging new business and revenue models, and the impact of disruptive technologies and media drivers. More and more people in the industry were looking to us for guidance and insights, and we realized we had to shift our view more solidly towards the future and start to walk the talk of adopting new models. We decided to create our own "open innovation" project.

The Advertising 2020 Project

Backed by Jerry's extensive knowledge and research on open innovation and challenging mental models, we landed on what we thought could bring some focus and clarity while offering a new way of thinking about, and dealing with, the tremendous changes our community was experiencing. We decided to tap the collective wisdom of our growing network of innovative thinkers. We challenged them to imagine a best possible scenario for the future and then go even further by suggesting actions that would make that future a reality. As the saying goes, the best way to predict the future is to create it, and we hoped to do so by inspiring and generating a diverse mix of fresh insights from around the world and across disciplines. By changing what we see is possible, we have the opportunity to co-create a future that is better for business, better for people, and by extension, better for society.

What we decided to do:

1. Gather great and willing minds from around the globe

2. Make sure to include traditional (often vested) and nontraditional (often barrier-breaker) perspectives

3. Reach beyond blaming, beyond prediction, to aspiration and inspiration

4. Identify what to do *now*

5. Share and distill insights to empower business leaders and inspire the next generation

Gather Great and Willing Minds from around the Globe

First, rather than an ivory tower exercise or even a one-time event, we knew we wanted to tap into the collective wisdom of the global community of visionaries, innovators, and executives who had become involved with WFoA through our roundtables, conferences, and speaking engagements. We began by reaching out to our Global Advisory Board (by that point over 80 thought leaders from top agencies and advertisers) and our broader network, asking them to recommend and introduce us to others in their network whose opinion they would value to amplify our access to the most innovative thinking. We ended up with contributions from over 200 thought leaders from over 22 countries, and we continue to solicit entries and input from our growing community.

Make Sure to Include Traditional (Often Vested) and Nontraditional (Often Barrier-Breaking) Perspectives

Second, we wanted to ensure that we gained the perspectives from those in traditional advertising and marketing fields, and those who could shed light on the newly emerging areas, as we described in our original invitation:

> "Ideally, who else should we invite to contribute from around the world? (Though not necessary, please indicate if you can make an introduction)—advertisers, CEOs, CMOs, CIOs, and CFOs; traditional, new, and emerging advertising agencies; traditional, new and emerging media; science and technology; advertising researchers; entertainment; gaming; government; academics from marketing, communications, psychology, cultural anthropology, sociology, behavioral economics, or others?"

As the entries rolled in we kept track of which perspectives were underrepresented and did our best to seek those out, across geographies and generations, titles, and talents.

Reach beyond Blaming, beyond Prediction to Aspiration and Inspiration

Third, and perhaps the most important decision we made, was in framing the questions that would define the project.

Question 1: What Could/Should Advertising Look Like in 2020?

Rather than trying to *predict* the future, we would ask the community to think more aspirationally: What *could* it be? What *should* it be? In essence, what would we *want* it to be if it could be anything we wanted? How do we take what is good or desirable about advertising and leave behind that which is undesirable, problematic, and just downright annoying? What can we imagine if all the forces that we are seeing emerge resulted in the best possible outcome?

We also didn't want to spend too much energy focusing on what other players are doing wrong.

> "Agencies are stuck in the past."
>
> "Brand managers are too short term focused and won't try anything new."
>
> "The best talent is being stolen by Silicon Valley."
>
> "Traditional media is in denial."
>
> "Analytics are anathema to creative."

Instead we wanted to ask, what would it look like if everyone was doing it "right"?

This approach celebrates Idealized Design, popularized by beloved and legendary Wharton Professor Russ Ackoff wherein seemingly intractable problems are solved by starting with a "future desired vision"—rather than being bogged down with what is—then working backward from there to find a path forward.

When we launched the project in early 2012, we were asking people to look ahead eight years to 2020. A quick look back eight years suggested just how difficult it would be to try to predict the breadth and depth of change another eight years hence. Here's what we wrote to try to give some context in our initial April 2012 invite to the project participants.

"Imagine that since 2004 (within eight years):

- World Internet usage grew from 11 to 33 percent of the global population
- Facebook was launched and now has 845 million active monthly users
- DVR users grew sixfold from 7 to 44 million users
- Twitter was launched and there are now 177 million tweets a day
- The iPhone and the iPad were launched and now there are more than 500,000 apps"

What's amazing about this list is twofold. First, how those numbers have jumped in three years. Here are the new stats:

- Since 2012, world Internet usage has reached a penetration of 42 percent of the global population as of January 2015, up from 33 percent in 2012.
- As of late 2014, "Almost as many people use Facebook as live in the entire country of China," a cool 1.35 billion people.
- DVR usage is still up, with usage in 47 percent of U.S. TV households.
- Today, 500 million tweets are sent per day. If Twitter were a country, it would be the twelfth largest in the world.
- The iPhone and iPad are still top competitors, though the market has diversified, making for a highly competitive smartphone market. As of July 2014, Android users can access 1.3 million apps, and Apple users can access 1.2 million.

But even more to the point are the stats that we didn't mention then that are so compelling as we write this book in 2015.

- Whereas in April 2012, DVR was the star of the show, in 2015, things are radically different. DVR has become old news to video on demand services and subscription services like Netflix, Hulu, and Amazon Instant Video. "62 percent of digital cable subscribers, and 57 percent of Telco video subscribers, used on-Demand in the past month. 29 percent of Netflix subscribers stream video daily, and 70 percent weekly—up from 10 percent daily, and 43 percent weekly in 2010." "Cutting the cord" is becoming a more prominent possibility.
- In April 2012, Instagram had only been launched 18 months prior. Today, Instagram boasts a user base made up of 20 percent of global Internet users between the ages of 16 and 64. This amounts to 75 million users per day.
- Although the iPhone 6 and iPhone 6 Plus made waves, more pressing considerations for the future include wearable tech and the Internet of Things: Apple Watch, Fitbits, and self-driving cars. Although only 0.06 percent of "things" are currently connected—10 billion out of 1.5 trillion "things" total—by 2020, Cisco estimates that we will have over 200 billion connected things.
- Native advertising started gaining momentum in 2012, with yearly native ad spend growing rapidly. In 2012, $1.5 billion; in 2013, $2.2 billion; in 2014,

$3.2 billion; in 2015 $4.3 billion. It's projected that by 2018, this number will swell to $8.8 billion.

- The programmatic advertising field was still relatively young in April 2012. Today, it has become standard. The United States is the largest representative accounting for 60 percent of global ad spend in 2013. Magna Global predicts, however, that the U.S. portion of the pie will shrink to 50 percent of global spend by 2017, with expenditures reaching $32.6 billion, up from $16.6 billion in 2014.

Simply put, we don't know what will be the "next big thing." And that is not our goal. Instead of a contest to see who is best at predicting the future, we've been more interested in tapping the creative DNA of a profoundly creative industry. And our contributors embraced the opportunity to put their creative juices toward thinking truly differently.

What to Do Now

Finally, we required that within the 1,000-word-or-less essays and entries, our contributors address the second question of the project:

Question 2: What Should We Do Now to Get Ready for that Future?

We wanted this project to be practicable, so we challenged our contributors to take their future concepts and suggest concrete, actionable steps to take now to prepare for their desired future.

As powerful as this action-oriented approach proved to be, we also found an important, serendipitous aspect of this second question that we didn't foresee at the outset. As soon as the first responses began pouring in, we knew we had hit on something even bigger. When we received the submissions, we sent a thank-you note to executives for taking the time and energy to articulate their contribution, what we heard back was surprising.

"No, actually, thank YOU. Now that I have taken the time to step away from the day to day and think seriously about these two questions, I am already in the process of convening my teams and making changes to how we are going forward."

We discovered that there was a deep desire among our participants to engage in this exercise and start figuring out ways to be proactive in the face of overwhelming change.

Share and Distill Insights to Empower Business Leaders and Inspire the Next Generation

Our first priority has been to ensure access to the complete, unabridged collection of 200+ Advertising 2020 entries, which resides for all to access on the Wharton Future of Advertising website. Second, we wanted to leverage Jerry's decades of research, teaching, and work with scores of executives. Catharine has since then led the charge to tackle the task of distilling these ideas into a cohesive *framework*—a model and roadmap—as well as curate what our contributors see as the compelling evidence that would motivate business leaders throughout organizations to take a new approach. Hence, three years since we started this project, this book seeks to achieve these triple objectives.

As readers of this book, you know all too well the fire hose of information that flows past unabated. We cannot assimilate all of the emerging research, examples, statistics, forecasts, explanations, insights, and innovations that continue to emerge to illuminate the way forward in these pages. Instead our role, along with our contributors, has been to take a step back and describe a future state that we can use as a true north (or pretty close) to head toward, no matter how frequently we are buffeted by the short-term changing winds.

In 2020, we look forward to celebrating the successes of all those individuals and teams and networks around the world, regardless of size or scope, who have envisioned a better future, who have articulated what that means for them and their organizations, and who have made choices and resource allocations to co-create a future we are truly proud of and that attracts an awe-inspiring cadre across disciplines, cultures and generations.

Can't wait, and please let us know how the journey unfolds.

Appendix 2
Advertising 2020 Contributors

			AT TIME OF CONTRIBUTION (VARIES)		AT TIME OF PRESS (JULY 2015)	
NO.	**NAME**	**COUNTRY**	**TITLE**	**ORGANIZATION**	**TITLE**	**ORGANIZATION**
1	**Kevin Allen**	UK	*Founder & CEO*	rekap Inc.	*Founder & CEO*	rekap Inc.
2	**Frederik Andersen**	DENMARK	*COO*	Vice Media Group	*COO, Strategy & Operations*	VICE Media Group + VIRTUE Worldwid
3	**Chris Arnold**	UK	Creative Director & Co-Founder	Creative Orchestra	Creative Director & Co-Founder	Creative Orchestra
4	**Adnan Azad**	USA	Jr. Statistical Analyst	KPMG Boston	Business Analyst, Global Tenders & Pricing	DHL Global Forwarding Asia-Pacific
5	**John M. Baker**	USA	President	dotJWT	CMO	Mirum Agency
6	**Kamini Banga**	UK	Author, Columnist	New Dimensions Consultancy	Founder, Director	Dimensions Consultancy
7	**Robert L. Barocci**	USA	President & CEO	Advertising Research Foundation (ARF)	Former President & CEO	Advertising Research Foundation (ARF)
8	**Steve Bellman**	AUSTRALIA	Research Associate Professor & Deputy Director	Audience Labs, Murdoch University	Researcher	MediaScience
9	**Lori Billey**	CANADA	CEO & Founding Partner	RED The Agency	CEO & Founding Partner	RED The Agency
10	**Keith Blanchard**	USA	Chief Content Officer	Story Worldwide	Owner & CEO	Teamstream Productions
11	**Marc Blanchard**	USA	Executive Creative Director	Euro RSCG Worldwide	Executive Creative Director	Havas Worldwide
12	**Jeff Boehme**	USA	Chief Research Officer	Kantar Media North America	Chief Client Officer	Rentrak
13	**Frederic Bonn**	USA	Executive Creative Director	Razorfish	Chief Creative Officer, North America	Mirum Agency
14	**Michelle Bottomley**	USA	President	Zinio, LLC	Chief Marketing & Sales Officer	Mercer
15	**Jacques Bughin**	BELGIUM	Director	McKinsey & Company, Brussels	Director	McKinsey & Company, Brussels
16	**Cheryl Burgess**	USA	CEO & CMO	Blue Focus Marketing	CEO & CMO	Blue Focus Marketing
17	**Mark Burgess**	USA	President	Blue Focus Marketing	President	Blue Focus Marketing
18	**Chris Burggraeve**	USA	Founder	Vicomte LLC	Founder	Vicomte LLC
19	**Thomas Burkhardt**	USA	VP Global Marketing	COTY Inc.	Global Brand Builder	Thomas Burkhardt Branding & Strategy
20	**Adam Cahill**	USA	Co-Media Director	Hill Holiday	Founder	Anagram LLC
21	**Rob Campbell**	CHINA	Regional Head of Strategy	Wieden + Kennedy	Head of planning	Wieden + Kennedy
22	**Mac Cato**	UK	Chairman	Cato Consulting Group	Chairman	Cato Consulting Group
23	**Michele Cerwin**	USA	President	HL Group	Principal	mCerwin Consulting
24	**Guy Champniss**	UK	Creative Media Strategist	Meltwater Consulting School, UK Associate Professor	VP Marketing & Consumer Behavior	Enervee; Henley `Business
25	**Kirk Cheyfitz**	USA	Co-CEO + Chief Storyteller	Story Worldwide	Co-CEO + Chief Storyteller	Story Worldwide
26	**Adrian Chiu**	USA	Senior Product Planner	Microsoft	Senior Product Manager/ Senior Business Strategy Manager for Measurement & Insights	Microsoft
27	**Brent Chudoba**	USA	VP, General Manager	SurveyMonkey	SVP & Chief Revenue Officer	SurveyMonkey
28	**Lisa Colantuono**	USA	Co-President	AAR Partners	Co-President	AAR Partners
29	**Amy-Willard Cross**	USA	Founder & Editor	Vitamin W	Founder & Editor	The BUY UP Index
30	**Dean Crutchfield**	USA	Founder	Dean Crutchfield Associates	Advisor	Amy J Weiner LLC
31	**Brian d'Allesandro**	USA	VP, Data Science	Media6Degrees	SVP	Digital Intelligence at Dstillery
32	**Craig Davies**	USA	Apprentice	Y&R	Apprentice	Y&R

			AT TIME OF CONTRIBUTION (VARIES)		AT TIME OF PRESS (JULY 2015)	
NO.	**NAME**	**COUNTRY**	**TITLE**	**ORGANIZATION**	**TITLE**	**ORGANIZATION**
33	**Allen Debevoise**	USA	Chairman & CEO	Machinima	Chairman	Machinima
34	**Oliver Deighton**	USA	VP of Marketing	VigLink	Co-Founder & CEO	Nickel Labs
35	**Yasir Dhannoon**	USA	Apprentice	WPP-Deliver	Product Manager	HarperCollins Publishers
36	**Pete Doe**	USA	Media Research & Data Expert	Nielsen	SVP Data Science	Nielsen
37	**Mike Doherty**	USA	President	Cole & Weber United	President	Cole & Weber United
38	**Simon Dolsten**	USA	Student	Syracuse University Newhouse School	Copywriter	Momentum Worldwide (McCann Worldgroup)
39	**Matthew Don**	USA	Chief Innovation Officer	Doremus	Chief Innovation Officer	Doremus
40	**Mike Donahue**	USA	EVP	4As	Founder	Connect the Dots
41	**Erik du Plessis**	SOUTH AFRICA	Chairman	Millward Brown South Africa	Author, Speaker and Consultant	
42	**Russell Dubner**	USA	President	Edelman NY	US CEO	Edelman
43	**Timothy Duquesne**	FRANCE	Screenwriter/Consultant	We Support Creators	Screenwriter/Consultant	We Support Creators
44	**Mark Earls**	UK	Writer & Consultant	Herd Consultancy	Writer & Consultant	Herd Consultancy
45	**David Edelman**	USA	Partner	McKinsey & Company, Boston	Global Co-Leader Digital & Marketing and Sales	McKinsey & Company, Boston
46	**Mike Ewing**	AUSTRALIA	Head, Department of Marketing	Monash University	Executive Dean & Pro-Vice Chancellor	Deakin University
47	**Mel Exon**	UK	Managing Partner, Co-Founder	BBH, BBH Labs	Managing Director; Co-Founder	BBH London; BBH Labs
48	**Peter Field**	UK	President	Field Consulting	President	Field Consulting
49	**Tim Flattery**	AUSTRALIA	Creative Director	Grainey Pictures	Executive Creative Director	MEC
50	**Arthur Fleischmann**	CANADA	President/Partner	john st. advertising	President/Partner	john st. advertising
51	**David Fogel**	ISRAEL	Head of Strategic Research & Business Consulting Department	McCann Tel-Aviv	Head of Strategic Research & Business Consulting Department	McCann Tel-Aviv
52	**Brendan Foley**	USA	Principal Program Manager	Microsoft	Divisional VP, Online Business Unit	Sears Holdings Corporation
53	**Mike Follett**	UK	Managing Director	Lumen Research	Managing Director	Lumen Research
54	**Jez Frampton**	UK	Global CEO	Interbrand	Global CEO	Interbrand
55	**Maria Luisa Francoli Plaza**	SPAIN	Global CEO	Havas Media	ISP	Digital Advisory Board
56	**Morten Gad**	DENMARK	Strategic Planner	Gorm Larsen & Zornig	Creative Director & Partner	Gorm Larsen & Zornig
57	**Cindy Gallop**	USA	Founder & CEO	IfWeRanTheWorld	Founder & CEO	MakeLoveNotPorn, IfWeRanTheWorld, Behance
58	**Georgia Garinois-Melenikiotou**	USA	SVP Corporate Marketing	The Estée Lauder Companies	SVP of Corporate Marketing	The Estée Lauder Companies
59	**Matthew Godfrey**	SINGAPORE	President	Y&R Asia	President	Y&R Asia
60	**Seth Godin**	USA	Author & Entrepreneur	Squidoo	Author & Entrepreneur	
61	**Julia Gometz**	USA	Founder & Author	The Brandful Workforce	Founder & Author	The Brandful Workforce
62	**Scott Goodson**	USA	CEO + Founder	StrawberryFrog	CEO + Founder	StrawberryFrog
63	**Tom Goodwin**	USA	Founder	Tomorrow Group	SVP Strategy & Innovation	Havas Media NA
64	**Bob Greenberg**	USA	Executive Director	Advertising Week Experience (AWE)	Executive Director	Advertising Week Experience (AWE)
65	**Loren Grossman**	USA	Chief Global Strategy Officer	RAPP	Chief Experience Officer & President of the CXM	Annalect
66	**Craig Gugel**	USA	President/CEO	Gugelplex TV, Inc.	President/CEO	Gugelplex TV, Inc.
67	**Scott Hagedorn**	USA	CEO	Annalect	CEO	Annalect
68	**Alex Hall**	USA	President, The Americas	TigerSpike	President, The Americas	Tigerspike
69	**Tim Hanlon**	USA	Founder & CEO	The Vertere Group, LLC	Founder & CEO	The Vertere Group, LLC
70	**Sam Hanna**	USA	International Director	Athenaeum Worldwide	International Director	Athenaeum Worldwide
71	**Thomas Harrison**	USA	Chairman, DAS	Omnicom Group	Chairman Emeritus, DAS	Omnicom Group
72	**Carl Hartman**	USA	E-Commerce Practice Lead	Ogilvy & Mather	Global Client Leader	Geometry Global NA, WPP
73	**Bill Harvey**	USA	Vice Chair, Chief	TRA, Inc. Research Officer	CEO	Bill Harvey Consulting, Inc., The Human Effectiveness Institute
74	**Karl Heiselman**	USA	CEO	Wolff Olins	Senior Director	Apple

			AT TIME OF CONTRIBUTION (VARIES)		AT TIME OF PRESS (JULY 2015)	
NO.	**NAME**	**COUNTRY**	**TITLE**	**ORGANIZATION**	**TITLE**	**ORGANIZATION**
75	**Alain Heureux**	BELGIUM	President & CEO	IAB Europe	Founder & Partner	Creative Ring, Your Own Lab
76	**Jason Hill**	USA	Director, Global Media Strategy	GE	Global Head of Media	BlackRock
77	**Nancy Hill**	USA	President & CEO	4As	President & CEO	4As
78	**Donna Hoffman**	USA	Professor; Co-Director	University of California, Riverside; Sloan Center for Internet Retailing	Louis Rosenfeld Distinguished Scholar & Professor of Marketing	The George Washington University School of Business
79	**Mark Holden**	UK	Strategy & Planning Director	PHD UK	WW Strategy & Planning Director	PHD Media
80	**David Hoo**	USA	Principal	Effective Marketing Mangement	Principal	Effective Marketing Mangement
81	**Michael Hussey**	USA	CEO	PeekAnalytics	CEO & Founder	StatSocial
82	**Leszek Izdebski**	USA	Managing Director, Internet Business Solutions Group Global Media & Entertainment Practice	Cisco Systems, Inc.	Managing Director, Service Provider Transformation Group	Cisco Systems, Inc.
83	**Michael Jacobs**	USA	Chief Digital Officer	Voyr	Managing Partner, Executive Creative Director; Chief Creative Officer	Our True North; iRGONOMIC
84	**John Philip Jones**	USA	Emeritus Professor of Advertising	Syracuse University	Emeritus Professor of Advertising	Syracuse University
85	**John Jordan**	USA	Clinical Professor, Supply Chain & Information Systems	Penn State Smeal College of Business	Clinical Professor, Supply Chain & Information Systems	Penn State Smeal College of Business
86	**David Jowett**	UK	President	Cossette Media	President, Europe	DAC Group
87	**Max Kalehoff**	USA	VP Product Marketing	Syncapse	CMO	SocialCode
88	**Bob Kantor**	USA	Chief Marketing & Business Development Officer	MDC Partners	Chief Marketing & Business Development Officer	MDC Partners
89	**Michael Kassan**	USA	Chairman & CEO	MediaLink	Chairman & CEO	MediaLink
90	**Gareth Kay**	USA	Chief Strategy	Goodby Silverstein Officer/ Associate	Co-Founder & Partners	Chapter SF
91	**Christopher Kenton**	USA	CEO & Founder	SocialRep	CEO & Founder	SocialRep
92	**Thomas Hong-Tack Kim**	KOREA	Executive Creative Director	Cheil Worldwide Korea	Former Executive Creative Director	Cheil Worldwide Korea
93	**Yaakov Kimelfeld**	USA	Chief Research Officer	Kantar Media Compete	Chief Research Officer	Merkle
94	**Jon King**	UK	Managing Director	Story Worldwide	Content & Marketing Consultancy	Content Corporation
95	**Ravi Kiran**	INDIA	Co-Founder & Managing Partner	Friends of Ambition	Co-Founder & CEO	DazzleToday, VentureNursery, Friends of Ambition
96	**Karsten Koed**	DENMARK	Managing Partner & Chairman	Gorm Larsen & Zornig	Managing Partner & Chairman	Gorm Larsen & Zornig
97	**Peter Koeppel**	USA	Founder & President	Koeppel Direct	Founder & President	Koeppel Direct
98	**Akihiko Kubo**	JAPAN	EVP	Ogilvy & Mather GK	Chairman, Group Repre-sentitive	Ogilvy & Mather Japan
99	**Claudia Lagunas**	USA	Marketing Director	PepsiCo	Senior Director Global Digital Marketing	Visa
100	**Alok Lall**	INDIA	Executive Director	McCann Worldgroup	Executive Director	McCann Worldgroup
101	**Steve Landsberg**	USA	Founding Partner & Chief Creative Officer	Grok	Founding Partner & Chief Creative Officer	Grok
102	**Laurent Larguinat**	BELGIUM	Director, Mars Marketing Lab	Mars Inc.	Director, Mars Marketing Lab	Mars Inc.
103	**Alessandra Lariu**	USA	Co-Founder	SheSays	Executive Creative Director; Co-Founder	frog design; She Says
104	**Denise Larson**	USA	President	Leap Media Investments	President	Leap Media Investments
105	**Everlyn Lee**	CHINA	Research Analyst	Z Graduate Program, Wunderman	Digital Planner	McCann Health Greater China
106	**Richard Lee**	CHINA	CMO	PepsiCo China	CMO	PepsiCo China
107	**Noam Lemelshtrich Latar**	ISRAEL	Founding Dean	Sammy Ofer School of Com-munication, IDC Herzliya	Founding Dean	Sammy Ofer School of Communication, IDC Herzliya
108	**Yoram Levanon**	ISRAEL	Chairman & Founder	Exaudios	Chief Science Officer	Beyond Verbal Communication

			AT TIME OF CONTRIBUTION (VARIES)		AT TIME OF PRESS (JULY 2015)	
NO.	**NAME**	**COUNTRY**	**TITLE**	**ORGANIZATION**	**TITLE**	**ORGANIZATION**
109	**Ayal Levin**	ISRAEL	Lead Digital Strategist	McCann Tel-Aviv	Strategy Associate	Designit
110	**Doug Levy**	USA	CEO	MEplusYOU	CEO; CEO; Chairman of the Board	TapGoods, MEplusYOU Agency, Conscious Capitalism, Inc.
111	**Ruth Lim**	SINGAPORE	Z Graduate	Wunderman	Digital Strategist	Wunderman
112	**Wonya Lucas**	USA	President & CEO	TV One	President & CEO	Public Broadcasting Atlanta
113	**Camila Lucena**	BRAZIL	Account Coordinator	Wunderman	Account Executive	BNP Paribas Cardif
114	**Carl Marci**	USA	CEO & Chief Science Officer	Innerscope Research, Inc.	Chief Neuroscientist	Nielsen Consumer Neuroscience
115	**Mzamo Masito**	SOUTH AFRICA	Managing Executive: Brand & Comms Africa Group	Vodacom	Managing Executive:	Vodacom Brand & Comms Africa Group
116	**Michael Maslansky**	USA	CEO	Maslansky Luntz + Partners	CEO	Maslansky Luntz + Partners
117	**Bill Maurer**	USA	Dean of the School of Social Sciences & Professor	University of California, Irvine	Dean of the School of Social Sciences & Professor	University of California, Irvine
118	**Pearse McCabe**	USA	CEO	Dragon Rouge New York	CEO	Dragon Rouge New York
119	**Duncan McCall**	USA	CEO & Co-Founder	PlaceIQ	CEO & Co-Founder	PlaceIQ
120	**Bob McCurdy**	USA	President	Katz Marketing Solutions	Consultant	Katz Radio Group
121	**Walter McDowell**	USA	Assoc. Professor of Communications	University of Miami	Professor Emeritus	University of Miami
122	**Jonathan Mildenhall**	USA	VP of Global Advertising Strategy	The Coca-Cola Company	CMO	Airbnb
123	**John Miller**	USA	President & Founder	Scribewise	President & Founder	Scribewise
124	**David Moore**	USA	Chairman & CEO	24/7 Media, Inc.	Chairman; President	Xaxis; WPP Digital
125	**Robert Morais**	USA	Principal	WeinmanSchnee Morais	Principal	Weinman Schnee Morais
126	**Mark Morris**	USA	Former Chairman	Bates North America	International Partner; Trustee	The FiftySeven; The Bogliasco Foundation
127	**Nigel Morris**	USA	CEO	Aegis Media Americas and EMEA	CEO	Dentsu Aegis Americas and EMEA
128	**Tom Morton**	USA	Chief Strategy Officer	Goodby Silverstein & Partners	Director of Strategy	co: collective
129	**Howard Moskowitz**	USA	President	Moskowitz Jacobs Inc.	Founding Partner and Chief Scientist	Mind Genomics Advisors
130	**Jo Muse**	USA	CEO	Muse Communications, Inc.	CEO	Muse Communications, Inc.
131	**George Musi**	USA	Head of Cross-Media Analytics	DG-Mediamind	Managing Partner, Analytics, Insights & Attribution	Mindshare
132	**Miles Nadal**	USA	CEO	MDC Partners	Former CEO	MDC Partners
133	**Evelyn Neill**	USA	Executive Creative Director	Doremus	Chief Creative Officer	Doremus
134	**Bruce Neve**	USA	CEO	Starcom MediaVest Group	Former CEO	Starcom MediaVest Group
135	**Ken Nisch**	USA	Architect & Chairman	JGA	Chairman	JGA
136	**Rob Norman**	USA	Chief Digital Officer Global	GroupM	Chief Digital Officer Global	GroupM
137	**Tom Novak**	USA	Albert O. Steffey Professor of Marketing; Co-Director	University of California, Riverside; Sloan Center for Internet Retailing	Denit Trust Distinguished Scholar & Professor of Marketing	The George Washington University School of Business
138	**Ralph Oliva**	USA	Executive Director of IBSM & Marketing	Penn State Smeal College of Business	Executive Director of IBSM & Marketing Professor	Penn State Smeal College of Business
139	**Shelly Palmer**	USA	Managing Director	Advanced Media Ventures Group	Managing Director, Digital Media Group; Managing Director; Commentator/Host	Landmark Ventures; Advanced Media Ventures Group LLC; Fox Television
140	**Alessandro Panella**	GERMANY	Managing Director Grey	Group Worldwide	Chief Strategy Officer	Grey Germany
141	**Daniel Parmar**	USA	Director, Digital Strategy	Merkle	Director, Digital Strategy	Merkle
142	**Robert Passikoff**	USA	Founder & President	Brand Keys, Inc.	Founder & President	Brand Keys, Inc.
143	**Greg Paull**	CHINA	Co-Founder & Principal	R3	Co-Founder & Principal	R3
144	**Bryan Pearson**	CANADA	President & CEO	LoyaltyOne	President	LoyaltyOne at Alliance Data
145	**Mark Pollard**	USA	VP Brand Strategy	Big Spaceship	EVP, Director of NY Planning	Edelman
146	**Faith Popcorn**	USA	Founder & CEO	Faith Popcorn's Brain-Reserve	Founder & CEO	Faith Popcorn's BrainReserve

			AT TIME OF CONTRIBUTION (VARIES)		AT TIME OF PRESS (JULY 2015)	
NO.	**NAME**	**COUNTRY**	**TITLE**	**ORGANIZATION**	**TITLE**	**ORGANIZATION**
147	**Chandramouli Prasad**	INDIA	VP Client Servicing	Cheil Worldwide	Client Service Director	FITCH
148	**Hamish Pringle**	UK	Partner	Pringle and Pringle LLP	Non Executive Director	23 Red
149	**Scott Puopolo**	USA	VP, Global Practices Lead, Internet Business Solutions Group	Cisco Systems, Inc.	VP, Global Lead, Service Provider Transformation Group	Cisco Systems, Inc.
150	**Isabelle Quevilly**	UK	Head of Digital	venturethree	Director, Brand Services	Brilliant Noise (UK)
151	**Zain Raj**	USA	CEO	Hyper Marketing	Chairman & CEO	Shapiro+Raj
152	**Thomas Zoega Ramsoy**	DENMARK	Professor of Marketing	Copenhagen Business School	Founder & CEO; Adjunct Faculty	Neurons Inc; Singularity University
153	**Anant Rangaswami**	INDIA	Editor	Haymarket Publishing	Editor	Storyboard
154	**Arvind Rangaswamy**	USA	Professor of Marketing	Penn State Smeal College of Business	Professor of Marketing	Penn State Smeal College of Business
155	**Annaliese Rapp**	USA	Corporate Communications Coordinator	72andSunny	Strategist	72andSunny
156	**Steve Rappaport**	USA	Knowledge Solutions Director	Advertising Research Foundation (ARF)	Senior Consultant; Senior Digital Advisor	Stephen D. Rappaport Consulting LLC; Sunstar
157	**Paul Reilly**	CANADA	SVP, Executive Managing Director	BBDO Toronto	SVP, Executive Managing Director	BBDO Toronto
158	**Vinicius Reis**	BRAZIL	Group Account Director/ New Business Director	Africa Propoganda	Partner, Chief Operating Officer	CP+B Brasil
159	**Lynda Resnick**	USA	Co-Chairman	Roll Global	Vice Chair & Co-Owner	The Wonderful Company
160	**Robbert Rietbroek**	AUSTRALIA	Managing Director & CEO; Corporate VP	Kimberly-Clark Australia Australia and New Zealand; Kimberly-Clark Corporation	Managing Director & CEO; Corporate VP	Kimberly-Clark Austrailia and New Zealand; Kimberly-Clark Corporation
161	**Martin Riley**	FRANCE	CMO	Pernod Ricard	CMO	Pernod Ricard
162	**Malcolm Roberts**	CANADA	Founding Partner	Corktown Seed Co.	Founding Partner	Corktown Seed Co.
163	**Lynne Robinson**	UK	Research Director	IPA	Research Director	IPA
164	**Richard Robinson**	UK	Managing Partner	Oystercatchers	Managing Partner	Oystercatchers
165	**Hayes Roth**	USA	CMO	Landor	Partner; Principal & Founder	Relationship Audits; HA Roth Consulting LLC
166	**Randall Rothenberg**	USA	President & CEO	Interactive Advertising Bureau (IAB)	President & CEO	Interactive Advertising Bureau (IAB)
167	**Joel Rubinson**	USA	President & Founder	Rubinson Partners	President & Founder	Rubinson Partners
168	**Vincent Schiavone**	USA	Chairman & CEO	ListenLogic	Founder & CEO	AKUDA LLC, ListenLogic
169	**Alan Schulman**	USA	VP, Chief Creative Officer	SapientNitro	National Director, Creative Experience & Content Marketing	Deloitte Digital
170	**Don E. Schultz**	USA	Professor Emeritus in Service	The Medill School, Northwestern University	Professor Emeritus in Service	The Medill School, Northwestern University
171	**Doc Searls**	USA	Author	UCSB	Instigator	ProjectVRM
172	**George Shababb**	USA	President	Kantar Media Audiences	Board Member	SQAD LLC
173	**Ron Shachar**	ISRAEL	Dean	Arison School of Business, IDC Herzliya	Professor; Professor	Duke; Arison School of Business, IDC Herzliya
174	**Saurabh Sharma**	CHINA	Planning Partner	Ogilvy & Mather	Head of Planning	Ogilvy & Mather Beijing
175	**Mike Shaw**	USA	VP Sales, Media	comScore, Inc.	VP Sales, Media	comScore, Inc.
176	**Amy Shea**	USA	Global Director of Brand Development	Brand Keys, Inc.	President	Amy Shea Consultancy, Inc.
177	**Howard Sherman**	USA	Global CEO	Doremus	Global CEO	Doremus
178	**Baba Shetty**	USA	Chief Strategy & Media Officer	Hill Holiday	Chief Strategy & Media Officer	Digitas
179	**Maria Sipka**	USA	CEO, Founder	Linqia	CEO, Founder	Linqia
180	**Calle Sjoenell**	SWEDEN	CEO	Ogilvy & Mather New York	CEO	Lowe Brindfors
181	**JR Smith**	SWITZERLAND	CEO	AVG Technology	Executive Chairman; Partner	NURO; Evolution Equity
182	**J. Walker Smith**	USA	Executive Chairman	The Futures Company	Executive Chairman	The Futures Company
183	**Lawrence Snapp**	USA	Principal Business Strategist	Microsoft	Principal Business Strategist	Microsoft
184	**Herb Sorensen**	USA	Scientific Advisor	TNS Global	Adjunct Senior Research Fellow; Scientific Advisor	Ehrenberg-Bass Institute for Marketing Science; TNS Global
185	**Pierre Soued**	UAE	CEO; Regional Managing Director	Havas Middle East; Havas Worldwide Middle East	CEO; Regional Managing Director	Havas Middle East; Havas Worldwide Middle East

			AT TIME OF CONTRIBUTION (VARIES)		AT TIME OF PRESS (JULY 2015)	
NO.	**NAME**	**COUNTRY**	**TITLE**	**ORGANIZATION**	**TITLE**	**ORGANIZATION**
186	**Horst Stipp**	USA	EVP, Global Business Strategy	Advertising Research Foundation (ARF)	EVP, Global Business Strategy	Advertising Research Foundation (ARF)
187	**Steve Stoute**	USA	Founder/CEO	Translation	Founder/CEO	Translation
188	**Rory Sutherland**	UK	Executive Creative Director; Vice-Chairman	OgilvyOne; Ogilvy Group UK	Executive Creative Director; Vice-Chairman	OgilvyOne; Ogilvy Group UK
189	**Michelle Taite**	USA	Associate Brand Manager	Unilever	Senior Global Brand Manager	Unilever
190	**Kai Hui Tan**	SINGAPORE	Z Graduate	Wunderman	User Interface Developer	Wunderman
191	**Art Tauder**	USA	Founding Partner	Thunderhouse	Founding Partner	Thunderhouse
192	**Sanjay Thapar**	INDIA	CEO	Bates India	CEO	India Today
193	**Richard Ting**	USA	EVP, Global Executive Creative Director	R/GA	EVP, Global Chief Experience Officer	R/GA
194	**Rishad Tobaccowala**	USA	Chief Strategy & Innovation Officer	VivaKi	Chief Strategist	Publicis Group
195	**Mark Tomblin**	CANADA	Chief Strategy Officer	TAXI	Chief Strategy Officer	Taxi
196	**Amelia Torode**	UK	Partner, Strategy/Innovation Head	VCCP	Chief Strategy Officer	TBWA London
197	**Zachary Treuhaft**	USA	Managing Director	VML New York	Chief Digital Officer	Grey Group
198	**Vicente Valjalo de Ramón**	CHILE	Founding Partner	Objectivo	CEO	JWT Chile
199	**Steven Van Belleghem**	BELGIUM	Advisor, Author, Professor	Vlerick Business School	Partner	Nexxworks
200	**Duane Varan**	AUSTRALIA	Director	Audience Labs, Murdoch University	CEO	MediaScience
201	**Venu Vasudevan**	USA	Murdoch University	Motorola Mobility	Senior Director, Media Analytics & Systems	ARRIS
202	**Uli Veigel**	GERMANY	Chairman & CEO	Grey G2 Group Germany & CEE	EVP	Grey Group New York & Frankfurt
203	**Marc Violo**	SINGAPORE	Senior Digital Lab Manager	Ogilvy & Mather	Partner	K1ND
204	**Kip Voytek**	USA	SVP	MDC Partners	CEO; SVP, Director of Digital Innovation	Rumble Fox; MDC Partners
205	**Watts Wacker**	USA	Founder, Director	Firstmatter	Founder, Director	Firstmatter
206	**Barry Wacksman**	USA	EVP, Global Chief Growth Officer	R/GA	EVP, Global Chief Growth Officer	R/GA
207	**Khayyam Wakil**	USA	Chief Innovation Officer	Immersive Media	Chief Belief Officer	Thynk Taynk
208	**Justin Williams**	USA	President	nuMVC	President	nuMVC
209	**Sally Williams**	USA	Global President, Business Development & Client Relations, DAS	Omnicom Group	Global President, Business Development & Client Relations, DAS	Omnicom Group
210	**John Willshire**	UK	Founder	Smithery	Founder	Smithery
211	**Russell Winer**	USA	Professor of Marketing	Stern School of Business, NYU	Professor of Marketing	Stern School of Business, NYU
212	**John Winsor**	USA	CEO	Victors and Spoils	CEO	Victors and Spoils
213	**Richard Wise**	UK	Global Head of Strategy	G2 Worldwide	Brand Anthropologist	Geometry Global
214	**Ian Wishingrad**	USA	Senior Manager	Vimeo	Founder & Creative Director	BigEyedWish
215	**Paul Worthington**	USA	Strategic Advisor	Wolff Olins	Independent Advisor	Brand Specialist
216	**Michael Wu**	USA	Chief Scientist	Lithium Technologies	Chief Scientist	Lithium Technologies
217	**Faris Yakob**	USA	Chief Innovation Officer	MDC Partners	Founder & Principal	Genius Steals LLC
218	**Nikao Yang**	USA	SVP of Business Development & Marketing	AdColony	SVP of Global Marketing & Business Development	Opera Mediaworks
219	**Judy Yeh**	USA	Global Media Director	Mars Inc	Global Media & Integrated Marketing Executive Director	SC Johnson
220	**Chris Yeh**	USA	VP Marketing	PB Works	VP Marketing; Co-Founder and Partner	PBworks; Allied Talent
221	**Terry Young**	USA	Founder & CEO	Sparks & Honey	Founder & CEO	Sparks & Honey
222	**Ken Younglieb**	USA	Senior Writer	The Wonderful Agency (formerly known as Firestation Agency)	Associate Creative Director	Apple
223	**Shelley Zalis**	USA	CEO	Ipsos OTX	CEO	Ipsos OTX
224	**Artem Zhiganov**	RUSSIA	Head of Planning	Red Keds	Brand Planner	Independent

Appendix 2
Advertising 2020 Contributors: Countries

1	Australia	12	Japan
2	Belgium	13	Korea
3	Brazil	14	Russia
4	Canada	15	China
5	Chile	16	South Africa
6	China	17	Spain
7	Denmark	18	Sweden
8	France	19	Switzwerland
9	Germany	20	UAE
10	India	21	UK
11	Israel	22	USA

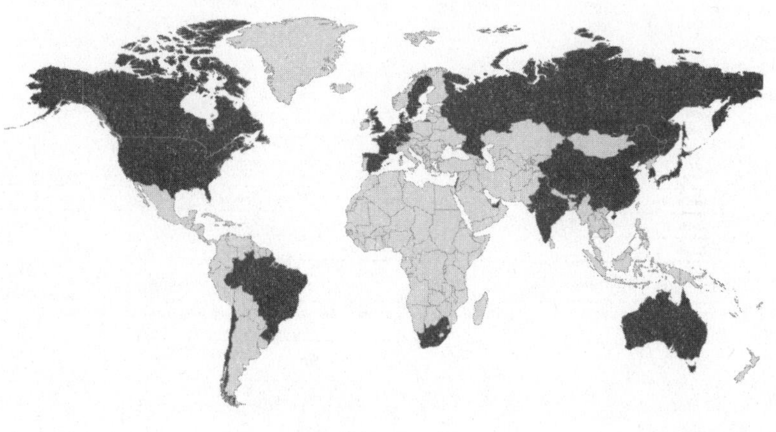

Appendix 2 Advertising 2020 Contributors: Organizations (Former and Current)

A
AAR Partners
AdColony
Advanced Media Ventures Group
Advertising Research Foundation (ARF)
Advertising Week Experience (AWE)
Aegis Media Americas and EMEA
Africa Propoganda
Airbnb
AKUDA LLC
Allied Talent
American Association of Advertising Agencies (4As)
Amy J Weiner LLC
Amy Shea Consultancy, Inc.
Anagram LLC
Annalect
Apple
ARF
Arison School of Business at IDC Herzliya
ARRIS
Athenaeum Worldwide
Audience Labs, Murdoch University
AVG Technology

B
Bates India
Bates North America
BBDO Toronto
BBH
BBH Labs
BBH London
Behance
Beyond Verbal Communication
Big Spaceship
BigEyedWish
Bill Harvey Consulting, Inc.
BlackRock
Blue Focus Marketing
BNP Paribas Cardif
Brand Keys, Inc.
Brand Specialist
Brilliant Noise (UK)

C
Cato Consulting Group
Chapter SF
Cheil Worldwide
Cheil Worldwide Korea
Cisco Systems, Inc.
co: collective
Cole & Weber United
comScore, Inc.
Connecting the Dots
Conscious Capitalism, Inc.
Content Corporation
Copenhagen Business School
Corktown Seed Co.
Cossette Media
COTY Inc.
CP+B Brasil
Creative Orchestra
Creative Ring, Your Own Lab

D
DAC Group
Dazzle Today
Deakin University
Dean Crutchfield Associates
Deloitte Digital
Dentsu Aegis Americas and EMEA
Designit
DG-Mediamind
DHL Global Forwarding Asia-Pacific
Digital Advisory Board
Digital Intelligence at Dstillery
Digitas
Dimensions Consultancy
Doremus
dotJWT
Dragon Rouge New York
Duke

E
Edelman
Edelman NY
Effective Marketing Mangement
Ehrenberg-Bass Institute for Marketing Science
Enervee
Euro RSCG Worldwide
Evolution Equity
Exaudios

F
Faith Popcorn's BrainReserveField Consulting
The Fifty Seven
Firstmatter
FITCH

Fox Television
Friends of Ambition
frog design

G
G2 Worldwide
GE
Genius Steals LLC
Geometry Global
Geometry Global NA
Goodby Silverstein & Partners
Gorm Larsen & Zornig
Grainey Pictures
Grey G2 Group Germany & CEE
Grey Group New York & Frankfurt
Grey Group Worldwide
Grok
GroupM
Gugelplex TV, Inc.

H
HA Roth Consulting LLC
HarperCollins Publishers
Havas Media
Havas Middle East
Havas Worldwide
Haymarket Publishing
Henley Business School, UK
Herd Consultancy
Hill Holiday
HL Group
Hyper Marketing

I
IAB Europe
IfWeRanTheWorld
Immersive Media
Independent
India Today
Innerscope Research, Inc.
Interactive Advertising Bureau (IAB)
Interbrand
IPA
Ipsos OTX
iRGONOMIC

J
JGA
john st. advertising
JWT Chile

K
K1ND
Kantar Media Audiences
Kantar Media Compete
Kantar Media North America
Katz Marketing Solutions
Katz Radio Group
Kimberly-Clark Australia and New Zealand; Kimberly-Clark Corporation
Koeppel Direct
KPMG Boston

L
Landmark Ventures/ShellyPalmer
Landor
Leap Media Investments
Linqia
ListenLogic
Lithium Technologies
Lowe Brindfors
LoyaltyOne at Alliance Data
Lumen Research

M
Machinima
MakeLoveNotPorn
Mars Inc
Maslansky Luntz + Partners
McCann Health Greater China
McCann Tel-Aviv
McCann Worldgroup
mCerwin Consulting
McKinsey & Company, Boston
McKinsey & Company, Brussels
MDC Partners
MEC
Media6Degrees
MediaLink
MediaScience
Meltwater Consulting
MEplusYOU
Mercer
Merkle
Microsoft
Millward Brown South Africa
Mind Genomics Advisors
Mindshare
Mirum Agency
Momentum Worldwide (McCann Worldgroup)
Monash University
Moskowitz Jacobs Inc.
Motorola Mobility
Muse Communications, Inc.

N
Neurons Inc
New Dimensions Consultancy
Nexxworks
Nickel Labs
Nielsen
Nielsen Consumer Neuroscience
nuMVC
NURO

O
Objectivo
Ogilvy & Mather
Ogilvy & Mather Beijing
Ogilvy & Mather Japan

Ogilvy & Mather New York
OgilvyOne; Ogilvy Group UK
Oglivy & Mather GK
Omnicom Group
Opera Mediaworks
Our True North
Oystercatchers

P

PBworks
PeekAnalytics
Penn State Smeal College of Business
PepsiCo
PepsiCo China
Pernod Ricard
PHD Media
PHD UK
PlaceIQ
Pringle and Pringle LLP
ProjectVRM
Public Broadcasting Atlanta
Publicis

R

R/GA
R3
RAPP
Razorfish
Red Keds
RED The Agency
rekap Inc.
Relationship Audits
Rentrak
Rubinson Partners
Rumble Fox

S

Sammy Ofer School of Communication, IDC Herzliya
SapientNitro
SC Johnson
Scribewise
Sears Holdings Corporation
72andSunny
Shapiro+Raj
SheSays
Singularity University
Smithery
SocialCode
SocialRep
Sparks & Honey
SQAD LLC
Squidoo
Starcom MediaVest Group
StatSocial
Stephen D. Rappaport Consulting LLC
Stern School of Business, NYU
Story Worldwide
Storyboard
StrawberryFrog
Sunstar
SurveyMonkey
Syncapse
Syracuse University

T

TapGoods
TAXI
TBWA London
Teamstream Productions
The Bogliasco Foundation
The Brandful Workforce
The BUY UP Index
The Coca-Cola Company
The Estée Lauder Companies
The Futures Company
The George Washington University School of Business
The Human Effectiveness Institute
The Medill School, Northwestern University
The Vertere Group, LLC
The Wonderful Company (formerly known as Roll Global)
Thomas Burkhardt Branding & Strategy
Thunderhouse
Thynk Taynk
TigerSpike
TNS Global
Tomorrow Group
TRA, Inc.
Translation
TV One
24/7 Media, Inc.
23 Red

U

UCSB
Unilever
University of California, Irvine
University of California, Riverside; Sloan Center for Internet Retailing
University of Miami

V

VCCP
VentureNursery
Venturethree
Vice Media Group
Vicomte LLC
Victors and Spoils
VigLink
Vimeo
VIRTUE Worldwide
Visa
Vitamin W
VivaKi
Vlerick Business School

VML New York
Vodacom
Voyr

W
We Support Creators
Weinman Schnee Morais
Wieden + Kennedy
Wolff Olins
WPP
WPP Digital
Wunderman

X
Xaxis

Y
Y&R

Appendix 3
WFoA Global Advisory Board

Doug Alexander
President, Actua

Ryan Anderson
Director of Marketing, ESPN

Bob Arnold
Digital Media & Strategy Lead, NA Google

Dave Balter
Head of Transactions, Pluralsight

Paul Bascobert
President of Local, Yodle

Jeff Bell
CEO LegalShield Partner NCT Ventures; Chairman of the Board of Directors DOMedia

Celia Berk
Chief Talent Officer, Y&R Group

Saul Berman
Partner & VP, IBM Global Business Services

Les Binet
Head of Effectiveness Adam & Eve DDB; Founder, DDB Matrix

Thomas Burkhardt
Global Brand Builder, Thomas Burkhardt Branding & Strategy

Alex Butler
Managing Director, The EarthWorks

Lou Capozzi
President, PRSA Foundation

Yubo Chen
Professor, Marketing Dept. Deputy Chair, Tsinghua University

Kirk Cheyfitz
CEO/Chief Editorial Officer, Story Worldwide

Howard Courtemanche
Global CEO, J. Walter Thompson Health

Phil Cowdell
North American CEO & Global COO, MediaCom

Mike Donahue
Former EVP, 4As

Tomas Emmers
VP Consumer & Market Insights, Homecare Unilever

Andrew Essex
Former CEO/Vice Chairman, Droga5

Mike Follett
Managing Director, Lumen Research

Matt Freeman
Partner, Bain Capital

Robert Friedman
CEO, Bungalow Horizons

Gayle Fuguitt
President & CEO, Advertising Research Foundation (ARF)

Gian Fulgoni
Chairman Emeritus, comScore Inc.

Bob Garfield
Co-host, NPR's On the Media

Georgia Garinois-Melenikiotou
SVP Corporate Marketing, The Estée Lauder Companies

Vaasu Gavarasana
Head of Digital Marketing, AXA

Matthew Godfrey
President, Y&R Asia

Mark H. Goldstein
Managing Partner, Efficient Capacity LLC

Scott Goodson
CEO, StrawberryFrog

Sanjay Govil
Chairman, Infinite Computer Solutions

Gillian Graham
CEO, Institute of Communication Agencies, Toronto, Canada

Richard Guest
President, North America Tribal DDB Worldwide

Alan Hallberg
CMO, BAE Systems Applied Intelligence

Tim Hanlon
Founder & CEO, Vertere Group

Karl Isaac
Head of Brand Strategy & Innovation, Adobe

Paran Johar
CEO & Founder, Mobile Media Summit

George John
Chairman & Founder, Rocketfuel

Max Kalehoff
CMO, SocialCode

Madhukar Kamath
Group CEO & Managing Director, DDB Mudra Group

Michael Kassan
Chairman & CEO, MediaLink

Ed Keller
CEO, The Keller Fay Group

Courtney Kelso
VP Enterprise, Growth Strategy American Express

Stephen Kim
General Manager, Global Creative Solutions Microsoft

Karsten Koed
Chairman & Partner, Gorm Larsen & Zornig

Akihiko Kubo
Group Representative, O&M Group Japan

Laurent Larguinat
Director, Mars Marketing Lab

Alessandra Lariu
Executive Creative Director frog; Co-Founder, SheSays, Broadli

Denise Larson
Principal & Co-Founder, NewMediaMetrics Inc.

William Lauder
Executive Chairman, The Estée Lauder Companies

Jim Lecinski
VP Customer Solutions for the Americas, Google

James R. Lee
Founder, Lee & Partners

Meredith Kopit Levien
EVP Advertising, The New York Times

Tara Walpert Levy
Managing Director, Americas Agency Solutions, Google

Sébastien Lion
Global Consumer & Market Insight Director, Mars Petcare

Christopher Lyons
President/CRO Marketing Group, Napco Media

Rob Malcolm
Chairman AMA; Executive in Residence Center for Consumer Insight & Marketing Strategy, McCombs School of Business

Mark Morris
International Partner The FiftySeven; Trustee, The Bogliasco Foundation

Tom Morton
Director of Strategy, co: collective

Graham Mudd
Director, Ads Product Marketing, Facebook

Alan Murray
Partner, Coriolis Ventures [Media 6°]

Miles S. Nadal
Chairman & CEO, Peerage Capital Group

Wes Nichols
CEO, MarketShare

Martin Nitsche
President, German Direct Marketing Association; Managing Partner, Solveta Ltd

Rob Norman
Chief Digital Officer Global GroupM; Non-Executive Director, BBC Global News

Kelly O'Keefe
Professor & Chair of Creative Brand Management VCU Brandcenter; Chief Creative Strategy Officer, PadillaCRT

Jim Oliver
VP Member & Business Intelligence, Sam's Club

Joseph T. Plummer
Adjunct Professor, Columbia Business School; President, Sunstar Foundation

Chuck Porter
Chairman CP+B; Chief Strategist, MDC Partners

Penry Price
VP Marketing Solutions, LinkedIn

Babs Rangaiah
VP Global Media Innovation, Unilever

Mitchell Reichgut
CEO, Jun Group

Gary Reisman
CEO & Co-Founder, LEAP Media Investments

Randall Rothenberg
President & CEO, IAB

Mark Samuels
CMO, SEI

Alejandro Segura
EVP (ret.), Grupo Vale Euro RSCG Mexico

Byron Sharp
Director, Ehrenberg-Bass Institute; Professor of Marketing Science, University of South Australia

Baba Shetty
Chief Strategy & Media Officer, Digitas

Andres Siefken
Principal, The New England Consulting Group

Clive Sirkin
CMO, Kimberly Clark Corporation

Jim Speros
EVP & Chief Brand Acceleration Officer, Fidelity Investments

Daniel Stein
Founder & CEO, EVB

Mark Stewart
EVP Chief Strategy Officer, Townsquare Media

Raymond Tao
Senior VP of Global Marketing Partnerships, NBA

Rishad Tobaccowala
Chief Strategist, Publicis Groupe

Uli Veigel
EVP & Managing Director of Global Client Services, Grey Group New York & Frankfurt

Roel de-Vries
Corporate VP, Global Head of Marketing, Communications & Brand Strategy, Nissan

Jack Wakshlag
Chairperson, US Advisory Board, Ehrenberg-Bass Institute

Tristan Walker
Founder & CEO, Walker & Company Brands

Kevin Werbach
Associate Professor, The Wharton School

John Winsor
CEO & Co-Founder, Victors & Spoils

Shelley Zalis
Chairwoman TFQ Ventures; Founder, The Girls' Lounge

Appendix 4
Planning and Conducting an Experiment

Below, we expand on the process of experimentation we discussed in Chapter 7, outlining the 10 steps that will ensure your experiment is a success. Remember, "success" does not mean positive results, it means results we can learn and iterate from. We hope this expanded section will help you think through your question and develop the most effective and exciting experiment for your organization.

We also suggest you consider a free online Coursera course (Coursera.org), such as Design Thinking for Business Innovation (offered through the University of Virginia), or Interaction Design (offered through the University of California) to develop your understanding and experience with experimentation.

1. **Decide on the Objective of the Experiment**
   The number and complexity of questions facing today's advertisers is immense. Whether you are trying to determine optimal budget allocation, gain a competitive edge through improved product design, decide whether to explore new marketing channels, or make customer service more efficient, applying principles of adaptive experimentation.

2. **Innovative Experimental Variable (ATP, R.A.V.E.S., M.A.D.E.^{5}, etc.)**
   Use the All Touchpoint Value Creation Model to identify the variables with which one should experiment. First, modify the model based on the unique characteristics of the firm: What touchpoints are frequently used? Which ones remain elusive? Which do you normally overlook? Assess the modified model against what the firm is doing now, and identify the gaps between the "ideal" and the current delivery model. Once the gaps are identified, evaluate them and decide where improvement would yield the greatest benefit. Use those as the experimental variables. We recommend using multiple experimental variables at once.

3. **Select a Control Group**
   Having a control is critical to help establish causality. Effective experimental designs compare a "control" group, selected through randomization, with one or more "treatment" groups. Randomization is necessary to ensure that those in the control group are similar to those in the test groups. Make sure to use a large enough sample of test subjects so that differences in performance between the two groups can causally linked with the differences in test conditions. Expose the control group

to normal conditions and the treatment group to a different condition. Good experiments will have a concurrent control group—that is, the control group will be tested alongside the treatment group. Comparing results from a control group with those from a treatment group at different times may produce inaccurate results.

4. **Decide on the Unit of Analysis (Country, State, City, Store, Individual)**
Experiments can be conducted at any level in different countries or states, cities within and across countries, stores, or at the individual level. For example, if you are testing the same creative executions across multiple cities, you might find that a certain type of execution fails or succeeds geographically. For the next phase of the experiment you could allocate more budget toward the sites that appear promising.

5. **Decide on the Performance Measures and Length of Experiment**
What are you looking to measure—traditional AIDA measurements? Attention, interest, desire, action? Or is it engagement? Actions, intent to purchase, actual purchase? Word of mouth as a brand ambassador? Will you only measure after the launch of the experiment, or will measure the change in each variable using a before and after design? Determine the natural length of time to run the experiment depending on the buying cycle of the product or service—a week, a few weeks, a month, a year, a few years.

6. **Decide on the Experimental Design Including the Execution of the Test and Control Stimuli**
It is important to present the experimental design graphically, as illustrated in figures in Chapter 7. This is key—presenting the experiment visually ensures we have truly innovative options and the right measures.

7. **Design the Implementation**
Iron out all the details, including who is going to design and present the stimuli; select the unit of analysis; the creative execution of the All Touchpoint Value Creation model; the budget; the time period. In short, implement the 10 steps outlined here.

8. **Analyze the Results (ANCOVA)**
Conduct statistical analysis of the results. Are the differences between the test groups and control group statistically significant? Complete an analysis of covariance (ANCOVA), which controls for the impact of unexpected events (a labor strike, a snow storm, etc.). To the extent that the firm is conducting multiple experiments, or is aware of other experiments being conducted, undertake meta-analysis to assess the impact across all the available studies.

9. **Present the Results as a Story and as an Integral Part of the Dashboard**

To be integrated in the business process, the results should be presented as part of the dashboard used by management. The ideal dashboard should include "what if" capabilities and be visually attractive and easy to use—many such dashboard templates are available online. Creating a story around the results increases the effectiveness of a presentation to the relevant decision makers.

10. **Decide on the Required Actions (Scale Up, Kill, Something Else); Develop the Next Round of Experiments**

The results will clarify the needs of the business. And this will lead to the decision about what to experiment with next when moving forward, which reveals what to experiment with next. Continued experimentation is critical.

References

Allen, Kevin. "The Future of Advertising." Wharton Future of Advertising Program (WFoA) Advertising 2020 Project, October 12, 2012. http://wfoa.wharton.upenn.edu/perspective/kevinallen/.

Andersen, Frederick. "Thinking of Running an Agency in 2020?" WFoA Advertising 2020 Project, October 12, 2012. http://wfoa.wharton.upenn.edu/perspective/frederikandersen/.

AOL and BBDO. Research presented by Christian Kugel at the Wharton Future of Advertising Program Annual Meeting, Philadelphia, PA, November 6–7, 2013.

AOL, BBDO, and InsightsNow. "Seven Shades of Mobile: The Hidden Motivations of Mobile Users," AOL Case History, October 2012. https://advertising.aol.com/sites/advertising.aol.com/files/insights/research-reports/downloads/aol-bbdo-7-shades-mobile-abstract-final.pdf.

Ard, Hayley. "Beyond Wearables: New Frontiers in Interactive Tech." *WIRED*, February 25, 2015. http://www.wired.com/2015/02/beyond-wearables-new-frontiers-in-interactive-tech/.

Arnold, Chris. "Now That's Advertainment." WFoA Advertising 2020 Project, September 15, 2013. http://wfoa.wharton.upenn.edu/perspective/now-thats-advertainment/.

Baker, John M. "Future of Advertising 2020." WFoA Advertising 2020 Project, October 12, 2012. http://wfoa.wharton.upenn.edu/perspective/johnbaker/.

Banga, Kamini. "Advertising 2020." WFoA Advertising 2020 Project, November 13, 2012. http://wfoa.wharton.upenn.edu/perspective/kaminibanga/.

Barocci, Bob. "Bob Ogilvy Dinner Speech," WFoA Advertising 2020 Project, November 2012. http://wfoa.wharton.upenn.edu/perspective/robertbarocci/.

Belani, Eshwar. Presented at the Wharton Future of Advertising Program Annual Meeting, Philadelphia, PA, October 22–23, 2014.

Bellman, Steven, and Duane Varan. "Advertising 2020." WFoA Advertising 2020 Project, October 12, 2012. http://wfoa.wharton.upenn.edu/perspective/stevenbellman/.

Berger, Jonah. *Contagious: Why Things Catch On*. NY: Simon & Schuster, 2013.

Billey, Lori. "What Could/Should Advertising Look Like in 2020?" WFoA Advertising 2020 Project, December 13, 2013. http://wfoa.wharton.upenn.edu/perspective/lori-billey/.

Binet, Les, and Peter Field. *The Long and Short of It: Balancing Short- and Long-Term Marketing Strategies*. London: Institute of Practitioners in Advertising, 2013.

Blanchard, Keith. "Advertising 2020." WFoA Advertising 2020 Project, October 12, 2012. http://wfoa.wharton.upenn.edu/perspective/keithblanchard/.

Bodine, Kerry and Moira Dorsey: "The Business Impact of Customer Experience." Forrester Research, Inc., 2013. http://solutions.forrester.com/customer-experience-t/prove-roi-cx-report-84QT-1623IB.html.

Bonn, Frederic. "What Could/Should Advertising Look Like in 2020?" WFoA Advertising 2020 Project, October 12, 2012. http://wfoa.wharton.upenn.edu/perspective/fredericbonn/.

Bottomley, Michelle. "The Future of Advertising in 2020: Are You Experienced?" WFoA Advertising 2020 Project, October 12, 2012. http://wfoa.wharton.upenn.edu/perspective/michellebottomley/.

Brown, Bruce, and Scott Anthony. "How P&G Tripled Its Innovation Success Rate." *Harvard Business Review*, June 2011. https://hbr.org/2011/06/how-pg-tripled-its-innovation-success-rate&cm_sp=Article-_-Links-_-Top%20of%20Page%20Recirculation.

Bughin, Jacques. "Advertising in 2020: The Demand for Marketing On-Demand." WFoA Advertising 2020 Project, November 13, 2012. http://wfoa.wharton.upenn.edu/perspective/jacquesbughin/.

Burgess, Cheryl. "Advertising Flight 2020: Destination 'The Future.'" WFoA Advertising 2020 Project, November 13, 2012. http://wfoa.wharton.upenn.edu/perspective/cherylburgess/.

Burgess, Mark. "The New Integrated Advertising Approach in 2020: Advertising in a Hyper-Real Time World." WFoA Advertising 2020 Project, November 13, 2012. http://wfoa.wharton.upenn.edu/perspective/markburgess/.

Burggraeve, Chris. "Why, Who, What, and How of Marketing by 2020." WFoA Advertising 2020 Project, October 12, 2012. http://wfoa.wharton.upenn.edu/perspective/chrisburggraeve/.

Burkhardt, Thomas. "My View of the Future." WFoA Advertising 2020 Project, June 12, 2013. http://wfoa.wharton.upenn.edu/perspective/thomasburkhardt/.

Cahill, Adam, and Baba Shetty. "The Emergence of Choice-Based Impressions." WFoA Advertising 2020 Project, January 7, 2013. http://wfoa.wharton.upenn.edu/perspective/adamcahill/.

Campbell, Rob. "Thoughts on How to Create the Future Rather Than Just Talk About It." WFoA Advertising 2020 Project, October 12, 2012. http://wfoa.wharton.upenn.edu/perspective/robcampbell/.

Cannes Lions Archive. "Gold: Lions: Breathe Again," June 2015. http://www.canneslionsarchive.com/winners/entry/591286/breathe-again.

Cannes Lions Archive. "Gold: Lions: Proud Whopper," June 2015. http://www.canneslionsarchive.com/winners/entry/591286/proud-whopper.

Cannes Lions Archive. "Gold: Lions: The Salt You Can See," June 2015. http://www.canneslionsarchive.com/winners/entry/566412/the-salt-you-can-see.

Cardona, Mercedes. "Study: CEOs Who 'Get' Marketing a Boon to CMO and the Business." *CMO*, June 1, 2015. http://www.cmo.com/articles/2015/5/8/2015-cmo-impact-study.html.

Cato, Mac. "There Will Be Advertising in 2020—But Not As We Know It." WFoA Advertising 2020 Project, October 12, 2012. http://wfoa.wharton.upenn.edu/perspective/maccato/.

Cerwin, Michele. "Advertising 2020." WFoA Advertising 2020 Project, October 12, 2012 http://wfoa.wharton.upenn.edu/perspective/michelecerwin/.

Champniss, Guy. "Advertising 2020." WFoA Advertising 2020 Project, April 26, 2013. http://wfoa.wharton.upenn.edu/perspective/guychampniss/.

Chansanchai, Athima. "Fake Facebook couple faces backlash from duped supporters." *Today*, April 18, 2011, accessed April 2014, http://www.today.com/news/fake-facebook-couple-faces-backlash-duped-supporters-123827.

Cheyfitz, Kirk. "Getting to the Last 3 Feet." WFoA Advertising 2020 Project, October 12, 2012. http://wfoa.wharton.upenn.edu/perspective/kirkcheyfitz/.

Chudoba, Brent. "Advertising 2020." WFoA Advertising 2020 Project, December 16, 2012. http://wfoa.wharton.upenn.edu/perspective/brentchudoba/.

Colantuono, Lisa. "Human Experience: The New Media Channel." WFoA Advertising 2020 Project, April 26, 2013. http://wfoa.wharton.upenn.edu/perspective/lisacolantuono/.

Cone, Carole. "Trust and the Corporations' Role in Society." Edelman, February 10, 2014, accessed September 14, 2014, http://www.edelman.com/post/trust-and-the-corporations-role-in-society/.

Costello, John, on "CMO Spotlight: Talent Today." Marketing Matters Radio Program, June 22, 2015. http://wfoa.wharton.upenn.edu/talent-today/.

Cross, Amy-Willard. "Brands: Why She's Just Not That Into You (And What You Can Do to Improve)." WFoA Advertising 2020 Project, April 26, 2013. http://wfoa.wharton.upenn.edu/perspective/amycross/.

d'Allesandro, Brian. "Advertising 2020." WFoA Advertising 2020 Project, October 12, 2012. http://wfoa.wharton.upenn.edu/perspective/briandalessandro/.

Debevoise, Allen. "My View of the Future." WFoA Advertising 2020 Project, November 13, 2012. http://wfoa.wharton.upenn.edu/perspective/debevoiseallen/.

Dhannoon, Yasir. "Where Will the Advertising Industry be in the Year 2020?" WFoA Advertising 2020 Project, October 12, 2012. http://wfoa.wharton.upenn.edu/perspective/yasirdhannoon/.

Diaz, Ann-Christine. "Zappos Turns Baggage Carousel into Wheel of Fortune-Style Game." *Advertising Age*, November 27, 2013. http://adage.com/article/news/zappos-baggage-claim-houston-airport-wheel-fortune-game/245454/.

Doe, Pete. "2020 Vision?" WFoA Advertising 2020 Project, October 10, 2012. http://wfoa.wharton.upenn.edu/perspective/petedoe/.

Doherty, Mike. "Marketing in 2020: What Will It Look Like and What Do We Need to Do Now to Be Ready for This Future?" WFoA Advertising 2020 Project, October 12, 2012. http://wfoa.wharton.upenn.edu/perspective/mikedoherty/.

Dolsten, Simon. "R.I.P. Storytelling, Hello Storysharing!" WFoA Advertising 2020 Project, October 12, 2012. http://wfoa.wharton.upenn.edu/perspective/simondolsten/.

Donahue, Mike. "Back to the Future." WFoA Advertising 2020 Project, February 14, 2013. http://wfoa.wharton.upenn.edu/perspective/mikedonahue/.

Dove, Jackie. "3D Scanner App for iPad Can Now Fashion Full-body Scans for Cute Figures and More." *The Next Web*, February 3, 2015. http://thenextweb.com/apps/2015/02/03/3d-scanner-ipad-app-can-now-produce-full-body-scans-for-creating-cute-figurines-and-more/v.

Dubner, Russell. "Advertising 2020: Where Hyper-Relevance Rules." WFoA Advertising 2020 Project, December 9, 2013. http://wfoa.wharton.upenn.edu/perspective/russelldubner/.

DuPlessis, Erik. "The Brand Feelings." WFoA Advertising 2020 Project, October 12, 2012. http://wfoa.wharton.upenn.edu/perspective/erikduplessis/.

Duquesne, Timothy. "United to Build Meaningful Media Ecosystems." WFoA Advertising 2020 Project, April 25, 2013. http://wfoa.wharton.upenn.edu/perspective/timothy-duquesne/.

Earls, Mark and John Willshire. "What is Advertising in 2020?" WFoA Advertising 2020 Project, October 12, 2012. http://wfoa.wharton.upenn.edu/perspective/markearls/.

Econsultancy with Adobe. "Why Marketing Should Be Personal." *Econsultancy Quarterly Digital Intelligence Briefing*, November 2014.

Edelman, David. "The Demand for Marketing On-Demand." WFoA Advertising 2020 Project, December 16, 2012. http://wfoa.wharton.upenn.edu/perspective/davidedelman/.

"Edelman Trust Barometer Global Results 2014." Edelman, January 2014. http://www.edelman.com/insights/intellectual-property/2014-edelman-trust-barometer/about-trust/global-results/.

Ewing, Mike. "Content, Context, Channels and Commerce in 2020." WFoA Advertising 2020 Project, October 12, 2012. http://wfoa.wharton.upenn.edu/perspective/mikeewing/.

Exon, Mel. "Advertising Is Dead, Long Live Advertising." WFoA Advertising 2020 Project, October 12, 2012. http://wfoa.wharton.upenn.edu/perspective/melexon/.

"EY—Announcing: An Institute for Purpose," EY. Accessed July 27, 2015. http://www.ey.com/GL/en/Services/Advisory/EY-announcing-an-institute-for-purpose.

Facebook Marketing Science. "Wharton Personalization at Scale." Presentation at Wharton Personalization@Scale Kickoff Call, Virtual, May 13, 2015.

Ferrier, Adam, and Lach Hall. "Art Series Hotels: The Overstay Checkout." Warc Case Study, 2013. www.warc.com/Content/ContentViewer.aspx?MasterContentRef=e3a4540f-4138-4695-9a6f-45abf86197a9.

Field, Peter. "The Future of Advertising—A Call of Common Sense." WFoA Advertising 2020 Project, October 12, 2012. http://wfoa.wharton.upenn.edu/perspective/peterfield/.

Fisher, Lauren. "U.S. Programmatic Ad Spend Tops $10 Billion This Year, to Double by 2016." *eMarketer*, October 16, 2014. www.emarketer.com/Article/US-Programmatic-Ad-Spend-Tops-10-Billion-This-Year-Double-by-2016/1011312.

Flattery, Tim. "Advertising 2020." WFoA Advertising 2020 Project October 12, 2012. http://wfoa.wharton.upenn.edu/perspective/timflattery/.

Fleischmann, Arthur. "Handling Democracy in Advertising." WFoA Advertising 2020 Project, December 13, 2013. http://wfoa.wharton.upenn.edu/perspective/arthur-fleischmann/.

Foley, Brendan. "Permission-Based Marketing in 2020." WFoA Advertising 2020 Project, November 13, 2012. http://wfoa.wharton.upenn.edu/perspective/brendanfoley/.

Follett, Mike. "Grow Up!" WFoA Advertising 2020 Project, October 12, 2012. http://wfoa.wharton.upenn.edu/perspective/mikefollett/.

Frampton, Jez. "The Future of Brand Building?" WFoA Advertising 2020 Project, October 12, 2012. http://wfoa.wharton.upenn.edu/perspective/jezframpton/.

Funaro, Vincent. "Samsung Galaxy S3 'Next Big Thing' Ad Launches." *Christian Post*, June 22, 2012. http://m.christianpost.com/news/samsung-galaxy-s3-next-big-thing-ad-launches-77072/.

Fung, Victor K., William K. Fung, and Yoram (Jerry) Wind. *Competing in a Flat World: Building Enterprises for a Borderless World*. Upper Saddle River, NJ: Pearson Education, 2008.

Gallop, Cindy. "Blow Yourselves Up and Start Again." WFoA Advertising 2020 Project, October 12, 2012. http://wfoa.wharton.upenn.edu/perspective/cindygallop/.

Garinois-Melenikiotou, Georgia. "Key Challenges in Advertising Around the World." WFoA Advertising 2020 Project, November 13, 2012. http://wfoa.wharton.upenn.edu/perspective/georgiagm/.

Gertner, Jon. "The Truth about Google X: An Exclusive Look behind the Secretive Lab's Closed Doors." *Fast Company*, May 2014. www.fastcompany.com/3028156/united-states-of-innovation/the-google-x-factor.

Gianatasio, David. "Adobe Live-Photoshops People into Bus-Stop Ads in Ambush That's Actually Not Awful; Erik Johansson Makes You Smile." *Adweek*, June 10, 2013. www.adweek.com/adfreak/adobe-live-photoshops-people-bus-stop-ads-ambush-thats-actually-not-awful-150167.

Gianatasio, David. "Virgin Atlantic Turns NYC Park Bench into the Lap of Luxury: Bringing Sky-High Service down to Earth." *Adweek*, July 3, 2013. www.adweek.com/adfreak/virgin-atlantic-turns-nyc-park-bench-lap-luxury-150984.

Gioffre, Maria. "Chobani: #PlainInspiring." Warc Case Study, last modified 2015, http://www.warc.com/Content/ContentViewer.aspx?MasterContentRef=6c3940c0-3889-47f9-95c7-2f537dea3a18&q=Chobani+PlainInspiring&CID=A104356&PUB=WARC-PRIZE-SOCIAL.

Godfrey, Matthew. "The End of Lazy Marketing." WFoA Advertising 2020 Project, October 12, 2012. http://wfoa.wharton.upenn.edu/perspective/matthewgodfrey/.

Godin, Seth. "The Future of Marketing & Advertising." WFoA Advertising 2020 Project, December 16, 2012. http://wfoa.wharton.upenn.edu/perspective/sethgodin/.

Gometz, Julia. "The Future of Advertising in 2020." WFoA Advertising 2020 Project, December 11, 2013. http://wfoa.wharton.upenn.edu/perspective/juliagometz/.

Goodson, Scott. "Change the Model, Change the World." WFoA Advertising 2020 Project, October 12, 2012. http://wfoa.wharton.upenn.edu/perspective/scottgoodson/.

Goodson, Scott. *Uprising: How to Build a Brand—and Change the World—By Sparking Cultural Movements*. McGraw-Hill Education, 2012.

Goodwin, Tom, on "'How To' with Havas Media." Marketing Matters Radio Program, May 6, 2015. http://wfoa.wharton.upenn.edu/havas-media-marketing-matters/.

Goodwin, Tom. "Advertising beyond Engagement." WFoA Advertising 2020 Project, August 22, 2014. http://wfoa.wharton.upenn.edu/perspective/tom-goodwin/.

Graham, Gillian. Presented at Wharton Future of Advertising Program Annual Meeting, Philadelphia, PA, October 22–23, 2014.

Grant, Ari, and Kang Zhang. "Airlock—Facebook's mobile A/B testing framework." Facebook, January 9, 2014, accessed January 9, 2014, https://code.facebook.com/posts/520580318041111/airlock-facebook-s-mobile-a-b-testing-framework/.

Greenberg, Bob. "Two Letters from 2020." WFoA Advertising 2020 Project, November 13, 2012. http://wfoa.wharton.upenn.edu/perspective/bobgreenberg/.

Griner, David. "Laphroaig Scotch Doesn't Mind If You Think It 'Tastes Like a Burning Hospital.'" *Adweek*, June 2, 2014. http://www.adweek.com/adfreak/laphroaig-scotch-doesnt-mind-if-you-think-it-tastes-burning-hospital-158069.

Grossman, Loren. "Advertising 2020." WFoA Advertising 2020 Project, October 12, 2012. http://wfoa.wharton.upenn.edu/perspective/lorengrossman/.

Hagedorn, Scott. "Vertical Integration and You." WFoA Advertising 2020 Project, October 12, 2012. http://wfoa.wharton.upenn.edu/perspective/scotthagedorn/.

Hall, Alex. "Adspotting." WFoA Advertising 2020 Project, October 12, 2012. http://wfoa.wharton.upenn.edu/perspective/alexhall/.

Hanna, Sam. "Advertising 2020." WFoA Advertising 2020 Project, February 12, 2013. http://wfoa.wharton.upenn.edu/perspective/samhanna/.

Harrison, Thomas. "Advertising 2020." WFoA Advertising 2020 Project, October 12, 2012. http://wfoa.wharton.upenn.edu/perspective/thomasharrison/.

Hartman, Carl. "Advertising 2020." WFoA Advertising 2020 Project, October 12, 2012. http://wfoa.wharton.upenn.edu/perspective/carlhartman/.

Harvey, Bill. "Digital Integration of Media, Advertising, Gaming, and Philanthropy." WFoA Advertising 2020 Project, October 12, 2012. http://wfoa.wharton.upenn.edu/perspective/billharvey/.

Heiselman, Karl and Paul Worthington. "Advertising in 2020: The New Brand Building Reality." WFoA Advertising 2020 Project, October 12, 2012. http://wfoa.wharton.upenn.edu/perspective/karlheiselman/.

Hepburn, Aden. "Qualcomm Mobile: Best Bus Stop Ever." *digitalbuzz blog*. Last modified February 26, 2013, http://www.digitalbuzzblog.com/qualcomm-mobile-best-bus-stop-ever/.

Heureux, Alain. "Advertising 2020." WFoA Advertising 2020 Project, October 12, 2012. http://wfoa.wharton.upenn.edu/perspective/alainheureux/.

Hill, Jason. "On Building Global Brands." WFoA Advertising 2020 Project, May 28, 2014. http://wfoa.wharton.upenn.edu/perspective/jason-m-hill/.

Hill, Nancy. "My View of the Future." WFoA Advertising 2020 Project, October 12, 2012. http://wfoa.wharton.upenn.edu/perspective/nancyhill/.

Hoffman, Donna L., and Thomas P. Novak. "How the Digital Future Killed Traditional Advertising." WFoA Advertising 2020 Project, December 16, 2012. http://wfoa.wharton.upenn.edu/perspective/thomasnovak/.

Holden, Mark. "Advertising 2020." WFoA Advertising 2020 Project, October 12, 2012. http://wfoa.wharton.upenn.edu/perspective/markholden/.

Hoque, Faisal. "What Zara, P&G, and Berlitz Know about Agility." *Fast Company*, September 21, 2012. http://www.fastcompany.com/3001444/what-zara-pg-and-berlitz-know-about-agility

IBM Corporation. "IBM Jam Events." Accessed on September 14, 2014, https://www.collaborationjam.com/.

IBM Corporation. "Capitalizing on Complexity: Insights from the Global Chief Executive Officer Study." Last modified 2010, http://www-935.ibm.com/services/us/ceo/ceostudy2010/.

IBM Corporation. "The Customer-Activated Enterprise: Insights from the Global C-suite Study." Last modified 2013, http://public.dhe.ibm.com/common/ssi/ecm/gb/en/gbe03572usen/GBE03572USEN.PDF.

InnoCentive. "What We Do." Last modified 2015, http://www.innocentive.com/about-innocentive.

Irwin, Neil. "Uber's Travis Kalanick Explains His Pricing Experiment." *New York Times*, July 11, 2014. http://www.nytimes.com/2014/07/12/upshot/ubers-travis-kalanick-explains-his-pricing-experiment.html.

Jacobs, Michael. "What Could Advertising Look Like in 2020?" WFoA Advertising 2020 Project, October 12, 2012. http://wfoa.wharton.upenn.edu/perspective/michaeljacobs/.

Jordan, John. "Advertising 2020: New Options for Video." WFoA Advertising 2020 Project, October 12, 2012. http://wfoa.wharton.upenn.edu/perspective/johnjordan/.

Jowett, David. "How Agencies Should Start Preparing to Support Clients in the World of Real-Time Marketing." WFoA Advertising 2020 Project, December 12, 2013. http://wfoa.wharton.upenn.edu/perspective/david-jowett/.

Kahneman, Daniel. *Thinking, Fast and Slow*. New York: Farrar, Straus and Giroux, 2013.

Kalehoff, Max. "Eleven Big Trends That Will Reshape Advertising in 2020 and Beyond." WFoA Advertising 2020 Project, November 13, 2012. http://wfoa.wharton.upenn.edu/perspective/maxkalehoff/.

Kantor, Bob. "What Could/Should 'Advertising' Look Like in 2020?" WFoA Advertising 2020 Project, October 12, 2012. http://wfoa.wharton.upenn.edu/perspective/bobkantor/.

Kassan, Michael. "What Could/Should "Advertising" Look Like in 2020." WFoA Advertising 2020 Project, December 1, 2012. http://wfoa.wharton.upenn.edu/perspective/michaelkassan/.

Kay, Gareth. "The Future of Advertising Could Be Small." WFoA Advertising 2020 Project, April 26, 2013. http://wfoa.wharton.upenn.edu/perspective/garethkay/.

Kelly, Tim. "Consumers Are in the Connected Car's Driver Seat in 2015." *WIRED*, January 28, 2015, accessed January 29, 2015, http://www.wired.com/2015/01/consumers-are-in-the-connected-cars-driver-seat-in-2015/.

Kenton, Christopher. "Seeing Beyond Waves: Have We Reached the Point of Terminal Efficiency?" WFoA Advertising 2020 Project, October 12, 2012. http://wfoa.wharton.upenn.edu/perspective/christopherkenton/.

Kimelfeld, Yaakov. "Advertising—and the Future—Are in the Consumers' Control." WFoA Advertising 2020 Project, October 12, 2012. http://wfoa.wharton.upenn.edu/perspective/yaakovkimelfeld/.

Kim, Thomas Hong-Tack. "My View of the Future." WFoA Advertising 2020 Project, November 12, 2012. http://wfoa.wharton.upenn.edu/perspective/thomashongtackkim/.

King, Jon. "The Irresistible Rise of Meaning." WFoA Advertising 2020 Project, October 12, 2012. http://wfoa.wharton.upenn.edu/perspective/jonking/.

Kiran, Ravi. "Advertising in 2020: The Rise-Again of Message." WFoA Advertising 2020 Project, October 12, 2012. http://wfoa.wharton.upenn.edu/perspective/ravikiran/.

"Kmart: Ship My Pants." Warc Case Study, last modified 2014, http://proxy.library.upenn.edu:4902/Content/ContentViewer.aspx?MasterContentRef=32af0dd5-8248-42d5-bf58-a5b4d9f44886&q=Ship+my+Pants&CID=A102039&PUB=EFFIES.

Koed, Karsten, and Morten Gad. "The Rewarding Customer." WFoA Advertising 2020 Project, October 12, 2012. http://wfoa.wharton.upenn.edu/perspective/karstenkoed/.

Ku, Ryan, Presented at the Wharton Future of Advertising Program Annual Meeting, Philadelphia, PA October 22–23, 2014.

Kubo, Akihiko. "Advertising in 2020." WFoA Advertising 2020 Project, October 12, 2012. http://wfoa.wharton.upenn.edu/perspective/akihikokubo/.

Kumparak, Greg. "Nike's Secret New York Vending Machine Trades Free Swag for FuelBand Points." *TechCrunch*, July 17, 2014, accessed July 17, 2014. http://techcrunch.com/2014/07/17/nikes-secret-new-york-vending-machine-trades-free-swag-for-fuelband-points/.

Lagunas, Claudia. "Advertising in 2020." WFoA Advertising 2020 Project, October 12, 2012. http://wfoa.wharton.upenn.edu/perspective/claudialagunas/.

Lall, Alok. "The End of Advertising, As We Know It." WFoA Advertising 2020 Project, October 12, 2012. http://wfoa.wharton.upenn.edu/perspective/aloklall/.

Landsberg, Steven. "Advertising in 2020." WFoA Advertising 2020 Project, October 12, 2012. http://wfoa.wharton.upenn.edu/perspective/stevenlandsberg/.

Larguinat, Laurent, and Judy Yeh. "Advertising 2020." WFoA Advertising 2020 Project, October 12, 2012. http://wfoa.wharton.upenn.edu/perspective/judyyeh/.

Lariu, Alessandra. "When Customers Control Their Data." WFoA Advertising 2020 Project, October 12, 2012. http://wfoa.wharton.upenn.edu/perspective/alessandralariu/.

Larson, Denise. "What Will Advertising Look Like in 2020?" WFoA Advertising 2020 Project, October 12, 2012. http://wfoa.wharton.upenn.edu/perspective/deniselarson/.

Lee, Everlyn. "Breaking Down Data Silos." WFoA Advertising 2020 Project, October 12, 2012. http://wfoa.wharton.upenn.edu/perspective/everlynlee/.

Lee, Richard. "My View of the Future." WFoA Advertising 2020 Project, October 12, 2012. http://wfoa.wharton.upenn.edu/perspective/richardlee/.

Legorburu, Gaston and Darren McColl. *Storyscaping: Stop Creating Ads, Start Creating Worlds*. Hoboken, NJ: Wiley, April 2014. http://www.wiley.com/WileyCDA/WileyTitle/productCd-1118823281.html

Lemelstrich-Latar, Noam. "Advertising 2020." WFoA Advertising 2020 Project, February 13, 2013. http://wfoa.wharton.upenn.edu/perspective/noamlatar/.

Levanon, Yoram. "Creating Influence." WFoA Advertising 2020 Project, October 12, 2012. http://wfoa.wharton.upenn.edu/perspective/yoramlevanon/.

Levin, Ayal, and David Fogel. "Advertising for Partners." WFoA Advertising 2020 Project, September 25, 2013. http://wfoa.wharton.upenn.edu/perspective/ayal-levin-advertising-for-partners/.

Levy, Doug. "My View of the Future." WFoA Advertising 2020 Project, March 21, 2013. http://wfoa.wharton.upenn.edu/perspective/douglevy/.

Levy, Tara Walpert. E-mail message to Catharine Hays, November 10, 2014.

Libert, Barry, Yoram (Jerry) Wind, and Megan Beck Fenley. "What Airbnb, Uber, and Alibaba Have in Common." *Harvard Business Review*, November 20, 2014, accessed November 20, 2014. https://hbr.org/2014/11/what-airbnb-uber-and-alibaba-have-in-common.

Lim, Ruth, and Kai Hui Tan. "Advertising 2020." WFoA Advertising 2020 Project, October 12, 2012. http://wfoa.wharton.upenn.edu/perspective/ruthlim/.

Lorenz, Taylor. "Soon You Can Order a Pizza by Tweeting the Pizza Emoji at Domino's." *Business Insider*, May 12, 2015, accessed May 12, 2015. http://www.businessinsider.com/dominos-emoji-pizza-order-2015-5?op=1.

Lowe, Mullen. "American Greetings: The World's Toughest Jobs." Warc Case Study, last modified 2015, http://www.warc.com/Content/ContentViewer.aspx?MasterContentRef=8a3e3c5c-c6dd-42ce-85f2-e91a7d6e061e&q=worlds+toughest+job&CID=A104701&PUB=CANNES.

Manabe, Nagisa. "The Role of the CMO in Leading the Organization's Capability and Talent Transformation," Presented at ANA/Wharton Leadership Program, Philadelphia, PA, May 12, 2015.

Marci, Carl. "Advertising 2020." WFoA Advertising 2020 Project, October 12, 2012. http://wfoa.wharton.upenn.edu/perspective/carlmarci/.

Masito, Mzamo. "The Power of Real Life." WFoA Advertising 2020 Project, October 23, 2013. http://wfoa.wharton.upenn.edu/perspective/mzamomasito/.

Maslansky, Michael. "A Day in the Life—2020." WFoA Advertising 2020 Project, October 12, 2012. http://wfoa.wharton.upenn.edu/perspective/michaelmaslansky/.

McCabe, Pearse. "Storytelling: The Marketing of 2020 and Beyond." WFoA Advertising 2020 Project, September 22, 2013. http://wfoa.wharton.upenn.edu/perspective/pearse-mccabe-storytelling-the-marketing-of-2020-and-beyond/.

McCall, Duncan. "The Future of Advertising 2020." WFoA Advertising 2020 Project, November 13, 2012. http://wfoa.wharton.upenn.edu/organization_type/technology/.

McDowell, Walter. "Biology-Based Measurement and the Future of Advertising." WFoA Advertising 2020 Project, October 12, 2012. http://wfoa.wharton.upenn.edu/perspective/waltermcdowell/.

McGee, Matt. "Google Glass Reveals Its First 5 'Glass at Work' Certified Partners." *Marketing Land*, June 16, 2014. http://marketingland.com/google-glass-reveals-first-5-glass-work-certified-partners-87593.

"Meaningful Brands," Havas Media Group, Accessed July 19, 2015 http://www.meaningful-brands.com/.

MediaBistro. "McDonald's: Free Wifi," June 26, 2013. http://adsoftheworld.com/media/ambient/mcdonalds_free_wifi.

MediaBistro. "Nike: Step Back in Time 2015," March 2015. http://adsoftheworld.com/media/outdoor/nike_step_back_in_time_2015?size=original.

Mildenhall, Jonathan. "Coca-Cola Content 2020." WFoA Advertising 2020 Project, October 12, 2012. http://wfoa.wharton.upenn.edu/perspective/jonathanmildenhall/.

Miller, John. "Advertising 2020: A Matter of Trust." WFoA Advertising 2020 Project, March 21, 2013. http://wfoa.wharton.upenn.edu/perspective/john-miller/.

MillwardBrown Vermeer. "Insights2020: Driving Customer-Centric Growth." http://mbvermeer.com/insights2020/.

Montague, Ty. Presented at "Emerging Orchestrators and New Business and Revenue Models," Wharton Future of Advertising Program Meeting, Philadelphia, PA, October 27, 2011.

Moore, David. "Advertising in 2020." WFoA Advertising 2020 Project, October 12, 2012. http://wfoa.wharton.upenn.edu/perspective/davidmoore/.

Morais, Robert. "Advertising Anthropology." WFoA Advertising 2020 Project, October 12, 2012. http://wfoa.wharton.upenn.edu/perspective/robertmorais/.

Morris, Mark. "What's on the Horizon and What Do We Do About It?" WFoA Advertising 2020 Project, November 13, 2013. http://wfoa.wharton.upenn.edu/perspective/markmorris/.

Morris, Nigel. "Convergence Is Shaping the Future of Communications." WFoA Advertising 2020 Project, October 12, 2012. http://wfoa.wharton.upenn.edu/perspective/nigelmorris/.

Morton, Tom. "Advertising 2020: A point of View From Euro RSCG New York." WFoA Advertising 2020 Project, October 12, 2012. http://wfoa.wharton.upenn.edu/perspective/tommorton/.

Musi, George. "The Era of the Empowered Consumer." WFoA Advertising 2020 Project, December 5, 2013. http://wfoa.wharton.upenn.edu/perspective/georgemusi/.

Nadal, Miles. "My View of the Future." WFoA Advertising 2020 Project, October 12, 2012. http://wfoa.wharton.upenn.edu/perspective/milesnadal/.

Neill, Evelyn and Howard Sherman. "Agency 2020." WFoA Advertising 2020 Project, October 12, 2012. http://wfoa.wharton.upenn.edu/perspective/evelynneill/.

Neve, Bruce. "24 Hours in 2020." WFoA Advertising 2020 Project, December 11, 2013. http://wfoa.wharton.upenn.edu/perspective/bruce-neve/.

Nisch, Kenneth. "Advertising Equals Experience." WFoA Advertising 2020 Project, October 12, 2012. http://wfoa.wharton.upenn.edu/perspective/kennethnisch/.

Norman, Rob. "Advertising 2020." WFoA Advertising 2020 Project, October 12, 2012. http://wfoa.wharton.upenn.edu/perspective/robnorman/.

Ogilvy, David. *Confessions of an Advertising Man*. New York: Ballantine Books, 1963, 96.

O'Hear, Steve. "GoButler, The Magic Clone Founded By Ex-Rocket Internet Execs, Launches Virtual Assistant in NYC." *TechCrunch*, April 13, 2015.

O'Keefe, Kelly. Presented at Wharton Future of Advertising Program Annual Meeting, Philadelphia, PA. October 22–23, 2014.

Olis, Eric, Marcus Martin, and Amy Goldstein. "America's Navy: Project Architeuthis—Engaging the Cyber Warrior." Warc Case Study, 2015. www.warc.com/Content/ContentViewer.aspx?ID=1d0f848c-d706-4a52-8770-706ee74dc755&CID=A104349&PUB=WARC-PRIZE-SOCIAL&MasterContentRef=1d0f848c-d706-4a52-8770-706ee74dc755.

Oliva, Ralph. "What Could/Should Advertising Look Like in 2020." WFoA Advertising 2020 Project, October 12, 2012. http://wfoa.wharton.upenn.edu/perspective/ralpholivia/.

"Our Culture." SEI, last modified 2015, https://www.seic.com/enUS/about/13336.htm.

"Oscar Meyer: Wake Up & Smell the Bacon." Warc Case Study, 2015. http://www.warc.com/Content/ContentViewer.aspx?MasterContentRef=653a01dd-6557-4784-96d8-67917c1cfbed&CID=A104366&-PUB=Warc-Prize-Social.

Palmer, Shelly. "Fundamentally the Same; Technically Different." WFoA Advertising 2020 Project, May 30, 2013. http://wfoa.wharton.upenn.edu/perspective/shellypalmer/.

Panella, Alessandro and Uli Veigel. "A GREY Perspective on 'Advertising 2020'." WFoA Advertising 2020 Project, June 14, 2013. http://wfoa.wharton.upenn.edu/perspective/alessandro-panella-a-grey-perspective-on-advertising-2020/.

Parmar, Daniel. "Taking the Road Less Traveled—Disciples for Future Marketers." WFoA Advertising 2020 Project, January 26, 2015. http://wfoa.wharton.upenn.edu/perspective/daniel-parmar/.

"Pantene Weather Program." Warc Case Study, last modified 2014, http://www.warc.com/Content/ContentViewer.aspx?MasterContentRef=516202bb-ce1f-48c7-9f67-b49350a5e056&CID=A102040&PUB=EFFIES.

Pearson, Bryan. "Advertising 2020: Using Data to Create Demand for the Actual Ad (Cats Optional)." WFoA Advertising 2020 Project, December 11, 2013. http://wfoa.wharton.upenn.edu/perspective/bryan-pearson/.

Plaza, Maria Luisa Francoli. "What Could/Should 'Advertising' Look Like in 2020?" WFoA Advertising 2020 Project, October 12, 2012. http://wfoa.wharton.upenn.edu/perspective/mlfplaza/.

Plummer, Joe. Presented at Wharton Future of Advertising Program Annual Meeting, Philadelphia, PA, October 22–23, 2014.

Pollard, Mark. "The Future of Advertising Is Inside Out." WFoA Advertising 2020 Project, October 12, 2012. http://wfoa.wharton.upenn.edu/perspective/markpollard/.

Popcorn, Faith. "FutureSight Advertising: 2020." WFoA Advertising 2020 Project, November 13, 2012. http://wfoa.wharton.upenn.edu/perspective/faithpopcorn/.

Prindle, Scott. Presented at "The Future of Creatives and Creative Ideas in a Digital World," Wharton Future of Advertising Program, New York, NY, March 18, 2011.

Pringle, Hamish. "Advertising 2020." WFoA Advertising 2020 Project, October 12, 2012. http://wfoa.wharton.upenn.edu/perspective/hamishpringle/.

Publix.com, "Publix Announces Fourth Quarter and Annual Results for 2013," March 2014. http://publix.com/about/newsroom/NewsReleaseItem.do?newsReleaseItemPK=6835.

Pundyk, Jeff, and Sanjay Dholakia. "The Rise of the New Marketer: The Economist's Findings on Key Trends." *Marketo*, March 18, 2015. http://www.chiefmarketer.com/webinars/rise-new-marketer-economists-findings-key-trends/.

Puopolo, Scott, and Leszek Izdebski. "The Future of Advertising: Looking Ahead to 2020." WFoA Advertising 2020 Project, October 12, 2012. http://wfoa.wharton.upenn.edu/list/innovations-in-technology/.

Quevilly, Isabelle. "Welcome to the 7.6 Billion Target Market." WFoA Advertising 2020 Project, April 5, 2013. http://wfoa.wharton.upenn.edu/perspective/isabellequevilly/.

Ramos, Laura. "B2B Marketing Budgets to Increase by 6% in 2014," *Laura Ramos' Blog*, Accessed February 2015. http://www.forrester.com/B2B+Marketing+Budgets+To+Increase+By+6+In+2014/-/E-PRE6644.

Raj, Zain. "Advertising 2020." WFoA Advertising 2020 Project, October 12, 2012. http://wfoa.wharton.upenn.edu/perspective/zainraj/.

Ramsoy, Thomas. "The Brain Buzz: Harvesting the True Impacts of Neuromarketing." WFoA Advertising 2020 Project, October 12, 2012. http://wfoa.wharton.upenn.edu/perspective/thomasramsoy/.

Rangaswami, Anant. "The World of Advertising in 2020." WFoA Advertising 2020 Project, October 12, 2012. http://wfoa.wharton.upenn.edu/perspective/anantrangaswami/.

Rangaswamy, Arvind. "Advertising 2020: Big Role for Big Data." WFoA Advertising 2020 Project, October 12, 2012. http://wfoa.wharton.upenn.edu/perspective/arvindrangaswamy/.

Rapp, Anneliese. "The Individual as the Next Big Advertising Medium." WFoA Advertising 2020 Project, October 12, 2012. http://wfoa.wharton.upenn.edu/perspective/annelieserapp/.

Rappaport, Steve and Howard Moskowitz. "Mindsets, Messages, Money." WFoA Advertising 2020 Project, March 21, 2013. http://wfoa.wharton.upenn.edu/perspective/stephenrappaport/.

Reis, Vinicius. "Advertising 2020." WFoA Advertising 2020 Project, October 12, 2012. http://wfoa.wharton.upenn.edu/perspective/viniciusreis/.

Resnick, Lynda, and Ken Youngleib. "The Glass Factory." WFoA Advertising 2020 Project, October 12, 2012. http://wfoa.wharton.upenn.edu/perspective/lyndaresnick/.

Rietbroek, Robbert. "2020 Advertising: Dynamic and Responsive." WFoA Advertising 2020 Project, October 27, 2014. http://wfoa.wharton.upenn.edu/job_title/ceopresident/.

Rifkin, Jeremy. *The Zero Marginal Cost Society*. New York: Palgrave Macmillan, 2014.

Rivers, Anne. Presented at Wharton Future of Advertising Program Annual Meeting, Philadelphia, PA, October 22–23, 2014.

Roberts, Malcolm. "Brand Stewardship in the Future." WFoA Advertising 2020 Project, December 11, 2013. http://wfoa.wharton.upenn.edu/perspective/malcolm-roberts/.

Robinson, Richard. "Fix My Business – Not My Marketing." WFoA Advertising 2020 Project, October 10, 2014. http://wfoa.wharton.upenn.edu/perspective/richard-robinson/.

Roth, Hayes. "Advertising 2020." WFoA Advertising 2020 Project, February 14, 2013. http://wfoa.wharton.upenn.edu/perspective/hayesroth/.

Rothenberg, Randall. "Advertising in 2020." WFoA Advertising 2020 Project, October 12, 2012. http://wfoa.wharton.upenn.edu/perspective/randallrothenberg/.

Schiavone, Vince. "Leveraging the Social Revolution." WFoA Advertising 2020 Project, November 13, 2012. http://wfoa.wharton.upenn.edu/perspective/vinceschiavone/.

Schulman, Alan. "Storyscaping 2020." WFoA Advertising 2020 Project, July 2, 2013. http://wfoa.wharton.upenn.edu/perspective/alan-schulman-storyscaping-2020/.

Schultz, Don E. "What Will Advertising Be Like in 2020?" WFoA Advertising 2020 Project, October 12, 2012. http://wfoa.wharton.upenn.edu/perspective/donschultz/.

Seligman, Martin. *Flourish: A Visionary New Understanding of Happiness and Well-being*. New York: Simon and Schuster, 2011.

Senge, Peter M. *The Fifth Discipline: The Art and Practice of the Learning Organization*. New York: Doubleday Currency, 1990, 8.

Shachar, Ron. "Advertising 2020." WFoA Advertising 2020 Project, October 12, 2012. http://wfoa.wharton.upenn.edu/perspective/ronshachar/.

Sharma, Saurabh. "Drivers of Change and the Advertising Company of the Future." WFoA Advertising 2020 Project, November 13, 2012. http://wfoa.wharton.upenn.edu/perspective/saurabhsharma/.

Shreffler, Melanie. "Working for a Living." *MediaPost*, May 21, 2015. http://www.mediapost.com/publications/article/250476/working-for-a-living.html?print.

Sidhu, Inder. *Doing Both: Capturing Today's Profit and Driving Tomorrow's Growth*. New Jersey: FT Press, June 6, 2010.

Sipka, Maria. "The Future of Advertising: Online Interest Communities." WFoA Advertising 2020 Project, October 12, 2012. http://wfoa.wharton.upenn.edu/perspective/mariasipka/.

Sjoenell, Calle. "The Year 2020." WFoA Advertising 2020 Project, November 13, 2012. http://wfoa.wharton.upenn.edu/perspective/callesjoenell/.

Smith, J. Walker. "The Future of Advertising Is Social." WFoA Advertising 2020 Project, December 16, 2012. http://wfoa.wharton.upenn.edu/perspective/jwsmith/.

Smith, J. R. "2020: The Promise of Advertising in the Coming Age of Privacy." WFoA Advertising 2020 Project, November 13, 2012. http://wfoa.wharton.upenn.edu/perspective/jrsmith/.

Sorensen, Herb. "My View of the Future." WFoA Advertising 2020 Project, October 12, 2012. http://wfoa.wharton.upenn.edu/perspective/herbsorensen/.

Soued, Pierre. "The Future of Advertising in the Middle East." WFoA Advertising 2020 Project, May 8, 2014. http://wfoa.wharton.upenn.edu/perspective/pierre-soued/.

Stewart, Mark. Presented at Wharton Future of Advertising Program Annual Meeting, Philadelphia, PA, October 22–23, 2014.

Stipp, Horst. "Advertising in 2020." WFoA Advertising 2020 Project, October 12, 2012. http://wfoa.wharton.upenn.edu/perspective/horststipp/.

Stock, Kyle. "Patagonia 'Buy Less' Plea Spurs More Buying." *Bloomberg Business*, August 28, 2013. http://www.bloomberg.com/bw/articles/2013-08-28/patagonias-buy-less-plea-spurs-more-buying.

Stoute, Steve. "Omniculturalism in 2020." WFoA Advertising 2020 Project, October 12, 2012. http://wfoa.wharton.upenn.edu/perspective/stevestoute/.

Sutherland, Rory. "Advertising 2020." WFoA Advertising 2020 Project, November 13, 2012. http://wfoa.wharton.upenn.edu/perspective/rorysutherland/.

Swift, James. "Comms Lab Launches to Help Ad Agencies Do Good." *Campaign*, June 19, 2015. http://www.campaignlive.co.uk/news/1352234/.

Taite, Michelle. "My View of the Future." WFoA Advertising 2020 Project, October 12, 2012. http://wfoa.wharton.upenn.edu/perspective/michelletaite/.

Tauder, Arthur. "What Could/Should 'Advertising' Look Like in 2020?" WFoA Advertising 2020 Project, October 12, 2012. http://wfoa.wharton.upenn.edu/perspective/arthurtauder/.

Teagarden, Pamela. "The Authentic Organization (TAO): The Tao of Positive Business in an Authentic Culture." *University of Pennsylvania Scholarly Commons*, 2012. http://repository.upenn.edu/mapp_capstone-abstracts/74/.

Terwiesch, Christian, and Karl Ulrich. Innovation Tournaments. Boston: *Harvard Review Press*, 2009.

Thapar, Sanjay. "The Future of Advertising-2020." WFoA Advertising 2020 Project, October 12, 2012. http://wfoa.wharton.upenn.edu/perspective/sanjaythapar/.

TheCognitiveMedia. "Coca-Cola Content 2020 Part One." *YouTube* video, 7:27, Accessed August 10, 2011, https://www.youtube.com/watch?v=LerdMmWjU_E.

"The 2012 IKEA Catalogue—A Roommate Worth Having." Warc Case Study, 2012. http://www.warc.com/Content/ContentViewer.aspx?MasterContentRef=eb0621e4-81b0-4bb5-9ada-1401f04a707e.

"The Global, Socially Conscious Consumer." Nielsen, last modified March 27, 2012, http://www.nielsen.com/us/en/insights/news/2012/the-global-socially-conscious-consumer.html.

Ting, Richard. " What Could/Should Advertising Look Like in 2020?" WFoA Advertising 2020 Project, November 13, 2012. http://wfoa.wharton.upenn.edu/perspective/richardting/.

Tobaccowala, Rishad. "Advertising 2020." WFoA Advertising 2020 Project, October 12, 2012. http://wfoa.wharton.upenn.edu/perspective/rishadtobaccowala/.

Tomblin, Mark. "On Laying Zombie Ideas to Rest." WFoA Advertising 2020 Project, December 12, 2013. http://wfoa.wharton.upenn.edu/perspective/mark-tomblin/.

Torode, Amelia. "Advertising 2020." WFoA Advertising 2020 Project, October 12, 2012. http://wfoa.wharton.upenn.edu/perspective/ameliatorode/.

Turnage, Will, on "Marketing Matters' Meets R/GA to Discuss the Connected Age." Marketing Matters Radio Program, February 17, 2015. http://wfoa.wharton.upenn.edu/rga_connected_age/.

Valjalo, Vicente. "What Could/Should 'Advertising' Look Like in 2020?" WFoA Advertising 2020 Project, October 12, 2012. http://wfoa.wharton.upenn.edu/perspective/vicentevaljalo/.

Vasudevan, Venu. "What Futures Will Technology Permit & Consumers Love?" WFoA Advertising 2020 Project, October 12, 2012. http://wfoa.wharton.upenn.edu/perspective/venuvasudevan/.

Vega, Marco. Presented at Wharton Future of Advertising Program Annual Meeting, Philadelphia, PA, October 22–23, 2014.

Voytek, Kip. "Advertising 2020." WFoA Advertising 2020 Project, October 12, 2012. http://wfoa.wharton.upenn.edu/perspective/kipvoytek/.

Wacksman, Barry. "From Horizontal to Vertical to Functional: A New Strategy for Growth in the 21st Century." WFoA Advertising 2020 Project, October 12, 2012. http://wfoa.wharton.upenn.edu/perspective/barrywacksman/.

Wakil, Khayyam. "The Cult(ure) of Innovation." WFoA Advertising 2020 Project, April 26, 2013. http://wfoa.wharton.upenn.edu/perspective/khayyamwakil/.

Wharton Social Impact Initiative, accessed March 2015. https://socialimpact.wharton.upenn.edu/about-wharton-social-impact/.

"Why Marketers Haven't Mastered Multichannel." e*Marketing*, July 24, 2015. http://www.emarketer.com/Article/Why-Marketers-Havent-Mastered-Multichannel/1012769?ecid=NL1001.

"Will the Future of Advertising Be a Blend of Old and New Media?" *Knowledge at Wharton*, September 30, 2009. http://knowledge.wharton.upenn.edu/article/will-the-future-of-advertising-be-a-blend-of-old-and-new-media/.

Williams, Lauren C. "The Psychology behind the Outrage at OK Cupid's User Experiments." *Think Progress*, July 31, 2014. http://thinkprogress.org/culture/2014/07/31/3466128/okcupid-psychological-experiments/.

Williams, Sally. "Communications in an Age of Connectivity." WFoA Advertising 2020 Project, October 12, 2012. http://wfoa.wharton.upenn.edu/perspective/sallywilliams/.

Wind, Yoram (Jerry). "Orchestration as the New Managerial Model in the Digital Age." *Think with Google*, April 2012. www.thinkwithgoogle.com/articles/orchestration-as-the-new-managerial-model.html.

Wind, Yoram (Jerry), and Colin Crook, with Robert Gunther. *The Power of Impossible Thinking: Transform the Business of Your Life and the Life of Your Business.* New Jersey: Pearson Education, 2005.

Wind, Yoram (Jerry) and Vijay Mahajan. "Convergence Marketing." Journal of Interactive Marketing. Wiley Periodicals, volume 16, issue 2, pages 64–79. Spring 2002.

Winer, Russell. "Advertising in 2020." WFoA Advertising 2020 Project, October 12, 2012. http://wfoa.wharton.upenn.edu/perspective/russellwiner/.

Winsor, John. "What Will Advertising Look Like in 2020?" WFoA Advertising 2020 Project, November 13, 2012. http://wfoa.wharton.upenn.edu/perspective/johnwinsor/.

Wise, Richard, and Watts Wacker. "The Future of Advertising." WFoA Advertising 2020 Project, December 16, 2012. http://wfoa.wharton.upenn.edu/perspective/richardwise/.

Wishingrad, Ian. "Advertising in Year 2020." WFoA Advertising 2020 Project, November 13, 2012. http://wfoa.wharton.upenn.edu/perspective/ianwishingrad/.

Wong, Danny. "NikeID makes $100M+: Co-Creation Isn't Just a Trend." *Huffington Post*, July 20, 2010. http://www.huffingtonpost.com/danny-wong/nikeid-makes-100m-co-crea_b_652214.html.

Wu, Michael. "The Future of Advertising." WFoA Advertising 2020 Project, October 12, 2012. http://wfoa.wharton.upenn.edu/perspective/michaelwu/.

Y&R. "Y&R History: A Look at the Early Years and Beyond." Y&R, 2015. http://www.yr.com/yr-history-look-early-years%E2%80%A6and-beyond.

Yakob, Faris. "Advertising 2020." WFoA Advertising 2020 Project, October 12, 2012. http://wfoa.wharton.upenn.edu/perspective/farisyakob/.

Yang, Nikao. "The Path to the Future Is Paved with Stones of the Past." WFoA Advertising 2020 Project, February 14, 2013. http://wfoa.wharton.upenn.edu/perspective/nikaoyang/.

Yarkoni, Tal. "In Defense of Facebook." Blog, 2014. http://www.talyarkoni.org/blog/2014/06/28/in-defense-of-facebook/.

Yeh, Chris. "The Future of Advertising Is Collaborative." WFoA Advertising 2020 Project, October 12, 2012. http://wfoa.wharton.upenn.edu/perspective/chrisyeh/.

Young, Terry. "Advertising 2020: Qualified Everywhere." WFoA Advertising 2020 Project, June 11, 2013. http://wfoa.wharton.upenn.edu/perspective/terryyoung/.

Zalis, Shelley. Presented at "WFoA Future Vision Breakfast Series," Los Angeles, CA, June 4, 2015.

Zhiganov, Artem. "Let's Prove Bill Hicks Wrong: The Role of Advertising in the Future of Planet Earth." WFoA Advertising 2020 Project, May 30, 2013. http://wfoa.wharton.upenn.edu/perspective/artemzhiganov/.

Zogby, John, and Dayna Dion. "Tribal Analytics." Zogby Analytics, last modified May 9, 2012, http://www.zogbyanalytics.com/news/295-tribal-analytics.

Index

Page references followed by *fig* indicate an illustrated figure.

G

J

K

L

M

N

P

U

V

X

Y

Z